TIMED TO PERFECTION

(A Memoir by Stan Greenberg)

"One way or another I seem to have timed the important things
in life just right.

Usually I consider it to have been sheer
blind luck, but sometimes I wonder....."

"It's probably correct to describe me as an analog man
in a digital world. However, this condition seems
to have caused more problems for other
people than it has for me"

Timed to Perfection

First published by TwigBooks in 2016
Paperback ISBN **978-1-907953-66-8**

TwigBooks

1-2 Biggs Lane, DINTON

Aylesbury, Buckinghamshire

UK, England HP17 8UH

(www.twigbooks.com)

TIMED TO PERFECTION
Stan Greenberg

Introduction

ave always liked books, and especially those with some sort of order to them. So I ve always enjoyed using dictionaries and encyclopaedias, in fact any form of erence work. Having spent most of my life, both private and working, putting things ɔ lists, files and classification systems, it seemed only natural for me to organise ऽ book in a similar way i.e. in an alphabetical order.

rtainly it should make it easier for the reader to dip in and out at will, perhaps ially only picking out items which seem to relate to their particular interests, or ich catch their immediate attention. Hopefully they will carry on and read, and oy, all of it. Although sport in general, and athletics in particular, has been, and nains, a very important part of my life, it is not all there has been of importance. My nily, friends, music, show business, school, various jobs, and my religion, have all yed their part in my make-up, and I think I have reflected these paramount ٤rests in these memoirs. Much of my attitude to life has been formed by ɔeriences, not always unhappy ones, from the World War II period, with its twin ɔmas, in my case, of evacuation and loss of an integrated family life. Also, I have ɔn intrigued to note that one's life continually 'bumps up' against others, often able in diverse fields of endeavour totally unconnected with one's own, and I have nd those contacts immensely interesting and mind-broadening.

ıvel has definitely broadened my horizons, and meeting many people from different tures around the world has further shaped my ideas. I have never been a political mal as such, but nevertheless have come into close contact with extremists, and ir attitudes, from both ends of the spectrum. I have developed strong views on ne social, educational and political issues - all these things affect one's psyche - J so all are represented here in one way or another.

; rare, in this day and age, for us to sit back and seriously contemplate our past, ɔple we have known, places we have been, things we have seen and done. A ınge mixture of pleasure and, one must admit, some torment, gets conjured up, it is well worth the trouble. Hopefully, my memories, descriptions, thoughts, and tings, will provide some similar entertainment for the reader. If it does, I will be ased. If it does not, then my apologies.

n Greenberg 2016

MY LIFE
(by Stan Greenberg)

For a person whose whole senior life has been practically governed by facts, figures and times, it is perhaps remarkable that I cannot be sure about the actual day and date that I was born. I normally state the day to be 8th July 1931, and I have a birth certificate to prove it. Except, in fact, it may not! The problem arose with my father being exceptionally excited when I was born, and him forgetting to inform the Registrar of the birth of his gorgeous (well I am writing this) son. After a week or so some friends told him that he could get into a lot trouble by not declaring my birth, or indeed declaring rather later than it should have been. So when he eventually went to see the official he gave him a more recent date, i.e. 14th July, which was a Tuesday, and received a certificate with that date on it. Five years later he plucked up the nerve to officially amend it, and gave the "new" date as the 8th, which it turns out was a Wednesday. So what, you may think. However, it does seem likely that in his first declaration he would have merely added a week to the original, instead of six days. Also, and more significantly, my mother always insisted that I was born on a Tuesday, and she should know I suppose. Therefore it is likely that I was actually born on the 7th of July, but there is no way of checking, as whatever "official" documents still exist, state that it is the 8th – so that's what it will remain. To really confuse the issue I still have the two birth certificates, with the two different dates.

My young life got even more disturbed at the age of eight, when the day before World War II was declared I was evacuated with my primary school to Peterborough in Cambridgeshire. As the *real* war hadn't started yet, the people we were billeted on didn't really want us, and in my case were not very nice about it. Happily, after about three months my father brought me home again. However, over the next four years I ended up attending a total of ten different schools, in London and various parts of the country. This not only mucked up my education to a degree, but also I became the victim of anti-Semitisms at most of them. The "best example" of this I can tell you about was when I was in Kings Lynn in Norfolk, with one of the best schools I attended. After school work we would cycle out to nearby farms to help with pea-picking and apples and strawberries. I preferred the peas, because (a) I didn't like them to eat, and (b) because of that I developed an ability to fill the requisite sacks remarkably fast – in fact I was told that only the fantastic gypsy women pickers were faster – and thereby earned quite a lot of pocket money. Over this time I developed a friendship with one of the local lads, which was quite pleasant, until the day I told the foreman that I would not be coming the following week because it was the Jewish New Year and Day of Atonement period. My friend overheard me and, looking me up and down, queried what he had heard with the words, "You can't be Jewish. You're no different". I asked him what he expected, "Perhaps horns?", and I left him still staring at me in a puzzled way. I often wonder what he had been told about people like me. Certainly our "friendship" was never the same again.

That rather special school was the Hackney Downs School (formerly Grocer's Company's School) originally based in East London. In fact, I was selected for it by taking the requisite examination while evacuated in Luton. That was rather odd in itself, as because I was the only boy taking the London Examination – all the locals presumably took the Bedfordshire one – I ending up as the only boy in the examination room, with about a hundred desks, that day. There were two invigilators just for me, which frankly was rather intimidating. Nevertheless, the results proved to be positive, and I joined the part of the school not evacuated, but that part temporarily based at Parminter's, in another part of Hackney. Getting there involved a bus ride and then a walk across the park, during which time one often would watch "dogfights" between British and German planes. Eventually I joined the main school in Kings Lynn and stayed there until the end of the war in Europe. During this peripatetic period of my life, I discovered two important things. One was that I was fast, i.e. I could run faster that most of those who wished me harm. It also meant I could do well at athletics and football, and I even made the school cricket team primarily as a deep fielder, as I usually was able to stop hits reaching the boundary for a four.

The second thing I realised was that I was "bouncing" up against people who were or became quite famous. Thus in the school sports in Kings Lynn, one of my younger housemates was Maurice Micklewhite who won the 12-year 100 yards. He gained much more fame later as Michael Caine. Another classmate in London was Harold Pinter, who gave me a right pasting when I called him a bighead – which he was despite being a brilliant actor, excellent cricketer and a good sprinter. He was to be awarded the Nobel Prize for Literature in 2005.

As I write this I have just heard of the passing of Lord Peston of Mile End, whose son Robert, formerly with the BBC, is currently the political editor for ITV. His father Maurice was also in my class at Hackney Downs, and I am fairly certain that he didn't finish ahead of me in most of our exams. However he stayed on to the sixth form, went to university and became a famed economist.

Although I passed the Matriculation exam, my family couldn't afford for me to stay on for the sixth form and try for a university. I hadn't any idea of what I wanted to work at, although I positively knew that it would have nothing to do with accounts or figures. In fact, following a close friend who had been given an application to join Lever Brothers, the soap and margarine company, I applied as well, and found myself one of about 100 well-educated young men who were accepted into that organisation. I eventually ended up in the shipping department, where I spent most of my time taking to and picking up from firms all over the city of London. The company had excellent sports facilities, and I helped revitalise the athletics section, as well as representing them at football and badminton – to my surprise I found I was surprisingly good at the latter.   The athletics section also flourished, and we did very well in

London business sports days with a very good medley relay team. At one point, Ken Wilmhurst, a great long and triple jumper, as well as a very good 440 yard hurdler, joined the firm. I persuaded him to join our relay team, and, of course offered him the captaincy of the firm team. He turned it down, so that I had the England team captain in my team, which, with him, went from good to excellent.

Although I was terribly shy for most of my younger life, I finally got around to meeting a girl to whom I was very attracted – and surprisingly seemed to like me too – and in 1960 we were married. From that union came a daughter, Karen, and a son, Keith, and, so far, 56 very happy years. Later in my career at the company, which became Unilever Limited, I transferred to the Economics & Statistics Department, where I became something of an "expert" on the new Common Market. Also, while there, I met up with, and became a friend of, Terry Higgins, a former international quarter-miler, now retired and a top-rate economist. He was later knighted, and then became a peer as Baron Higgins of Worthing.   After twenty years at the company I decided to leave, and ended up helping to set up a transportation library at the Greater London Council. At about the same time, in 1968, I began to be contracted by the BBC to help their athletics commentators, David Coleman, Ron Pickering and Norris McWhirter, with statistics. This continued for a remarkable 26 years, during which time I travelled to some 40 countries all over the world, attending every major, and some minor, athletics meeting, including six Olympic Games, seven Commonwealth Games, five World championships, and seven European championships. And this was mainly just my hobby!

At the end of 1976 I was offered the position of sports editor of the Guinness Book of Records, which to a person with my interests was ideal. While there I also authored a history of the Olympic Games, which I updated and republished a further seven times. I held the Guinness position until I gave it up in 1981, to finally work full time for the BBC. I officially retired in 1995, but my last actual job for them was at the 1998 African Championships in Mauritius – quite an interesting experience. Since then I have attended many more international meetings, but now as a part of a fan group, although I have been able to obtain press accreditation for most of them, which enables me to get the "paperwork" for the meet. In that area, I was especially fortunate to obtain a special IOC (International Olympic Committee) accreditation, apparently for "services to the sport", for the 2012 Games in London – a truly memorable occasion. Today, approaching the age of 85, I am still producing British and Commonwealth ranking lists, statistical booklets, and writing letters to the sports press.

***

TIMED TO PERFECTION
Stan Greenberg

CONTENTS

TIMED TO PERFECTION
Stan Greenberg

Fashion
Father
Fawlty Towers
Fear
Filing Systems
Finance
Financial Advice
First Job
Flying
Fogs
Food
Football (Playing)
Football
(Watching)
Foreign Travel
Friends
Frisked
Frustration

Gambling
Gamesmanship
Gastronomy
Genes
Genius
German
Gobbledegook
Ghost Train
Gone
Great Day
Greater London
Council
Greenbergs
Growling
Guinness Book of
Records

Hair
Hammered
Handwriting
Hate
Health
Hear, Hear
Helicopters
Heroes

Hire cars
Holidays
Honeymoon
Horror
Hospital
Hot and Cold
Hotels
How Are You
Feeling
Hugging
Humour
Husbandcide

Ice
Idiocy
Illegal
Illness
Imagination
Income Tax
Interviews
Intolerance
Inventions
Irish
Italy

Jellyfish
Jerusalem
Jobsworth
Jogging
Jury Service

Kamasutra
Kilograms etc
Kiss
Knock Down
Ginger
Knowledge

Languages
Legend
Level Playing Field
Libido
Life

Lifts/Elevators
Lim Lim
Listings
Lizards
Locusts
Loneliness
Longevity
Lords and Ladies
Love
Luck

Machu Picchu
Mangle
Manners Maketh
Man
Marriage
Meanings
Memory
Men and Women
Minor Disasters
and
Irritations
Modesty
Mother
Motor Vehicles
Movie Memories
Music

Naïveté
Names
Navy
Nerve Wracking
Newspapers
Nightclubs
Nobel Prizes
No Problem
Nostalgia
Nut by Name

Obsessive
Compulsive
Disorder
Occupation
Olympic Games

TIMED TO PERFECTION
Stan Greenberg

On Time
One of Us
Oops
Opera
Opinions
Orwell
Other Sports
(Playing)
Other Sports
(Watching)
Overheard
Oxymoron

Paradise
   or Luton
      Airport
Paris
Parties
Pea Picking
Pets
Philosophy
Pith
Places
Politeness
Politics
Psychiatry
Public Speaking
Public Transport
Punishment
Put-Downs

Queueing
Quizzes
Quotations

Racism
Rationing
Rechthaberei
Refrigeration
Regrets
Religion

Residence
Responsibility
Revenge
Royalty

Sailing
Salt Beef
School
Shaving
Sins
Skiing
Slowly Does It
Spoken Word
Specialisation
Speed
Spicy Food
Stamp of Approval
Stars
Stingy
Style
Suitcases
Swans
Sweet Tooth

Tactics
Talking To Oneself
Tarzan
Taxis
Tea
Technology
Telephone Boxes
Telephones
Television Times
Temper
Terrorism
Texas
Theatre

They
Time
Timewatch

Toilet Rolls
Towels
Trains
Travel
Travel in Britain
Twiddling

United States

Vanity
Vernacular
Victory

Wanderlust
Water
We Have Ways
What Might Have
   Been
Whisky
Whistling
White City Days
White Vans
Wilson of The
   Wizard
Window Gazing
Window Shopping
Winter Sports

Xenium
Xmas
X-Rays

Yiddish
Yin and Yang

Zeal
Zeitgeist
Zucchetto

TIMED TO PERFECTION
Stan Greenberg

AARDVARK
One has to start an alphabetical book somewhere, and what could be better than with a word like this. In fact it has some relevance. When I first obtained a word processor, and not being a particularly good typist, I had a bad habit of regularly hitting the key which brought up the dictionary word check onto the screen - the first word of which was...you guessed. My wife tells me that for weeks the peace and quiet in my study would be suddenly shattered by me shouting out "Aardvark, bloody aardvark", as time and again I hit the wrong key.

ABOMINATION
According to my dictionary, an abomination is an object of detestation. It seems to me that there only used to be a few prime ones, e.g. religious heresies, sexual aberrations, and suchlike, but nowadays there are so many more. Among those on my list are: metal coat hangers; American TV talk shows; large organisations with call centres in other countries, often India; directors of companies, often the same ones as the previous item, who get millions in bonuses while their workers are laid off; hair adverts on TV; phone calls from double-glazing firms; boiled cabbage. I am sure there are many more, but these are the main ones which immediately come to mind.

ACCOLADE
I am privileged to know a number of people who have been awarded various accolades, such as MBEs, OBEs, CBEs, knighthoods and peerages. However, to someone of my interests, the greatest accolade is one that has to be won - an Olympic gold medal. I have been lucky to know a number of Olympic champions, and it was a childhood dream of mine to be the world's greatest sprinter. The nearest I was to get to that honour was to hold the gold medal of such a man. It was that won by the late Harold Abrahams (of Chariots of Fire fame) in 1924, when he became the

first Briton, indeed the first European, to take the Olympic 100m title. I was visiting his house, and in his study I began looking around the room, especially the walls, and finally asked him where IT was. When he queried what I meant, I referred to the gold medal. He said that he wasn't sure where it was, but I insisted that I see it. He dug around in a glass dish on his desk, full of paper clips, elastic bands and fluff, and drew out a very tarnished medal. I was horrified, and told him so. If I had such a trophy, I would have it on the wall with searchlights aimed at it. He pointed out that it had never really meant all that much to him, as he had received it by mail some weeks after the Games had finished, and that there had not been the razzamatazz of presenting it in the stadium in the way such things are done now. Also, and I know he meant it, he said that he thought that the American attitude of "There's only the winner, or nothing" was nonsense, as a mere few centimetres sometimes separated the winner from, say, fourth place. Nevertheless, I still think he should have given his gold medal a little more 'honour'.

ACCOUNTS

Probably my worst subject, at school, at evening classes, and also at work, was accounting. My old friend and one-time accountant, Alf Wilkins, constantly expresses amazement that someone who makes his living from figures can be so bad at 'keeping books'. The main trouble is that, basically, I have never been interested in accounts. Also I have always had the sneaking suspicion that accountants and lecturers, who make their living from the discipline, deliberately make the subject difficult for the ordinary person to understand. I used to get more than just a sympathetic groan when I stood up at club AGMs and queried the Treasurer as to why the total on one side of the balance sheet was the same as on the other. The word 'obfuscating' always comes to mind relative to balance sheets.

However, in one area of the subject I appear to have been well ahead of its practitioners. Years before the banks brought in the concept of spreading bills over monthly payments, I had introduced the idea into my own household accounts. As soon as I got married, with a home of my own, I bought a small notebook in which I listed all my main projected outgoings for the coming year. Included were mortgage repayment, electricity, gas, water, insurances, TV hire etc. I then divided that total by twelve and allocated that monthly figure from my salary to a column headed "Musts". To another column I allocated the amount given to my wife for shopping - a different 'Must'. The last column, needless to say a very meagre one at first, was headed "Available money". That was the only column we ever looked at when thinking of buying something special or having a holiday. Simplistic, no question, but in 52 years of marriage we have never been in debt. At the time, I mentioned my 'system' to another accountant friend, who had a good laugh. However, I was gratified to receive a telephone call from him a few years later, when he got married, which began "Er, Stan, remember that accounts book you keep - what exactly do you do?"

ACCURACY
In my 'business', sporting statistics, in which tenths, hundredths, and even thousandths of a second can be vital, accuracy is paramount. However, sometimes it can be said to go too far. When I was the sports editor of The Guinness Book of Records in the late 1970s, I had occasion to contact the archivist of Edinburgh Academy about two of their former pupils who jointly held the record of being the youngest Scottish Rugby Union international, both having been 17 years and 36 days of age at the time of their respective first matches. The archivist answered my enquiry, and then commented that of course they were not really equal. When I queried this, he said that our dates of birth and dates of play were quite correct, but that we had never taken account of the number of leap years - as one of the boys had one leap year less in his 17 years the record should be allocated solely to him. I was staggered and delighted by this discovery, as was the editor, Norris McWhirter, but we decided to show them both, but with a footnote

about the leap year business.

AFFAIRS
My highly imaginative and with-it daughter always thought, and I understand still does, that when I travelled abroad with BBC television I indulged in 'extra-curricular activities', i.e. that I was having affairs, as such things are quaintly referred to in certain quarters. I found her attitude rather sweet, although I regret somewhat that it was not true, as it implied the suggestion that the opposite sex was, in some way, interested in me. Unfortunately, this was never the case, as I fear I missed out when the good Lord gave out looks and stature, and I was never particularly well-off, so I would have been a non-starter anyway. I say, unfortunately, not that I ever really wanted to 'play away', but I think I would have rather liked to have had the opportunity presented, even if I would never have taken it up. (Oh yes you would! Oh no I wouldn't!).

AGEING
One of the characters in the movie Citizen Kane says, "Old age is the one disease you don't look forward to being cured of". They say, whoever 'they' are, that every age has its compensations. I suppose, if you are lucky, ease and contentment are the compensations for getting old - but only if you are lucky. As you get older, you can, if you choose, get cleverer and, more importantly, wiser, but only if you want to. However, so many people obviously seem not to want to. They retain the same ideas, beliefs, and attitudes that they had in their youth and middle years, and though they have probably seen most of those ideas fail, proved wrong, or, at best, not do any good, still stick doggedly by them.

There are some wonderful quotations about old age, and I make no apologies for including a few here. The Russian revolutionary, Leon Trotsky, said in 1935 that "Old age is the most unexpected of all things that happen to a man ". In 1712, Sir Richard Steele, a playwright, wrote that "There are so few who can grow old with a good grace". The financier, Bernard Baruch, said, when he was 85, that "Old age is always 15 years older than I am ". Lastly, I particularly like the comment by the French singer, Maurice Chevalier, who said, "I prefer old age to the alternative". The first time I really thought about getting old was when I was 35. At work I received some birthday cards which I placed on my desk. One of the typists, a pleasant young girl, came in and inquired what age I was. When I told her, she suddenly looked quite sad. When I commented that it wasn't that old, she said "Oh, yes I know, but....you're halfway there". She was obviously referring to the biblical threescore and ten, and though she didn't mean it in a nasty way of course, in fact it was rather sweet, I suppose, it preyed on my mind for weeks.

One of the problems of getting older, for males anyway, is the 'dirty old man' syndrome. Now I don't mean that in the context of what one reads in the tabloid press, but in a man's perception of himself. I have come to realise, sometimes too late, that, at the age I am now, a mildly flirtatious remark made to a young lady is taken entirely differently than when the same remark was made as, say, a 25-year-old. The problem is, of course, that I don't think of myself as old, and my attitudes to many things still tend to be the attitudes I had when I was 25.

Other than the odd lapse referred to above, I trust that I am growing old gracefully. That is more than can be said for many people of my age, and especially those in the entertainment industry. I find nothing more ludicrous than "mutton dressed up as lamb"; exemplified by ladies who plaster more and more make-up on their faces in an attempt to hide the wrinkles, and by men who dye their hair jet black while their faces remain grey (certain American politicians come to mind). Certainly, fight old age as hard as possible, particularly via exercise and diet, but I can't go along with cosmetic surgery. Sooner or later it will go to pot, and the recipient will look twice as bad as he or she might have. A few years ago I met an ageing film star/singer who had obviously had 'things done' at some point, but now he looked like something out of an early horror movie.

Some people are born old it seems, while others become old before their time, not always because of ill-health or poverty. Apparently my father always felt more comfortable with old people, and would naturally gravitate to the more elderly in a room, even when he was quite young, much to the annoyance of my mother. In my youth I knew two boys who were cousins, and looked remarkably alike. I was friendly with one of them, but found the other one rather pompous. Even as a schoolboy he would always dress and act 'old' and 'proper', and it was no surprise to learn he intended to take up the law. Some years later, near the Law Courts in the City, I happened to see the cousins walking together, my former friend dressed normally, while the other one was in his lawyer gear. I drew the attention of my companion to them and asked if he could guess at their relationship. He immediately said that they were obviously father and son, even though the older-looking one was then only about 24, and some months younger than his cousin. I shudder to think how old he looks now.

One of the main delights of getting old is to have the time, and indeed the inclination, to look back, reflect, and savour the things one has done, the people one has met, and the places one has been. So I have had a wonderful time compiling this book. Totally unconnected, recently I have also met an unusually large number of acquaintances from my past, and it has proved to be very pleasant and interesting to discuss 'old times'.

AIRPORT LOUNGES
As a former BA Executive Club Silver card holder I used to use the Club lounges around the world. They were very useful for catching up on my statistical work, with lounge facilities usually very comfortable. Also it was interesting to note one's fellow passengers. One particular occasion brings a smile. I should state categorically that I have never been unfaithful to my wife - except, as President Carter put it, in my thoughts. However, when discussing the highly

unlikely possibility that I might want to, Carole kindly gave me a special dispensation for two particular ladies. They were the actresses Racquel Welch and Cyd Charisse, two of my all-time favourites. Undoubtedly she thought she was on fairly safe ground, as it was improbable I would ever meet them, let alone anything else. However, once, while in the lounge at Heathrow, I telephoned home to remind Carole of her concession, with the news that Cyd Charisse was sitting next to me. Needless to say, I never even spoke to her, but she looked wonderful in a quiet, refined way, albeit aged about 61.

Another time, on a trip to Newcastle, I shared a lounge with playwright Harold Pinter and actor Donald Pleasance. I introduced myself to a wary Pinter, as having been a class-mate of his some 40 or so years before. He greeted me pleasantly enough, but I don't think he remembered me really. Then, some years ago, while in the lounge at Nice airport, I noticed someone whose face struck a chord. What also drew my attention was the presence of an obvious 'minder', and the fussing of the female attendant. Only after he was gone did his name come to mind - it was Jean-Marie Le Pen, the leader of France's far-right National Front party. Good thing I wasn't wearing my yarmulke.

AIRPORTS
Airports are not the usual stuff of memory, but some have stayed in my mind for one reason or another. Particularly, I recall my stay at Indira Gandhi airport, New Delhi - and it really was a stay. I had stopped off for a few days in 1991, on the way to Tokyo, so that I could visit the Taj Mahal in Agra. Boarding my flight to continue my journey to Japan, via Hong Kong, I was relaxed and happy. The plane taxied out to the runway, and then stopped there for the next 7 hours, in order to change a faulty engine. Thankfully, I was in business class, courtesy of the BBC, but if you have never experienced such a wait you can have no idea of the excruciating boredom, let alone annoyance, one suffers. Eventually the landing at Kai Tak, the old airport in Hong Kong, made me feel quite

nervous, as it seemed to be literally next door to the main city. In fact, it was.

After the 1974 Commonwealth Games in Christchurch, New Zealand, I arranged to fly back via Hawaii. First we landed at Pago Pago on the island of Tutuila in American Samoa, where there had been a tragic crash only two days before, in which a couple of people that I had been talking to in the hotel only the night before, had been killed. Sadly, that in itself would have made the place unforgettable, but also it looked exactly like I had always imagined a South Sea island was supposed to look.

My favourite airport is, undoubtedly, at Tampa, Florida. My wife, Carole, and I always hope we will be delayed there, as its layout, shops and restaurants are just what we think such facilities should be, and we have never found time drag while waiting for a flight. Also there is very little walking involved, as there is a central hub from which people movers take you to your departure point. Mind you, it has been in the business for a long time apparently, as the first ever scheduled passenger flights in the world took place between Tampa and St Petersburg, Florida in 1914. Now, not many people know that, as my old schoolmate Michael Caine purportedly says. Also Tampa is in direct contrast to Miami airport, which, as far as Carole and I are concerned, is as close to "hell on earth" as one can get.

ALTITUDE

Quite early in my athletics statistics collecting career I became aware of the effects of altitude on performances. In 1955 the Pan-American championships were held in Mexico City, and there were some quite remarkable performances in the 'explosive' events. At the time I don't remember anyone making any particular comments on why that should be. However, when the 1968 Olympic Games were awarded to that city in 1963, there was a gradually increasing furore about the expected effects of the altitude (Mexico City is 2240m 7349ft above sea level) on competitors in distance events, especially those who came from low lying countries. By then athletes from Kenya and Ethiopia had begun to make their mark on the sport, and it was realised that there was a tremendous advantage to be had if you lived and/or trained at such high altitudes. Conversely, it was going to be a tremendous disadvantage in certain events if you did not. One famous British journalist even stated, in print, that "There will be those who will die!". Happily that did not happen, but one or two top class runners were never the same again.

Actually, the effects were first brought home to me by the reaction of an office colleague, who had been on a business trip to Ethiopia just prior to the Games. He was a youngish, fairly fit, chap, and had not given any thought to the question of altitude conditions. Arriving at Addis Ababa airport (2365m 7760ft), it seems that his aeroplane had unloaded on the tarmac, and, noticing an acquaintance just ahead of him, he began running after him – only to collapse and regain consciousness some time later in the airport lounge.

I myself called in at Mexico City on the way back from New Zealand in 1974, and don't especially recall having any particular difficulty in breathing, at the age of 43, despite a rigorous sight-seeing tour. My next experience of extreme height was on Tenerife, climbing the not too difficult final few hundred feet of Pico de Teide (3719m 12,200ft). I was then over 50 but, apart from a shortage of breath from the physical exertion; I can't say that I had too much trouble. Lastly, in 2003 when I went to Peru at the age of 71, I must admit to feeling the lack of air in Cuzco (3326m 11,000ft). Of course, while there I spent some time walking around and found that I had to pace myself very carefully. The locals tell you to drink the tea they make with coca leaves, but I found the concoction so awful that I only had it twice and then just suffered – although it wasn't that bad really. By the time I reached Machu Picchu, which is some 1066m 3500ft lower than Cuzco, the altitude (still about as high as Mexico City) didn't seem to worry me very much, even though there was some pretty vigorous climbing to be done around the ruins.

TIMED TO PERFECTION
Stan Greenberg

AMBITIONS

I have been very fortunate to have achieved most of the ambitions that I had as a youth - at least those that, in reality, I had the slightest hope of realising. Thus, Olympic gold medals, Rita Hayworth, Cyd Charisse and Raquel Welch, don't really count. However, even at 84 I have a few more I would like to experience. (Actually, if the truth be known, Racquel is still among them.) They include: (a) reaching a considerably older age, but with reasonable health; (b) spending most of the winter outside Britain; (c) reducing my weight; and (d) seeing some shares get back to the value at which we bought them (though this is probably bracketed in the same category of likelihood as Miss Welch). I have always believed that a person must aim at some goals in life even if they seem unattainable at the time. To quote Robert Browning "Ah, but a man's reach should exceed his grasp, or what's a Heaven for?"

ANIMALS

Unlike most of the inhabitants of the British Isles, I don't really like animals. I have a particular dislike of dogs in general, and, when they are allowed to foul the pavement, of their owners as well. However, I must admit to fond memories of a beautiful red setter that befriended me in Manchester during WWII. Cats arouse a certain grudging respect from me, and I can recall becoming quite attached to one that my parents had. I should stress that the cats they boarded were working cats, kept to keep down the mice which inhabited the spaces between the walls and floorboards of their old house. Our cats seemed to live quite happily and healthily, on leftovers and the odd special something bought from "the catsmeat man". Of course, they also had the mice. Nowadays, of course, people spend ridiculous amounts on gourmet meals for their pets, and our local Tesco even advertises health insurance for cats and dogs - costs are higher for the latter I notice. I often wonder if their owners are as well fed, or health protected, as these pampered animals are. Our old tabbies must be spinning in their graves - in the garden by the way and not in the specialised pet cemeteries of today.

TIMED TO PERFECTION
Stan Greenberg

A cat that impressed me greatly was one that lived nearby when I was young. It was the biggest domestic cat I have ever seen, and its owner would take the great fluffy-haired thing for a walk on a leash. Most dogs avoided it like the plague, and any that approached too near were met by wild hissing, spitting and scratching claws. They never came near a second time. In fact, most people avoided it as well.

I have always considered it odd, if not a national disgrace, that, in Britain, until comparatively recently, and sometimes even now, one had the impression that children could be illtreated with impunity, but woe betide anyone hurting a dog. In fact, the early prosecutions against child abuse were taken out under laws protecting animals.

I consider it shameful that the national society protecting children does not have the same Royal patronage in its name as that of the society protecting animals. What sort of message does that give to foreigners about Britain?

ANTHEMS
One of the most moving experiences I have ever had at an athletics championships medal ceremony was when an Israeli athlete, the Russian-born immigrant Alexander Averbukh, won the European indoor pole vault title at Ghent, Belgium in February, 2000. It should be explained that Israel is allowed to compete in European title events because the Arab nations refuse to allow them to compete in the Asian ones, which would be their correct geographical milieu. At the medal ceremony the national anthem is played, and so the Hatikvah rang out. The only other times I had ever heard it played was at Jewish weddings, and so the moment was quite emotional.

ARTISTIC THINGS
Painting has never raised great passion in me, but I am of the school that knows what it likes, and what it does not. I look on art

TIMED TO PERFECTION
Stan Greenberg

from a purely aesthetic point of view, and am not swayed by its monetary value. There are paintings which are worth millions, I am told, to which I would not give house room (not that I will ever have the chance), while there are others which please me immensely. What I call the 'Botticelli' type of work, with fat little angels, and equally fat men and women sprawled everywhere, I abhor. Similarly, most modern painting not only leaves me cold, but sometimes gets me angry that anyone can make a fuss over what is to me rubbish. I know this is considered a Philistine view by followers and collectors of Picasso, Braque et al, but I can never be convinced that Cubism, Dadaism and the like is not an out and out hoax, over which the perpetrators laugh hysterically on their way to the bank. Having made one of my usual generalisations, I should say that every so often representative works of these artists/movements do catch and please my eye.

The following two quotations say everything that I feel about modern art. The first is a definition of the subject by the American cartoonist Al Capp: "A product of the untalented, sold by the unprincipled, to the utterly bewildered". Then please consider the next quote by the famous artist, and one of the prime perpetrators, Pablo Picasso, who actually said, "The world today doesn't make sense, so why should I paint pictures that do". I rest my case

However, in 1986 in Madrid I had the opportunity to see the huge painting by Picasso named *Guernica*. Housed in a separate building near to the Prado, the exhibit also comprises preliminary drawings of the figures used in the painting, which help introduce you to the main work. But nothing can prepare you for *Guernica* itself. It is awe-inspiring, weird, horrific and powerful. I didn't like it, but I doubt that I will ever forget it. Perhaps that is what the artist intended. In the Prado itself, there is a magnificent collection of the Spanish masters, and I particularly liked the works of El Greco, Goya and Velazquez. The latter's *Las Meninas* still lingers in my mind.

While I am out on a limb giving my opinions of some of the world's

TIMED TO PERFECTION
Stan Greenberg

greatest treasures, I might as well go all the way. Perhaps the most famous painting of all is *La Gioconda* (better known as the *Mona Lisa*) by Leonardo da Vinci. It hangs in the Louvre, in Paris, and draws thousands every day. It is undoubtedly a marvellous piece of art, but frankly I wondered what all the fuss was about. One painting by the same artist that I do like, albeit I have only seen it in photographs, is *The Last Supper*. Twice I have tried to see it in the flesh, so to speak, in the church of Santa Maria delle Grazie, in Milan, but both times I tried, after a long walk, I found the building was closed. I had the same frustration, on some five occasions, when I tried to view the ceiling of the Sistine Chapel in Rome. I usually went there on a Monday, after a week-end's work at an athletics meeting, but invariably it was closed. It finally got through to me that the Chapel was not open at all on Mondays. Eventually, after years of trying, I made it, and was not disappointed. The modern cleaning and restoration work had just started, and one could compare the older, dirtier, parts with the newly cleaned area. Michelangelo would surely have been pleased with what the restorers have done. For the first time for hundreds of years the glorious colours can be seen, and the finished ceiling must surely overwhelm visitors even more than it had done before. I sat for a long time staring up, trying to take in the beauty and power of that place. How could the artist have created it, lying on his back only a couple of feet away from his work (or looking up from a standing position, as the current theory suggests), with little opportunity to actually see what he was doing overall. Now there is one of the world's wonders.

The same artist's sculpture of *Pieta*, in St Peter's, in Rome, was most moving, while his tremendous statue of *David*, in Florence, really took my breath away. Another wonder, even more monumental, this time by Bernini, is the Piazza of St Peter's, and specifically the remarkable semi-circular colonnades. The precision of the pillars is such that if one stands in a specially marked spot the three rows become one. The only structure to compare with this, that I have seen, are the pillars in the Temple of Karnak, in Luxor, Egypt. There, the vast columns are perfectly set in line, and an engineer, in our party of tourists, said that even today, with modern construction equipment and scientific skills, his colleagues would have trouble matching the precision of the ancient builders. I think it does modern man good, to see what our ancestors created without any of our amenities.

ATHLETICS (Competing)

When the good Lord gave out attributes I have always felt that I was short-changed somewhat. But one thing he did give me was speed. I was always able to run that little bit faster than most, and often it stood me in good stead. In one area of my life it meant I could get away from bullies and other tormentors, while in another area it meant that I could excel in something. That something was sport, and from an early age I was able to make my mark in school sports, races in the street, a winger at football, and a fielder in cricket. Being the youngest in my class at school - my July birthday inevitably resulted in that situation - stopped me from winning much in the school sports. However, usually I was one of the highest points scorers for my House. In my last year I was chosen to represent the school at the then-named Public School Sports at Motspur Park in April 1947. Unfortunately, I didn't do well, but, at least, I had run on one of the best cinder tracks in the country.

Two years later I captained a team from Lever Brothers, at the National Association of Boys Clubs championships at Chiswick. The company had such a large number of young staff then that it had its own affiliated club. I ran in the 220 yards event, and in my heat there was a youngster in the lane outside mine who had reportedly broken the British junior record just weeks before. When the race started he shot away and probably doubled the distance of the stagger by the end. His name was Derek Johnson, then only 16, and he was to win an Olympic silver medal over 800m in 1956. At that meeting, I had a tall youth in my team who ran the mile. He came up to the rest of us and said that his father, a pharmacist, had given him something that would give an extra boost to your energy. He produced a small bag of white powder. (In the light of current

TIMED TO PERFECTION
Stan Greenberg

sporting revelations I should point out that this was in 1949). We all tried a little and found it incredibly, and sickly, sweet. The rest of us declined any more, so my miler gulped down the lot. Incidentally, it was glucose, something we had never heard of in those days. He then made the major error, on a very hot day, of washing it down with lemonade. A while later in his mile race he fell to the track and was disgustingly ill.

Lest I give the idea that I never won anything, let me recount the story of my great triumph at a Butlins holiday camp. I was about 18 and had entered the camp sports at the urging of my friends. When I turned up for my event, which was approximately 300 yards around a rough, very rough, circular track marked off on extremely bumpy grass, I was horrified to see two or three other competitors wearing well-known club tracksuits and running spikes. I was dressed in a thin vest, PT shorts and plimsolls. As we got to our marks, not in lanes, they looked immaculate and very professional, while I must have looked a real novice. When the gun was fired I went off like the proverbial rocket and reached the first turn (more a corner really) well in the lead. Not daring to slacken I gave it everything I had all the way, and was paying the price as I approached the line. Apparently I was well ahead, as, despite their fine kit, the others were not very good. However, thinking they were close, I threw myself through the finishing tape, and felt a sharp pain around my chest as I fell to the ground. As my friends gathered round to cheer and help me up, one of the girls in the party let out a scream and pointed to my chest. I looked down and blood was pouring through my torn vest. I was too exhausted to appreciate what was wrong, but I realised that I was in some sort of trouble. The first thing that came to mind was that I had burst a lung or something. It transpired that the organisers of the sports had been unable to find ordinary finishing tape, so they had used thin parcel string. To compound the felony, the people holding the string had not let go immediately, so that in running into it, it had cut deep into my body, leaving a long weal right across my chest, cutting my vest and my skin like a knife. I was rushed to the medical section, where they quickly cleaned and bandaged me up, in time to return for the prize-giving. My prize was a very nice cigarette lighter, and though I have never smoked, I kept that lighter for years. One surprising side effect of my injury was that it made me a camp celebrity, and I was very gratified by the interest in my welfare shown by many young ladies that week. The scar remained for a long time, but eventually faded.

The statistics and history of the sport later became my abiding hobby, much to the chagrin of my father, who thought that I was wasting far too much time and energy on it. One of the few regrets I have in life is that he didn't live to see me make my living from my hobby. I cover this aspect further under 'Television'.

ATHLETICS (Watching)
One of the more horrendous athletic occasions I can remember was at the 1978 European Championships in Prague. Not the place itself, as Prague is one of my favourite places in Europe, but due to the circumstances that surrounded that particular six days at the end of August/ beginning of September. Firstly, the weather was basically terrible, often with freezing temperatures. The TV positions were set up in such a way that necessitated the commentary team sitting on cold, hard, stone steps. On the first day I was so cold that I found it almost impossible to hold my pen, let alone try to write with it. Cliff Morgan, the former Welsh Rugby player and at that time a BBC executive, who was with us on the trip, disappeared for a time, and when he returned he had blow-up cushions, blankets and bottles of something warming for each of us - a true lifesaver. To compound the 'injury', when we got back to our hotel after a long, hard, hungry day, we found that the kitchens were closed and no food was available. With the media close to revolution this state of affairs was quickly remedied by one of the waiters - who probably retired on the gratuities he received from the grateful members of the press. But the highlight of the trip was when the stadium broke! Somehow, the main electricity cable to the stadium went out of action, and nothing worked. All the lights went out. No indicator or results boards lit up. The starter's gun wouldn't

fire. No announcements could be made over the tannoy system. The TV monitors were blank, and all telephone and radio links went offline. As I say, the stadium broke. To be fair, it didn't last too long, but for about 30 minutes all we could do was sit there and wait.

You would not think that watching athletics could be very dangerous, would you. However, in Stockholm at the 1958 European Championships - one of Britain's most successful international engagements - I nearly suffered a serious injury. Sitting with other British fans in the middle of the last row of the back straight, I had my back against a brick wall, in which there was a porthole-like opening near me. We had expected that our team would do well, and hoped for an early success, which always sparks a team off. The first final on that first day was the 20km walk, an event contested outside on the roads, but finishing in the stadium. Now my athletics friends will tell you that I am not a walking event fan, but as the walkers approached the stadium for the finish, I looked out of my porthole and saw that our man, Stan Vickers, was well ahead, and seemed certain to win. I was so excited that I leapt up and down and ended up thudding my head back hard against the wall - and spent the next ten minutes in a daze, and the rest of the afternoon with a terrible headache.

For an athletics fan there is nothing like the annual Weltklasse meeting in Zurich. It has the largest budget of any one-day meet in the world, and the 'cast list' reflects that money. The athletes used to be put up at the InterContinental hotel - it was formerly, i.e. in my day, the Nova Park - about 200m from the track. The evening before the meet, the scene in the hotel lobby is one out of the most ardent fan's wildest dream. Wall-to-wall Olympic medalists, world record holders and past greats. The pens of local autograph hunters must run dry before they get everyone. I was lucky enough to go to the Weltklasse a dozen times, and was never less than overawed by that lobby extravaganza. It was in the coffee shop there that I first met Seb Coe, the morning after his 1500m record of 3min 32.1sec in 1979, when he came over and asked me, then a stranger, if I would mind if he sat at my table. The next time I spoke to him was in the following year, outside the Moscow Olympic stadium, soon after his defeat in the 800m. I doubt if he recognised me, as I congratulated him on his run. He looked at me sharply, perhaps thinking I was being sarcastic, but I explained that I thought he had run a remarkable, albeit rather stupid, race, and had still got the silver medal - and that couldn't be totally bad. He seemed to realise that I meant what I said, smiled, and thanked me, before getting into the athletes' bus. That seemed to be the start of a firm, friendship with him and his father/coach, Peter.

ATHLETICS (Personal Statistics)
No, don't worry; this isn't about my actual physical achievements, i.e. times and distances, which were not that good anyway. This is a quick compilation of some of the terrific things I have been privileged to see in over 60 years of watching the sport. I have seen - and I do mean seen, and not just been present on the occasion - 325 world athletics records, indoors and out, in nearly all events. (Additionally, I have witnessed about 10 swimming records and two weightlifting ones). I have attended 8 full Olympic Games (plus one day at another one); 10 Commonwealth Games; 12 World Athletics Championships; 16 European Champs; 11 World Indoor Champs; 26 European Indoor Champs; 8 World Athletics Cups; 17 European Athletics Cups; and lastly, but by no means least, over 50 AAA Championships. Without intending to boast (Oh, yes I am) there can't be too many people able to match that list of major meetings, and records.

ATTITUDE
The way you look at things has an important bearing on the way you consider life. What I am getting at can best be summed up in the following way. The optimist sees a glass of water half full; the pessimist sees the same glass of water half empty; the opportunist sees the same glass of water as something with which to quench his thirst. I think that most of my life I have been an opportunist.

AUGUST 1

This day in 1948 was when I first began collecting and collating statistics on the sport of athletics. It was the day after my first visit to an Olympic Games, held at Wembley that year, and immediately I had realised that to fully enjoy this new-found sport I needed to learn as much as possible about it and its stars. So began a pastime that has led to much greater involvement with governing bodies, television and writing. Sixty-four years on I am still involved, and, God willing, will continue as long as I am able. During those years I have been privileged to become well-known in the sport, both at home and around the world, and I am proud of the reputation that I have gained for expertise and accuracy. When I first started, there were not many people as interested as I was. However, in 1950 the ATFS (Association of Track and Field Statisticians) was formed to collate data worldwide. Eight years later I helped set up the NUTS (National Union of Track Statisticians) in Britain, and over the years various national and international groups of like-minded people have been formed. Today, in virtually every country in the world, and there are a lot more countries now than there used to be, there is at least one statistician beavering away collecting data on his nation's athletic performances.

AUTHORITY

The former Soviet Union was one of the most authoritarian regimes ever, so it is fitting that the following story emanates from there. I went to the 1980 Moscow Olympic Games, and fully expected to have great difficulty in obtaining the various data and bits of paper that I required to successfully perform my work for the BBC. The prime items that I was going to need were the start lists, i.e. the names of competitors in each heat or round of the event listed, in lane order, and their competition numbers. Ideally, these should always be available to athletes, coaches and journalists at least 24 hours before the competition, but very often this does not

TIMED TO PERFECTION
Stan Greenberg

happen. At an Olympics, with as many as ten heats of the 100m (with 8 athletes in each) in the first round alone, it is vital to get them as soon as possible.

With this in mind, I went to the press section of the athletics stadium a couple of days prior to the start of the programme, to make myself known to the staff, and try and find out how things were going to work. To overcome the obvious language problems of visitors from many countries, the Soviet organisers had brought in top-class graduates in all sorts of disciplines, from all over the country, if they could speak another language. Thus, the young man I first spoke to was an architectural student from the Ukraine, who had little or no knowledge of the sport, but who spoke excellent Englsh, and French as well. Very polite he tried to be helpful within the realms of what he perceived his job to be. Specifically, I began asking about the availability of start lists, and initially I had to explain to him exactly what they were. When I implied that I was expecting him to produce them soon, he shook his head and said that it was not his responsibility, but that of another colleague somewhere hidden in the offices behind. I explained that being English I was asking him nicely, but that soon the French and Italian journalists would be arriving, and that they would not be so polite, and would likely tear the place, and him, apart if the lists were not made available. I added a comment that "you know what they are like". I am sure that he didn't, probably never having met any foreigners before anyway, but he paled somewhat, and murmured that he would go and try to find out something. I suggested that in his position on the press desk he should "exercise his authority" – a concept that I am certain he had never contemplated before in his young life. Muttering to himself he went off.

After about 30 minutes, he reappeared, a little flustered and red-faced, but undoubtedly pleased with himself as he waved a few pieces of paper. Looking triumphant he handed me the first few start lists. Pulling himself to his full height, he stated, very proudly, that "I exerted my authority". It may well be that I created a monster, but whatever lists or results I needed for the period of the Games, that lad got them for me well in time. It was probably the best service that I have ever had at a major championships, and I often wonder what he went on to later in his life with that new-found ability to "exercise his authority". I only hope it didn't get him into trouble.

BABIES
One often hears young couples say that they intend to wait for three years, in my day usually after marriage, before having babies. Why three years particularly? What exactly is the mystique of 36 months? It would appear that nearly all young couples arrive at the same decision, and I find it rather puzzling. There is probably a very sound reason, although frankly it eludes me, to decide on three years instead of two or four, or even five. When I mentioned it to a relative, she said that she found it much easier to understand, as she had a sister who always bought a pound and a half of tomatoes at a time. Never one pound or two pounds, but always a pound and a half. Her reaction was that if someone was that strange, then nothing surprised her.

My wife and I made the same decision when we got married, but I don't really remember why. However, within a year or so I found that Carole was getting broody whenever we visited friends or relatives who had children, and often became quite upset. So we decided that fashion could go hang and we wouldn't wait any longer. After a few months nothing had happened and she became convinced that there was something wrong. To calm her I agreed that we should visit our doctor. Initially he showed sympathy and concern, noting that there were tests and suchlike which he could do to see that everything was okay with both of us. He then began to take notes and asked how long we had been 'trying'. When Carole replied that it was about three to four months he nearly exploded, and said that when it was three to four years then he would show some interest, and practically threw us out of his surgery. When I mentioned the episode to an older colleague at the office I got much more sympathy and indeed help. He said that we were probably getting too intense and would have better success if we relaxed more. He suggested getting both of us slightly tipsy. It so happens that neither Carole nor I are big drinkers, but our second anniversary was due. So I bought tickets for the Mermaid Theatre (where by fortunate circumstance the play was a rather bawdy Elizabethan comedy), and fixed up a meal in the theatre restaurant afterwards. I also made sure that we had a particularly good bottle of wine. Forty-two weeks later our first child (Karen) was born. It was a little short of the planned three years but we didn't mind really.

Unusually, I was able to pinpoint the conception of our second child (Keith) just as accurately. One of the first long drives that we made in our 'new' car was to the Welsh Games in Cardiff in the late summer of 1965. This was before the Severn Bridge was open, and we had to drive via Gloucester and round the Severn estuary. We stopped for the night at a pleasant inn at Newnham-on-Severn, where we had an enjoyable meal, followed by a romantic walk in the soft, summer evening air. A totally different occasion from the previous time, but happily it had the same effect.

BACKACHE
It is pure coincidence that this item follows on from the previous one, but they are very much connected. I was very active and sporting in my youth, and had never suffered any undue muscular problems. But both times my wife's pregnancy affected my back badly. No, it wasn't exactly sympathy pains, but something similar. In the early sixties there was the 'Thalidomide scare' - a period when horrifying abnormalities were found in babies whose mothers had been given the sedative drug. Although we were certain that Carole had not taken it, the frequent media references to, and pictures of, the poor malformed children weighed heavily on both our minds. I particularly worried about the effect of such a birth on Carole, and it became something of an obsession. Finally something gave, and it was my back. About 12 weeks prior to

TIMED TO PERFECTION
Stan Greenberg

Karen's birth, I undressed for bed one night. The only thing that I remember doing that could have had any bad effect was that I removed my shoes in a lazy manner, just bending over from the waist and pulling them off.

The following morning I awoke, apparently paralysed from the chest down, unable to move my back or legs. In her condition Carole couldn't help me, except to call the doctor. When he came he looked grave, and, surprisingly, suggested calling an osteopath. I didn't know what that was then but would have agreed to anything. When the gentleman arrived he was a very jolly character, with a breezy manner. "Let's see what's wrong shall we - now out of bed". Exasperatedly I said I couldn't move, to which he replied, "Come now, out you get", and, grabbing hold of me rolled me off the bed. I crashed to the floor and lay there dazed, wondering how to get away from this lunatic. However, he apologised, and explained that often people were suffering from hysterical paralysis, and by doing what he had done they would usually put out their arms and legs to prevent falling - thereby affecting a cure. He realised that that was not my case, and rolling me over on my front, proceeded to use what I can only call a horse syringe. He injected something bubbly into my back; it seemed to a depth of two or three feet. After a minute or so he grasped my lower back in both hands and twisted. I felt something give, and suddenly I could move my legs, in fact was able to climb, slowly, back into bed. A few days later I was back at work. A friend who had a similar problem was referred to a hospital by his doctor, and ended up in a plaster cast for about eight months. However, the business left me with a weakness in my back, which every now and again would manifest itself when I was under any stress. Some people have headaches, stomach pains or throat infections under such conditions - my Achilles heel was my back.

Remarkably, almost exactly the same period before my son was born, it happened again. This time I was at work, at lunchtime, alone, when I stood up and suddenly locked. With great difficulty, and pain, I got into the corridor. Nobody was about. Holding to

TIMED TO PERFECTION
Stan Greenberg

doorknobs and window ledges I somehow reached the lift area where someone helped me down to the medical department. I can recall the excitement which my condition engendered, with the nurse and doctor calling their colleagues to come and look at my back - which apparently was spasming quite spectacularly. I was given some pills to relax me and then they arranged for a company car to take me home. As I had to remain in a prone position, the only car which was suitable was the Chairman's Austin Princess. I wish I had been more conscious of the effect the arrival of that car must have had on my neighbours in our small, narrow, suburban road. At home, I lay on the dismantled top of a coffee table, placed on the bed, for three days before I could get up. When I did, I literally screamed, as the bones of my hips were so tender from lying on the wood. In the excitement, nobody had noticed that I was lying just on a thin sheet, laid on the wood, instead of a blanket.

Ever since, my back has given me trouble on and off, until now, at a fairly advanced age, it is something that I live with day to day, which only the occasional visit to an osteopath, not that original one, relieves. Most upsetting was that the problem seriously curtailed my sporting activities, before ending them altogether.

However, the most remarkable treatment that I have had was on a trip to Bangkok. No, it is not going to be that sort of story! Actually, I was visiting a local temple complex, and had come to one edifice which was adorned with small sculptures of what appeared to be ancient physiotherapists at work. Standing there, looking up at the walls, I was approached by one of the elderly monks, who said that it was obvious that I had a problem and that he could help. The tourist guide told me that these people were experts at massage, and recommended that I try it. With some trepidation I arranged for the chap to come to my hotel room that evening and do his worst. By the time he was due I was having second thoughts, but when he arrived he seemed harmless enough. I lay on the bed, very tense as you can imagine, just in my Marks and Spencer pants, and he went to work, with amazingly strong hands and fingers for a man of his age. It was incredible. For about an hour he kneaded, twisted, pulled and massaged virtually every muscle and bone in my body. As well as the obvious neck, back, shoulders, arms and legs, he also dealt with every finger and toe. At the end I was so loose and relaxed that I could hardly stand, and gladly paid over what seemed to be a very small fee for the amount of time, and the expertise involved. I awoke the next morning after the most relaxed sleep I think I had ever had. I wanted to tell people about the experience, but chickened out when I realised how implausible it sounded, and might cause them to question my reasons for having a complete stranger in my room, at night, in Bangkok - and what's worse, a man. So this is the first time I have mentioned it outside my family.

BADGES
There was one occasion abroad when I really did think I was going to get involved in something 'heavy'. It was during a BBC trip to Minsk, for the USA v USSR athletics match in 1973. On the day prior to the meet I was at the stadium watching the teams training, when a Russian TV man I knew slightly, motioned me to one side, and in a conspiratorial way asked me to come and meet a colleague of his. He led the way to a room under the main stand, being very careful, I noted, that we were not seen. Then in came an officious-looking gentleman, rather better dressed than the norm, holding a bulging briefcase. I wondered whether this was something to do with illegal currency or smuggling -and I seriously thought about making a run for it. Then the new man smiled broadly, introduced himself as a senior official in Soviet TV, and asked if I had any badges to swap. As I tried to hide my relief, he opened that briefcase to reveal sheets of paper on which were pinned thousands, literally, of Soviet pins and badges. It turned out that he was a major collector, and had seen the opportunity to obtain some rare foreign items. The secrecy was so that none of his colleagues would get the get the same idea. Gladly I gave him the few BBC and British team badges that I happened to have with me, and left one Soviet citizen with kinder thoughts towards Britain than perhaps he had held before.

TIMED TO PERFECTION
Stan Greenberg

BAGEL

Mainly through American influence the bagel has become quite common in baker's shops and restaurants around the world. I remember when, it seemed to me, that the only place you could buy, what was then pronounced as "a biegel", was from a little old lady in Petticoat Lane, London, who sold them for a farthing each from a large hessian sack, unhygienically stood on the pavement. Whatever, they had a wonderful taste, unfortunately not matched by the modern product. Also, in those far off days, you could only get a plain bagel, whereas, today, they come in all sorts of flavours and colours – not necessarily an improvement I think. Recently, at an airport bagel joint, I noted a fine piece of philosophy exhibited in a notice on a wall. It stated:

> As you go through life,
> Whatever your goal,
> Keep your eye on the bagel,
> And not on the hole.

BALLOONS

One of my greatest professional successes, when I was with the GLC Transportation library, came in connection with balloons. Not like those at a party, but big, really big, ones. In the 1970s, the media seemed to publish quite a lot of pieces, some trivial but intriguing, about the possibility of bringing back large Zeppelin-type balloons for commercial purposes, especially for the transport of goods between and within cities. The fire problems of the early part of the 20th century had been solved with the introduction of non-flammable helium gas, and various experts could see a future for them in our current traffic-jammed environment. Anyway, personally I found the articles interesting, and I made up a file. Came the day that a question was asked by a member of the Greater London Council about just such a possible development in London - probably asked more as a chance to catch out the hard-working planners and engineers, than for any serious reason. Thus, at the lunch break I received a worried visit from a senior planner asking me if it was possible to find out anything, urgently, about this weird item that had been raised, of which his staff virtually had no knowledge. I produced my fat little file and suggested that he read it over lunch. His face was a picture, and the following day it seemed that everybody in the building knew of my 'brilliant' stroke. It raised my status, in certain important quarters, to a remarkable degree, and I found that I was much more in demand in giving assistance to the senior planning staff.

BANKS

Happily, I have had very little to do with banks, other than retaining a current account with one or other over the years. The awful investment decisions, and the eventual calamitous results of those decisions, by some of the major banks in recent times, confirms me in my belief that it is better not to have more dealings with them than necessary. The fact that they rarely do anything of benefit for their customers, until forced to by the Government, or their competitors, merely reinforces my feelings.

I remember the time my father was asked to call on his bank manager. Dad was not a very good businessman, but had always provided adequately for his family. He never took risks, and lived by the dictum, 'save something for a rainy day'. This rule of life came to his rescue towards the end of his life when his earning capacity virtually disappeared. However, this story was set in the 1950s when his business was fairly sound, and the phone message from the bank upset him terribly. What could be wrong? He always kept a decent sum in the bank (for the rainy day). He didn't have an overdraft - he didn't believe in them. Worried out of his mind he asked me to go with him. We duly arrived at the bank premises and were ushered into the recently appointed manager, who greeted Dad warmly. After a few pleasantries, during which Dad grew more and more agitated, the manager finally broached the momentous matter of Dad's financial affairs. He had been checking on the bank's old customers, and did Mr Greenberg realise that in the thirty or so years he had had an account with them he, a successful businessman (sic), had never borrowed money from them. The bank manager looked incredulous. Dad looked bewildered. I was bemused. How could we explain to the poor man that, contrary to everything he had been taught in accountancy and banking studies, men like my father believed that if you don't have the money then you don't spend it. You most certainly don't borrow it.

Two totally different financial philosophies were clashing head-on. They eventually agreed to differ, and Dad never had a meeting with a bank manager again. He had, undoubtedly, an out-of-date, indeed old-fashioned, attitude to money, but it is one which I have kept to all my life, and I have never had any financial problems either. If we couldn't afford it then we never had it until we saved up for it. The one and only exception to that, and I think you will agree it is a rather special one, was with a house mortgage - and I paid that off as quickly as I could. I know accountants will shudder, or indeed laugh, but I honestly don't think I have ever had a sleepless night because of my financial situation.

As a corollary to the above, I remember that soon after we returned from our honeymoon, my parents came over to be shown round our new house. At one point Dad and I were in the garden alone, and he asked me how things were financially. I said that things were very tight, having had to buy so much, and that my savings were virtually at rock bottom. Horror-struck, Dad exclaimed, "But what about for a rainy day?". I tried to explain that this was my rainiest day ever, but I don't think he was convinced.

BARMITZVAH
In the Jewish religion a boy is regarded as a man - in religious ritual only - on reaching the age of thirteen. Normally, after his 'performance' in the synagogue, this is celebrated by a gathering of family and friends at a party. In recent years, this aspect of what is really a matter of religion has got totally out of hand, and some of the celebrations border on the obscene in terms of cost and ostentation. Now my attitude to this could be attributed to sour grapes on my part, as I missed out on any bash. My barmitzvah occurred during the war, and at very short notice - due to the

bombing - was transferred to Manchester. So it was that the only family in attendance were my grandparents.

When my son, Keith, came of age, my wife and I 'joined the parade' and arranged, by our standards, a big affair at a smart hall, with 200 guests. It cost us more than was really sensible, given our circumstances, but, what the hell, it was a terrific occasion, that some of our guests still talk about.

BATTERED WIVES (AND HUSBANDS)

I get very annoyed when I hear of men hitting their wives, and nearly as annoyed with the wives for staying with the men who do this. I would never dream of striking my wife, and never have. However, I claim to have been a battered husband. Soon after we were married, before the children came, we had not been out for a considerable time, due to our lack of finances and also due to poor quality cinema and theatre fare. One Saturday evening I proposed that we go to the West End to see a particular film we had been waiting for. It was late autumn, and the weather was diabolical, and Carole protested that she didn't want to go out in the wind and rain - we didn't have a car in those days. Finally, I persuaded her to come, and we struggled to the local bus stop and froze until the bus came. Tempers were somewhat frayed, I suppose, at least on one side. Halfway to town, ironically opposite the Whittington Hospital, I suddenly noticed from the evening newspaper I was reading that I had made a bad mistake, and that the film we were hoping to see wasn't on until the following week - and also that there was nothing else Carole would want to see. Nervously, I handed her the newspaper, and explained the situation, while gazing out of the window at the rain pouring down. Suddenly, I was struck repeatedly on the head with a rolled up newspaper, by a screaming 'banshee', who made it clear that she hadn't wanted to go out anyway. We got off the bus, and, as we crossed the road, to get one back home, I noticed that the other passengers were glued to the windows to watch any further entertainment. Happily, nothing similar has occurred since, but thereafter I did check cinema and theatre listings very carefully.

TIMED TO PERFECTION
Stan Greenberg

BATTERIES

Looking around my house, I realised just how many small batteries we use in this day and age. TV remotes, VCR controls, tape recorders, portable radios, smoke alarms, torches, pocket calculators, alarm clocks, stove lighters, etc, everything seems to need them. Happily they are easily obtainable, although somewhat expensive. It made me think back to my youth, in the late 1930s, when it was my job to take the acid-filled glass accumulator battery, which was used to power our wireless set in those days, around to the corner shop to be recharged. It was incredibly heavy, and I would struggle there with the old one, and then struggle home with a charged up replacement. Now, that was a battery – the only thing to compare with it today is probably your car battery.

BEAUTY

"Beauty is altogether in the eye of the beholder" - is a famous quotation by an almost totally unknown author, Margaret Hungerford. However, it is so very true. I have always had my own idea of what is beautiful, and what is not. When it concerns women, then I seem to be going against the general grain. The consensus today seems to be that blondes are best, but all the truly beautiful women that I can think of, have, without exception, been dark. I concede that many blondes are/have been highly attractive, sexy and exciting, but when it comes to out-and-out, knockout gorgeous, as far as I am concerned, it always comes back to the brunettes, and perhaps the occasional redhead. My mind goes immediately to Hedy Lamarr, Cyd Charisse, Raquel Welch, Rita Hayworth, Sophia Loren, Claudia Cardinale, Gina Lollobrigida, Elizabeth Taylor, and Maureen O'Hara. Now, I'll be the first to admit that it is/was not just the colour of their hair that caught my eye, but it was certainly one of the major things.

BEDROOMS

Some months before we were married, Carole come to my parent's house after work one evening. Needless to say, we had things to talk about that we didn't want others to hear, but Mum and

TIMED TO PERFECTION
Stan Greenberg

Dad wouldn't take the hint and leave us alone. So I suggested that we go up to my bedroom. This we did, but for propriety's sake left the door open. We were sitting on the bed merely talking - honest - when my father suddenly appeared at the doorway wishing us goodnight. We both leapt to our feet in fright, and it must have seemed, guiltily. My father was quite a big, heavy man, but was very light-footed, and I had never realised before that he did move remarkably quietly. Highly embarrassed, I suggested to him and my mother that in future they might give a little warning of some kind, not that we were doing anything that we were ashamed of, but that such sudden manifestations were something of a shock. The following week, when Carole and I were upstairs again - still only talking - there was a loud banging and coughing downstairs, followed by the sound of heavy, very heavy, footsteps on the stairs. Dad had taken my complaint to heart and really made sure that we heard him coming. When he appeared at the doorway, this time we really were rolling about the bed, curled up with hysterical laughter.

One year, on holiday in Tenerife, we were awakened by the most alarming noises outside our bedroom. When I opened the door, the corridor was filled with bleary-eyed guests discussing the disturbance. It seems that a drunken Norwegian had misplaced his very attractive wife, and had decided that she was being unfaithful to him in the room next to ours. He had knocked on the door, and not getting an answer, he had tried to break it down using the heavy metal wastebin/ashtray that stood next to the lift. Having smashed part of the door in, he reacted to cries from other guests by throwing the bin the length of the corridor, and ran out shouting wildly. We all stood there gazing at the damaged door, which slowly opened to reveal an elderly, timid, English couple, in their late sixties at least, who fearfully asked what was going on. The Norwegian man was eventually apprehended by the police and charged. The whole business left me wondering if the little old lady ever asked her husband why the man had thought it was he who was with his wife. No doubt he would have felt quite proud of the accusation.

BELLS

"And therefore never send to know for whom the bell tolls; it tolls for thee." In *The Hunchback of Notre Dame*, Quasimodo goes on quite a bit about "The bells, the bells." I have a certain sympathy with his point of view. The first time I visited Cologne, I stayed in the hotel just across the road from the famous cathedral, which initially I thought was a terrific plus. However, on the first morning, a Sunday, I was awakened by an incredible cacophony, as the cathedral bells were rung. It seemed that they were in the room with me, and it reminded me of a similar scene in the film Genevieve. Apparently, one of the Cologne bells is among the heaviest (25 tons) swinging bells in the world still in use, but that piece of information didn't make me feel any better at the time.

The largest bell I have ever seen is the Tsar Kolokol, which stands in the grounds of the Kremlin, in Moscow. It was cracked soon after it was cast, and is now an unrung tourist attraction. It stands 6.14m *20ft* high, is 6.60m *22ft* in diameter, and weighs a record 193 tons *196,000kg*. When I was in Beijing, I took the opportunity to ring one of those 'temple' bells, which are struck with a swinging wooden boom. It was in the gardens of the Lama Temple, famous for the enormous sandalwood carving of the Buddha, and which, to my surprise, had a *Guinness Book of Records* plaque on the post outside. Anyway, for a small charge I was invited to 'have a go' at the bell. My first try was rather half-hearted, as I was somewhat self-conscious, but, at the urging of the old chap in charge, I gave it a more powerful swing, and was rewarded with a very satisfying sound.

BEVERAGES

I have never drunk coffee in my life. This statement should be slightly amended in that I did drink it once, and then only a very small quantity, but found it so unpleasant that I never repeated the experiment. My earliest recollection of the drink was of the time when people used to have something out of what I thought was a sauce bottle. It was called, I believe, Camp coffee, and was a thick black liquid to which hot water was added. As a child, even if they

TIMED TO PERFECTION
Stan Greenberg

had allowed me to, I would never have drunk that. With the advent of war, or more properly, the advent of the GIs, coffee became much more prevalent in Britain, but I remained faithful to tea. When I went to work in 1947, coffee was available widely, and indeed had become the 'in' drink, but not for me. My one aberration, in a lifetime of utter constancy, occurred at an office do. It was my first time at such a grand occasion, and I was quite nervous. The dinner was held at a top London hotel, and I was dressed in my best suit - in fact my only suit - and on my best behaviour. I had not been to many such occasions in my 16 years, and I was eager not to show it. I spent a long time eyeing all the laid-out cutlery so that I would not make a fool of myself and use the wrong knife or fork. Also I hid my shyness as best I could when I found that the seating was arranged in a boy-girl-boy-girl arrangement, and made an effort at smart conversation. By the end of the meal I was feeling quite pleased with myself. Yes, I had acted very grown up and sophisticated, and surely none of the others would have realised that I was unaccustomed to this luxury. Then, came the coffee. I truly believe that up to that time I had never actually seen 'modern' coffee being served. My parents were primarily devotees of tea - I sometimes thought that my mother was a priestess of the cult considering the amount that she consumed. So when I saw the waitress advancing around the table holding two glass pots, my life flashed before my eyes. Then she was there, asking, "White or black, sir?". I looked at the two pots, and didn't like the look of the one with black stuff in it, and said, "White, thank you". To my surprise she began pouring the black liquid, so I quickly stopped her, and pointing at the other pot said, "No, the white please". After a moment's silence the table erupted into hearty laughter, with everyone saying how funny I was. The waitress continued pouring the black stuff, and then added some of the white. Covering my confusion by joining in the laughter, I wondered what on earth I had said or done. I tried the odd coloured stuff in the cup, added sugar, then more sugar, but still found it awful, and left it. It was not till much later that I learnt the truth. I had thought that the white coffee was going to be more pleasant than the black coffee.

TIMED TO PERFECTION
Stan Greenberg

As a youngster, one of my great treats was to be taken to a Lyons corner house in the West End for tea. I was usually taken there by my mother or an aunt on birthdays and suchlike. It was very grand - to my eyes - and made me feel very important. One of the things that fascinated me then was the presence of a tea-room orchestra. Such a group invariably consisted of a number of elderly ladies, playing the piano, violins and perhaps a harp. They played in the background while people were eating and drinking. A veritable Palm Court orchestra. The leader usually spent half her time nodding, bowing and smiling at acquaintances and newcomers, and this I found very amusing. In more recent times I have been taken back to those days by the appearance of the comedy duo, Hinge and Bracket, on television. They completely epitomize the sort of orchestra ladies I remember.

BICYCLING
Perhaps the first thing I really had a passion for was a bicycle. Most of my friends had one, but a combination of lack of the wherewithal, and an irrational fear of their young son hurting himself, stopped my parents getting me one. I learnt to ride by paying people a penny a time to use their machines. There was a certain poetic justice to it as I usually used their own money, which I had won from them playing marbles. I was exceptionally good at the game, and supplemented my pocket-money that way.

I finally got a bike when I was evacuated to Kings Lynn, Norfolk. I had just celebrated my thirteenth birthday, and had expected one as a present. But my parents just could not afford one then. Eventually, I found a second-hand machine for sale in the town and my father sent me the money. It was a pre-War machine, very heavy and old-fashioned, but I loved that bike, and was rarely off it. Suddenly the open road beckoned, and every weekend I would cycle to one of the many pleasant spots in that part of the country, my favourite being the resort of Hunstanton. At that time, before petrol became available again, the roads were virtually free of traffic. I lavished a lot of love and elbow-grease on that bicycle, and it stood me in good stead for many years.

TIMED TO PERFECTION
Stan Greenberg

On one occasion I had been pea-picking after school, and was cycling home, along the typical high-banked, open Norfolk roads, when a tremendous storm broke out. Thunder rolled and lightning lit up the sky like daylight, as I pedalled as fast as I could go. I suddenly realised that I was quite high in the landscape, and on a metal machine, and I was terrified. I must have smashed all speed records that night as I tore along the deserted roads, gingerly holding the handlebars by the rubber grips. Apparently, I arrived back at my billet in a crazed state, but I was never again unduly frightened by a storm. If it hadn't got me that night, it was never going to.

BIG OR SMALL

I am 1.72m *5ft 7½in* in height. I have never thought of myself as small, although I have a number of friends who are 10-15cm taller, and know many athletes considerably taller than that. However, when I was young, I always hoped, indeed prayed, that I would reach 1.83m *6ft* when I got older. To that end, for a time, I tried something that I had read about a famous hurdler. This chap, to keep his legs long and straight, tied them to the end of his bed at night, so that he would not curl up. I don't know what effect it had on him, but all it did for me was to give me a lot of sleepless nights, make my ankles very sore, and nearly suffocate me when I still curled up - but at the bottom of the bed under the bedclothes.

As a child, I was never conscious of being small among my contemporaries. In fact, I remember that during the war, when there was a special issue of clothing coupons for children of above average height and shoe size, I was eligible for both. Also, when I started work, I didn't seem to be overshadowed in bus queues or on underground trains. So I assume that I must have been of average height for the time. Nowadays, I sometimes feel like a midget. If I stand at a bus stop when the kids come out of school, I feel dwarfed - they must be some 5-8cm *2-3in* taller than in my time. And that is just the girls! Seriously, children are so much taller than their parents were. Look at your own, and those of your friends and neighbours. Rarely are parents bigger than their offspring.

One of the tallest men I have ever come across was Wilt 'The Stilt' Chamberlain, the former American basketball star, who stands 2.18m *7ft 2in*. That is a tremendous height, and is made to look even more by the fact that he is a big man in body as well, 135kg *300lb*. As a sports commentator, he caused some problems to the BBC athletics team at the Montreal Olympics in 1976. Sitting just in front of us, he appeared to be an ordinary chap standing up and obstructing the view. On being called at to sit down, in perhaps not the most courteous of terms, he uncurled himself and stood up, and up, and up, glaring frighteningly at my colleagues and I. Apologies were quickly made, and he fairly good-naturedly moved away - much to our relief. What does one do in a cinema or a theatre when someone like him sits in front of you? Move, I suppose. Actually my wife and I were once in the balcony of a local cinema, when the comic actor Bernard Bresslaw, who stood at least 2.03m *6ft 8in*, and big with it, came in with his family, and made his way towards where we were sitting. Happily, he was obviously considerate of others and made his way to the back row.

BIGOTRY

Perhaps the worst creation on God's earth is a bigot. If you believe that He created all things, then he must have created them as well, and when one thinks of the terrible things that have been said and done by bigoted minds, one wonders why. I, like so many of my co-religionists, have been on the receiving end of such bigotry for most of my life. It has come in all forms, often from people that one has trusted, and virtually always from those to whom I have done no wrong that I know of. At school, one could excuse it as blind ignorance, but as one got older, one realised that although ignorance is still a major part of the problem, it goes much deeper. Rudeness and disdain, being sworn at, even being spat at, can be attributed to poor education and intelligence, but outright hatred and physical abuse must be laid at the portals of something far more evil and sinister.

TIMED TO PERFECTION
Stan Greenberg

Most religious and ethnic bigotry, in England at least, has usually taken the form of jokes, albeit bad jokes in equally bad taste. What many of the tellers of these jokes do not seem to realise is that they are perpetuating certain racial myths which can cause serious problems. It is unlikely that most of the 'jokers' wish anyone any real harm, and often cannot understand when the butt of the joke gets upset. This is particularly true, in my experience, when the 'joker' is a WASP Liberal.(WASP - White, Anglo-Saxon, Protestant). Again, in my experience, which unfortunately has been only too wide, they have no conception or understanding of what it does to a person to be bullied and harried for years. To bear the brunt of derision and hatred from people who you do not even know. To hear of acts of violence and vandalism against friends and family, who you know would never hurt anybody. To have organised religions denounce you to their young, in current as well as historical terms. When I was evacuated at the beginning of World War II, I had the fortunate (sic) experience of being sent to Sunday School in the village where I was billeted. Having already had some years of (Hebrew) religious learning I quickly became teacher's pet, with my knowledge and quick answers to things. What disturbed me even then was some of the things that I was being told - about myself as it were - and apparently my reactions started to create some problems. Eventually I was called to the day school headmaster's study, where it became apparent that I was of the Jewish faith. Their reaction was that I obviously should not be attending a Christian Sunday School. They were astonished to learn that my father knew and approved - he took the view that any study was better than none. Nevertheless, and I am sure it was to cover their own embarrassment, I was excused. This caused me even more problems, as my Christian friends were jealous that while they had to attend Sunday School, I was able to play and go fishing. So yet again I copped it both ways.

Later in the war I used to go pea-picking after school during long summer evenings. While there I got to know one young village lad very well, and we became good 'mates'. That is until I made it known that I couldn't go to the fields on a particular few days because it was the Jewish New Year. I will never forget the look on his face. It wasn't nasty or offensive, but one of utter bewilderment, and looking at me with totally new eyes he actually said to me "You can't be a Jew. You're no different". My immediate reaction was to ask him what he had expected - perhaps horns? What had he been told or taught? For the rest of the evening he kept staring at me, and I am afraid that things were never the same between us. Over the years, in other out of the way places, I have encountered similar reactions.

Perhaps, even worse, is the reaction I have experienced from much better educated people. In their cases, I can only guess that either they have had a specifically bad experience with a Jew, or they have reason to be jealous or afraid. The bad experience syndrome doesn't really hold water on its own since I am sure that such people have had all manner of unfortunate experiences - we all do - but they rarely refer later to a lying Frenchman, or a cheating Bulgarian. They take it for whatever it was - a liar or a cheat. What is it in their makeup, or more likely their upbringing, that has to specify the religious affinity of the person, and then to apply the condemnation, rightful though it may be, not only to that particular individual, but to a whole group of people. With regard to jealousy, that is perhaps more easily understandable. There is no question that Jews, as a group, do, and will, work harder than the average. That, of course, is a rather wide generalisation, but let it be in our favour for a change. My father would often warn me about having too many Christian friends, as his experiences, especially in Russia, had not been happy. When I defended them as nice people, he would note that, yes they are always nice in good times, but beware of the bad times. And he has been proved right, of course. As so many Jews, and, more recently, Indians, Pakistanis and Blacks, have found out, when there is economic decline and unemployment they are the first to be targeted. If their critics are honest with themselves, what is it they dislike most about Indian and Pakistani shop-owners and workers? Almost certainly it is that they work exceptionally hard and long, and that they look after their own. That is the same outlook on life that former immigrants, the Jews, had, and suffered for. The only difference is that the more recent immigrants are more noticeably 'foreign'. Generations of Jewish immigrants hid their identities by changing their names. Not that those who wanted or needed to know didn't find out about them. Also the influx of non-Jewish immigrants from Eastern Europe after the War, helped make the foreign-sounding name much more acceptable in Britain. However, changing from Patel to Smith does little good when one's face remains dark, and is thus recognisable to bigots.

BIRTH

A couple of years before my birth, Jerome Kern wrote a song *Why was I born?* Perhaps he should have written one for me entitled, *When was I born?* Apparently, it was on the morning of Wednesday, 8th July 1931, in a nursing home in Newington Green, Islington, London, to my parents, Mary and Joseph. (Despite the obvious temptation, I was named Stanley). In fact, I was actually given the Hebrew name of Shlomo (Solomon), after my paternal grandfather, and wanting an English equivalent, my parents chose Stanley, probably after the former Prime Minister, Baldwin. I say 'apparently', because there is some uncertainty about the date. My father, in his excitement, forgot to register my birth for a couple of weeks. Having been told that he could get into trouble being late, he gave the registrar a more recent date,14th July, which was duly noted on my birth certificate. Later, in 1936, he officially amended it to what I have always assumed was the correct date - but retained copies of both certificates.

In 1952, when I made my first trip abroad, I applied for a passport and duly produced my birth certificate. That's right, the wrong one. Thus, my application showed the 8th July and the supporting document showed the 14th. This latter appeared on the passport. I explained the mistake and produced the amended certificate, and the passport entry was duly amended, in ink. But for years, whenever I went through Customs Control, I always got the impression that they would notice the crossed out date and think to themselves that I must be a right idiot not knowing my own date of birth. However, it may be even worse than that, as I am still not certain that I know my correct birthdate - a fundamental parameter of one's life.

To go back to the faux pas by my father - no, not me, the birth certificate. The 8th July 1931 was a Wednesday. However, my mother has always insisted that I was born on a Tuesday - and she ought to know I suppose. It seems to me that if father was going to lie originally to the registrar, he was more likely to add a week to the proper date. He actually gave the 14th July, apparently only six days after the correct date, but, interestingly, a Tuesday. So the thought does occur that it really was one week after, i.e. I was born on the 7th. But there is no way I can check it now. The nursing home no longer exists, and the usual way of checking one's birth, the birth certificate, is probably wrong anyway.

Some interesting things happened on the day I was supposedly born, some of them remarkably appropriate, with hindsight, given the jobs and interests I would have later in life. Particularly significant was the main letter in The Times, which was about the need for a ring road around London. (I was very involved with this very matter when I worked for the GLC). On the National Station - radio - the BBC Orchestra gave a concert of music by Beethoven and Stravinsky. The exchange rate was US $4.86 to the pound. In sport, the English ladies tennis team annihilated the German ladies by 10-0, while Oxford beat Cambridge at cricket. In the RAF athletics championships the 120yd hurdles was won by 22 year-old Leading Aircraftman Don Finlay. He was to take the oath on behalf of the athletes at the 1948 Olympic Games (the first that I attended), and won his eighth AAA title in 1949 at the age of 40 (I was among the spectators).

BLUE PILLS
Over the last few years I have been aware of 'odd' looks when I

have had lunch out at other people's houses and at restaurants. Originally, I thought I was probably being paranoiac, but I now realise that there was something that I was doing that was definitely drawing people's attention. I was taking one of my pills. The thing about the particular one I then took at lunchtime was that it is small, triangular and blue. Now, let me say straight away that the pill I was taking was something called finasteride, and I took it to control my PSA reading connected to my prostate cancer situation. However, apparently very similar pills, with the same shape and colour, are quite common with men around my age, and are taken for an entirely different reason. I refer, of course, to Viagra pills, and similar medication. It was only recently drawn to my attention, when I rather naively asked someone what were the pills mentioned in newspaper and magazine adverts, which were only referred to as 'little blue pills'. I would like to state categorically that though I take pills for regulating my blood pressure, and for controlling my cholesterol, as well as the above mentioned PSA ones, I have no need for these other blue pills – at least, not yet anyway.

BOATS

As I am not the sort to "mess about in boats" I haven't really got the hang of when to use the term 'ship' or 'boat', so excuse me if I make a mistake. My very first trip abroad, to Helsinki in 1952, was mainly by water transport. Another early smooth voyage was on a marvellous Hovercraft across the English Channel. Then I remember a trip on a romantic Bateaux-Mouche on the River Seine in Paris. However, I have been lucky to have had a few very interesting trips in unusual types of this form of transport in various places in the world. One of the most exciting was while in Christchurch, New Zealand, for the 1974 Commonwealth Games. A few of us were taken to a nearby very shallow river on which jetboats were used. These were small boats which literally skimmed over water often no more than a few centimetres in depth. It was a very exhilarating ride. Previously, stopping at Sydney on the way to New Zealand, I had taken the Hydrofoil ferry on Sydney harbour to Manly beach. Years later, on a visit to Aswan, in Egypt, I made a tranquil journey on the unique Nile vessel, a Felluca, which tacked back and forth continuously against the prevailing head wind. Although a wonderfully scenic and peaceful journey, I had unwisely forgotten to take a hat, and ended up with sunstroke. Just as peaceful, was a mini-cruise around Oslo harbour on one of the famous tall ships, the imposing white-hulled *Christian Radich*, a great way to spend a few hours. Then there was a remarkable sensation to being on one of the fast-moving riverboats on the Chao Phraya River in Bangkok. When in Hawaii, I still remember the exhilaration that came with being a member of an improvised 'crew' which paddled a large outrigger canoe which rode the surf in on Waikiki beach - very thrilling, but I soon realised that I was getting too old for this sort of thing, and my shoulders felt bruised for a week. On our first visit to Florida, Carole and I 'flew' across the Everglades on an airboat, which was propelled by a vast fan-like propeller, and later had a cruise on a large catamaran. Then there was the occasion, at Clearwater Beach, Florida, when we had a trip on the *Sea Screamer*, claimed to be the largest motorboat in the world. I think that the claim may not be correct, but certainly it was very fast, and very noisy, and we enjoyed it immensely. Ferry boats are usually much more peaceful, as illustrated by the Staten Island Ferry which Carole and I took on a trip to New York. However, the trips we made on the small, quick, ferry boats across the Dardanelles at Istanbul were slightly hair-raising, when one considers the phenomenal volume of traffic on that ultra-busy stretch of water.

In the last few years, we have succumbed to the very popular idea of cruising. The first time was in the newly-launched P & O liner, the *Azura*, a massive 3000 passenger ship on a cruise in the Mediterranean. We have since done a number of other cruises. All of them were most enjoyable.

BODY

I have always tried to look after my body. In my youth I competed regulary in a variety of sports, and was extremely fit, and, apart from the odd muscle pull, had virtually no physical problems. However, even at the time I realised that I had something of a breathing problem, which limited me to sprinting as opposed to middle or long distance running, but I didn't consider it important. It was only much later in life I found out that I had very narrow nasal passages, even though I have a fairly large nose, and thus was restricted in my lung capacity at any one time. Other than that everything seemed to work well, and, I thought, was setting me up well for later in life. I now find that that thought was not correct. In fact, talking to others who were as sporty when young, it seems that we are paying for that emphasis on sport with damaged knees and hips. The main problem seems to have been that in those far off days we wore very thin-soled sports shoes, i.e. plimsolls, and one's feet, legs and knees took a terrific pounding if we ran or played on hard surfaces. I must say that I get very cross with my body nowadays when it lets me down – not yet too seriously, but when my back, knees and ankles ache.

In most other ways, I believe I have led a healthy life: not having smoked; only drinking moderately, mainly wine and very little spirits; never consuming drugs, other than those prescribed by my doctor for an ailment. My diet, from when I was in my teens, has always contained large amounts of raw vegetables, fruit and nuts, and, for many years, hardly any red meat. In recent years I switched to semi-skimmed, and then, nowadays, skimmed, milk. On two occasions, when interviewed by hospital dieticians, I was told that my diet was extremely good, and that they had nothing to add to it. It is to be hoped that my body appreciates all that I do for it, and pays me back by continuing to function reasonably well for a few more years yet.

BOOKS AND OTHER WRITINGS

One of the greatest pleasures I have had in life has been the reading of books. Always an avid reader, the books that I took up during the first fifty years of my life were almost, exclusively, non-

TIMED TO PERFECTION
Stan Greenberg

fiction - history, geography, travel, sport, autobiographies and the like. What little fiction I read was done while at school, and consisted of the classics, i.e. Shakespeare, Dickens et al. Not that I didn't enjoy it, but when it was no longer a neccesity I found many other real-life topics to occupy my attention. However, as I have got older, and perhaps have a little more free time, I have begun to read much more contemporary fiction, though I confess a weakness for science fiction of a certain type, ie the works of Tolkien and Robert Jordan, and historical-based dramas.

Recently, I have been shocked to discover that not only are there large numbers of adults in Great Britain who cannot read, but I gather that practically the whole of the modern generation doesn't or wont. It seems that the culture of television, the mobile telephone, and, even worse in this respect, the computer, has almost destroyed the 'art' of reading books. I fear that it is a great loss for the individual, and a serious prospect for the future of our society.

Byron wrote "T'is pleasant, sure, to see one's name in print; A book's a book, although there's nothing in't", and I was very eager when young to get my 'name in print'. Having read a great deal, especially history and geography books, my head was full of all sorts of ideas and superfluous knowledge. At school, writing essays was always one of my strong points. In fact, in primary school, I was allowed to pick my own subjects, instead of those awful 'A day in the life of a postman' or 'What I did on holiday' things. I remember particularly writing about 'The Charge of the Light Brigade'. It must certainly have lifted the teacher from his boredom with the other above subjects, as he gave me an A+.

When it came to taking the equivalent of today's 11 plus exam, I ended up all alone in a vast room, as I was then evacuated to Luton, but wanted to take the London County exam. There were two invigilators just for me that afternoon, and I felt quite intimidated until the essay question came up. One of the half-dozen or so set subjects was *Monkeys*, something I reckoned I knew about, and I gleefully set to. After some time I suddenly realised that both invigilators were behind me avidly reading what I was writing, so I knew that it must be interesting rubbish, if nothing else.

My first athletics oriented writing was a letter to *Athletics* Weekly, then the top magazine in the sport, in the issue of 29 September 1956. Over the next few years I became embroiled in two famous arguments, via the letter pages, about time-keeping and front-running. These gave me something of a reputation in the sport, and I began to collaborate on compiling ranking lists, and then to write the odd article. (Sometimes, I am told, they were very odd). The first time I had my name connected with a proper book was when I was credited as the Associate Editor of *The Guinness Book of Olympic Records*, a paperback produced by the McWhirter twins in 1964. Two years later I produced a booklet entitled *Commonwealth Statistics*, which my old friend Charles Elliott published. Although it sold fairly well I believe, my total return for a truly intensive amount of work was - six copies of the publication, that's all. But I was so pleased to have it in print, that I didn't really care. You will note that I was also rather naive (okay, stupid then!).

As I got older the urge to write my own proper book became stronger. I had no idea of a subject, but I wanted to get myself into print - it seemed a way of grabbing a brief bit of immortality. Well, I was rather precocious in some ways. Meanwhile, I had joined the Greater London Council. As part of a specialist library, I had to compile guides to the literature on certain subjects, primarily to do with transportation. In that capacity, in the 1970s, I had my first entry in the publication, *Books in Print*, with a pamphlet about *Traffic Restraint: Selected References*. Not the most thrilling of titles, but it was well received in the field of interest at which it was aimed. The first hard back book I authored was *The Guinness Book of Sporting Facts* in 1982, which was produced on behalf of the Marks & Spencer organisation. Finally, in 1983, I produced my magnum opus, *The Guinness Book of Olympics Facts and Feats*. Happily it was quite successful, and has been updated and re-published in 1987, 1991, and 1995. At various times there have been foreign editions in Holland, Norway, Germany and Japan. I later revised and rewrote it for publication by, firstly, Whitaker's Almanack (1999 and 2003), and most recently by SportsBooks (2007 and 2012) – it is now called *Stan Greenberg's Olympic Almanac*, and let me state that the use of my name was the publisher's idea.

BOOMERANGS

Most encyclopaedias attribute the boomerang to Australia, which, of course, we all knew when we were at school. So I was quite surprised, when I visited the Cairo museum, with its wonderful collection of Egyptian antiquities, that there on a wall was a display of ancient Egyptian boomerangs. Further research gave me the information that forms of the boomerang - a v-shaped hardwood throwing weapon - were used by some American Indians as well as various tribes in northeastern Africa, and in Ancient Egypt. So there!

The first time I was in Australia I bought a souvenir boomerang, not thinking for a moment that it would work. However, my son and I took it to our local park and quickly discovered how to throw it correctly. Despite trees getting in the way, we eventually were throwing it about 45.70m *150ft* and, more importantly, having it return close to us. It was quite fascinating, and great fun, and I can heartily recommend the activity. I believe that experts can use it effectively over distances approaching 150m *500ft.*

BOREDOM/BORING

With the utmost honesty I can state that I cannot ever remember being bored - or at least not for any appreciable length of time. Far too many things have interested me. I have always look/read right through a newspaper or magazine, and not just the pages or sections that I know I want to see. So many people never look at the sports pages, or the business section, or the travel, etc etc. I peruse virtually every page, and stop and read anything that catches my eye. This has been almost a lifetime habit, and I pride myself on a good general knowledge, although currently I have to admit blanks of knowledge and interest in such areas as TV soap operas, cooking and celebrity programmes, and so-called pop music. There never seems to be enough time to watch, read or listen to all the things I want to.

Undoubtedly, as I have grown older, I have become something of a bore, as, my friends tell me, I keep repeating stories that I have told many times before. I don't think that it is because I like to hear the sound of my own voice, but more that I have found, or know, something that I think is exciting or interesting, and I want others to appreciate it as well. Perhaps, the only solution, at least from my point of view, is to get a load of new friends, although I am still absorbing lots of new stuff every week, which the old friends can hear about if they wish. However, I realise that I must really bore my wife, as she has heard all the stories so many times before, and then has to listen again whenever I find new listeners. From the look on her face at these times, I think she finds a way to 'turn off'.

BREATHING

While the act of breathing is probably the most basic act that you undertake, I find that it has also produced one of the most perplexing puzzles to assail me during my life. Consider the following. When your hands are cold, and when aren't they in the British climate, often you blow on them to warm them up - presumably with hot breath. When your tea or soup is hot, often you blow on them to cool them down - presumably with your cold breath. Now, what puzzles me is at what point, and how, do you instruct your system to use the hot or the cold breath? Answers please in a plain envelope.

BRIDGE OF SIGHS

In 1976 I took my family to Scotland for a holiday. We were based in Inverness on the east coast, and made wonderful daily forays by

TIMED TO PERFECTION
Stan Greenberg

car, mainly north into the highlands. One special trip was to Cape Wrath in the far north-west. Our first stop was the little town of Bonar Bridge, where we had a mid-morning snack, and I pacified my passengers by telling them that we would stop to eat something more substantial at somewhere called Laxford Bridge, which I noted on my map was on the west coast, well sited on the route to our ultimate destination. The journey across the highlands, amid rugged and magnificent scenery, took much longer than I had thought on the single track roads, and there were sounds of rebellion from the back where my children were seated. I calmed them, and Carole I should add, with the promise that we would have a really good meal when we reached Laxford Bridge. Eventually, when we did reach it, we were shocked to find that that was all it was – a bridge. Very picturesque, over Loch Laxford which stretched north-westward to the ocean, but just a bridge. The rebellion nearly became a bloody revolution, but I convinced them that there must be somewhere to eat nearby, although inwardly I was beginning to wonder if our emaciated bodies would ever be found. Quite a while later we finally came across what appeared to be a deserted hotel, overlooking the loch. Nevertheless, I stopped and knocked at the door. Thankfully, it was not deserted, and we were welcomed in and partook of what may have been the most excellent fish meal we have ever had - fresh too, taken from the loch that very morning. We were saved.

BUSES

When I was young, one method that I used to keep fit, and, unknowingly, improve my sprinting, was the way I got on and off the old Routemaster buses, with their permanently open doorways. I delighted in jumping off the buses before they had finally slowed down at stops, and the resulting 'whiplash' effect would propel me forward at a much greater leg speed than I could normally generate. Also, when intending to board a bus, I would deliberately wait until the bus was pulling away, and then make a 'desperate' run for it, leaping onto the running board as it reached a good speed – again running faster, albeit only for a few seconds, than I normally did. Now, I am talking about a time when I was in my middle to late teens, and when I was incredibly fit. At my current state of life I find that I have some trouble stepping onto the stationary vehicle.

For many years I went to work by bus. Luckily there was a route which went straight from my home, Stoke Newington, to work, at Blackfriars. When I started in 1947 the fare was, at the most, 3d (that is old pence) - now it is about a hundredfold more. On the way home after a hard day's work - and we did work hard then - I would often doze off on the bus. Sometimes when the conductor would stop and ask for the fare, I would wake with a start, jerk upright from my slumped position, and thud my head resoundingly on the metal upright which connected the back of the seat to the ceiling. The resulting 'dong' echoed through the bus, which added embarrassment to the headache.

Another time I jerked awake and offered the 3d fare to the conductor with a request for the "*Evening Standard* please", much to the amusement of other passengers. The following day I was telling the story against myself at the office, and one of the senior managers thought I was a real idiot. However, he told me later, that as he was leaving his office to go home that evening, he got change ready to buy his evening paper outside the main door of the building. As he entered the lift he remembered my story, chuckling, and thinking "what a clot young Greenberg is". The lift stopped, and the attendant announced it was the ground floor. My critic, aroused from his reverie, turned to the man, offered him the money and asked "*Evening Standard* please". It's dangerous to mess with Greenberg.

CABBAGE

I am sure my older readers will remember a music-hall song about the efficacy of *Boiled Beef and* Carrots. I can't say that I ever really liked the dish. However, one other, undoubtedly equally nutritious, favourite of the masses which I abhorred, and still abhor, is boiled cabbage. I find it difficult to look at it if it is on my plate, put there by some sadistic chef, and the smell positively churns my stomach. I have been able to pin down my revulsion of it to one of two sources. Firstly, when I was young, the preponderance of the vegetable in school dinners, which were the main origin of most of my culinary distastes. Secondly, and almost certainly the more likely reason, was that the upstairs tenants, who my parents had in their house for a time, seemed to live on the vile stuff, and the smell pervaded the whole house on most days of the week, month, year. Oddly perhaps, in view of the foregoing, I delight in raw cabbage of all varieties, red, green or white, and rarely miss a day without having some with at least one meal.

CARDS
When I was a young boy my parents would, invariably, visit my maternal grandparents at the weekends. It was the custom of other members of the family to be there too, and, without exception, cards would be played - usually the game of solo. Week in, month in, year in, my young cousins and I would sit, read or play, while the grown-ups took part in their game, and gradually, mainly by watching and listening, we became quite proficient ourselves. As we got older we were often asked to sit-in for a hand or two while the women made tea or supper, and more importantly, we were allowed to keep any winnings we made. Although the games were only played for pennies, I remember that I would regularly supplement my pocket money this way. The thing was that, over time, we youngsters had noticed all the foibles, habits and mistakes that the adults made consistently, and thus we were able to put this knowledge to good use when we were allowed to play. Strangely enough, or perhaps not when one considers those early years, I haven't played a game of cards for about fifty years.

When I started working as the BBC athletics statistician, I began to 'play' with a different form of cards. These were pre-printed pieces of stiff card 30cm x 21cm *11¾in x 8in* on which I would insert the various data about the events that were to be covered in the broadcast. I designed them to allow space for the various categories of records, the athlete's bib number, name, nationality, and, most importantly, any information that I could muster about the athlete. I carried large quantities of these cards on all my assignments, and for an Olympic Games or other major championships they would often number well into the hundreds. 'Stan's cards' became quite famous at athletics stadia around the world. Later, when I got computerised, I adapted the printout to fit these cards, and the tradition continued until I retired. I know that my original 'system' was adapted and copied by TV companies on every continent.

CAROLE

She is my wife, my friend, my lover, my companion. She laughs with me when I am happy, and cheers me up when I get depressed. I get withdrawal symptoms when we are apart, and enjoy holding her when we are together. When we walk along we usually hold hands, and do the same when we are sitting watching television. In some 52 years together I cannot ever remember regretting a moment of it. Of course, we have had our disagreements and arguments, and there have been times when she has driven me crazy, but the reasons have never been to do with money or jealousy. Neither have other people ever come between us, unless one counts the children as other people - and at times I have had serious doubts that they are people at all, but aliens from another planet. In fact, the only major arguments that I can recall have been about our two 'darlings', and happily most of them were when they were small. Most of the truly great moments of my life have been due to her, and/or spent with her. The last five decades would have been much lonelier and unhappy without her, and I thank whoever or whatever looks over me that I made that tentative phone call all those years ago, and fervently hope that we have a few more years together. However, she does have one major fault, which sometimes does put a strain on our marriage - she mangles toothpaste tubes.

CARPE DIEM

The early Roman poet, Horace, knew what he was talking about when he wrote "Carpe diem, quam minimum credula postero". Usually translated as "Seize the present day, trusting the morrow as little as you can", it is taken to mean that you should enjoy yourself while you can, i.e. you never know what the future may hold. Many people tend to leave doing things until a later date, and so often, that day never comes. My late mother-in-law was such a person. Whenever Carole and I suggested that she and my father-in-law should book such and such a holiday, or go to such and such a place, or do such and such a thing, she always replied that they would do all those things at a later time. Unfortunately, she didn't live until that time, and although he eventually did start doing those various things, they were with someone else. Carole and I agreed long ago that, given the wherewithal, time and opportunity, we would do what we wanted to, and go where we wanted to go, as soon as possible, and not wait until it was 'too late'. That we have done, and hopefully will continue to do so for a few more years yet.

CARROTS

The older of my readers will no doubt remember that during World War II the Ministry of Information (or was it Misinformation) announced that carrots were especially good for one's eyesight, and that it was consumption of them that enabled our night-time fighter pilots to destroy so many German planes. Only later was it revealed that, of course, it was Radar that was the prime reason for their success, and the carrot ruse had apparently worked quite well in hiding the secret from the enemy. Nevertheless, I was already 'hooked' on carrots, which became my favourite vegetable, and it is still so today. Actually, there is something in them that does have some slight effect on the potency of one's eyesight, and the fact that my own sight has been, and basically still is, surprisingly good, even into my eighties, seems to back up that premise. One of the things that I find puzzling about most restaurants is that they hardly ever use the vegetable in their salad dishes. Not only is it colourful and nutritious, but it is not very expensive either - so why don't they use it? (Answers in yet another plain stamped envelope please).

CARS

I hardly took any interest in cars until I was in my early 30s. When I was a small child I delighted in a the rare ride in a taxi, or even rarer trip in somebody's car - at that time, in the 1930s, no close friend or relative had one. Other than that, the mechanism of cars had no interest for me, and I never dreamed that I would have one of my own. It was only after I had got married, and our first child had arrived, that I realised the advantages that a car would provide. After sometimes traumatic learning experiences (of which I have written elsewhere), I passed my driving test at the second attempt. That was in 1964, at the time that my father was in hospital, and it made visiting him so very much easier. Sadly, it also helped enormously during the hectic time of his funeral.

Decisions about the type of car I bought have always been, primarily, based on financial considerations, but also I have been limited by the size of my garage. Thus, for one reason or another, my cars have usually comparatively small. In recent years I have been hooked on Renault Clios. Although my wife is able to recall nearly all the registration numbers of the cars I have owned, I always seem to have trouble with the number of the current car. I once spent a very worrying twenty minutes looking for my car in a large car park, having forgotten that I had changed it for a newer model and colour only a few months earlier. That, I think, puts in a nutshell my attitude to cars - or perhaps it shows that I am getting quite old.

CHANTS

Over the years I have learnt many forms of chant, usually religious, but perhaps the most enjoyable was that of the Maori haka, *Ka Mate*. Rugby followers will know it from the New Zealand All-Blacks, who always precede their matches with a stirring performance. My first contact with it was at the 1952 Olympic

TIMED TO PERFECTION
Stan Greenberg

Games in Helsinki. I had met two New Zealand supporters at Stockholm, just before I crossed the Baltic. These Kiwis were cycling, and went overland to Helsinki, travelling right up Sweden, almost to the Arctic Circle, and around the Gulf of Bothnia. In the stadium they were not sitting far away from the group I was in, and we made contact again. On the fourth day of the Games the women's long jump witnessed a tremendous battle between Yvette Williams of New Zealand and Alexandra Tchudina of the Soviet Union. Towards the end of the afternoon, with the issue still in doubt, the New Zealand couple climbed to the back of the stadium, where all of the competing countries' flags were flying, and lifted theirs from out of its socket. Bringing it back to their seats they gathered a small band of pro-Williams supporters around them. As the British girl, Shirley Cawley, had sown up third place, with no hope of winning, we switched our cheering to the Commonwealth athlete. The Kiwis taught us the words (or rather the sounds) of the Haka, and prior to the New Zealander's next jump we went into action. The Finns were quite surprised at all the "New Zealanders" in the stadium. It was thrilling to be part of such a chant, especially when Williams then made her winning jump, just 1cm short of the world record.

CHARACTERS
We all have come across odd characters at one time or another. There are two I encountered, when I was quite young, who made vivid impressions on me. The first was the well-known 1930s black racing tipster who called himself Prince Monolulu. He had a famous cry of "I've got a horse". He was a tall, colourful, figure, who wore a feathered headdress, and Arabian Nights garb of a bolero jacket and billowing pantaloons, and always carried an umbrella. I first recall seeing him was striding along our local high street, creating quite a stir, and I was doubly fascinated, as, almost certainly, he was the first black man that I had ever seen.

The second character, in the late 1940s, was the complete antithesis of the first. He was of medium-height and slim, with long, shoulder-length white hair - and men didn't have long hair in those days. He was of indeterminate age, but must have been in his 50s at least, but looked, and I believe was, amazingly fit. This was at a time when West End cinemas and theatres usually had long queues for every evening performance, and it seems that he would walk from the East End of London up to the theatre district every weekend, and perhaps also every weekday evening, irrespective of the weather. I know that whenever I was waiting in a cinema or theatre queue, he would appear. He would stop and stare disapprovingly at the people, never uttering a word, and then stride off, at quite a fast pace, using his ever-present umbrella as a walking stick. Apparently, he would tour the various cinemas and theatres, stare at the people - not with a threatening demeanour - and move on. From personal experience, I know he did this for some years in the post-War period. Often there would be rather offensive remarks made to him, but he never responded, just staring down the offender with his startlingly piercing eyes, and then go. I recall that one Sunday morning, when I was visiting Petticoat Lane market with my father, he suddenly appeared, dressed just the same, umbrella in hand. As he passed by, one of the stall-holders, a real big, tough-looking chap, made a rude remark. He stopped, stared, then slowly walked towards the man. Initially the stall-holder looked sheepish, but then the old chap grabbed him by the front of his coat, and just lifted him up off his feet, held him there for a minute, and then let him down again. The tough bloke had gone ashen, and my 'friend', without saying a word, just walked off at his usual brisk pace. The stall-holder busied himself with his goods, not wanting to face the impressed onlookers for a while. My father commented that it was one of the most impressive things he had ever seen. That man was something of a hero to me for a long time, and I really missed seeing him on my trips 'up West' when he no longer turned up.

CHEATING

That fount of bon mots, the American comedian and wit, W C Fields, said that "You can't cheat an honest man", and I think it may have been one of the truest sayings he ever made. Most cheating, whether at home, in the office, or on the sports field, is based on one or more of the Seven Deadly Sins – pride, wrath, envy, lust, gluttony, avarice, sloth – and a truly honest man, or woman, will be able to acknowledge which of these faults is prodding him, or her, towards dishonesty. I don't 'honestly' know just what I am getting at with this piece, although having just watched the football World Cup may have something to do with it, but I just liked writing it.

CHEMISTRY
The only school subject that I truly hated was chemistry. That was almost certainly due to my first teacher of the subject in grammar school, of which more anon. Nevertheless, I have found that the discipline has intruded into my life on a number of occasions. I think my first knowledge of chemical reaction came when I put some carbide into an ink bottle at school - not during a chemistry class I should add. The bottle began to jump about violently, and fearful of an actual explosion, I slightly loosened the screw top. With a whooshing noise a column of ink - it was a red ink bottle - shot up and splattered the ceiling. That took a lot of explaining, and I must have been in a lot of trouble.

I particularly remember one experiment that we were asked to perform in the lab. It involved using a pipette, a thin glass tube used to transfer liquids from one container to another. We had a mild acid solution, and it was necessary to suck up a certain measure of the stuff, so that it reached a preset mark on the tube. I tried first, not wholeheartedly I must admit, but failed to reach the point. So I let my experiment partner have a go. Full of enthusiasm he sucked too hard, and the liquid shot up the tube and into his mouth. With a loud scream he dropped the pipette, knocked over the glass container, and leapt about, with what appeared to be smoke coming out of his mouth. In fact, the solution was much too weak to have burnt him, but it did produce spectacular results. My 'nemesis', Mr. Tucker the chemistry master, went almost as berserk as my friend, as similar smoke rose from the workbench and the

TIMED TO PERFECTION
Stan Greenberg

floor where the liquid had spilled. Rather unfairly I thought, we both were kept in after school and given a lecture on proper laboratory procedures.

By the time the Matric examinations came round I was thoroughly disenchanted with chemistry. Tucker, was an uptight martinet and all-round fusspot, who took all the fun out of classwork. I think he disliked me from the start, and he was never able to stimulate in me any interest in the subject. Rather childishly, I suppose, I determined to 'get even' somehow, and I got my chance in those final exams. He was the invigilator for the chemistry paper, and after we were settled he gave permission to start. I wrote my name and the subject on my paper, and rising to my feet, moved slowly towards the door. Catching sight of me, and thinking that I needed to oblige the call of nature, he testily called out that I should wait while one of the other masters in attendance went with me. "Oh no", I said, "I'm finished", and swept out of the room. I am told that he stood there in shock for several minutes, before regaining his composure. It was worth the one failure that I ever scored in examinations.

Later in life I occasionally had stirrings of regret that I had not taken to science subjects more. I was especially impressed when I learnt that one of my favourite composers, Borodin, was a chemist by profession. Also I met a distant relative, Professor Sir Bernard Katz, a brilliant scientist, and found him a most friendly, pleasant man - the antithesis of Mr. Tucker. I was immensely proud when Professor Katz was awarded the Nobel Laureate for medicine in 1970.

Working as a tariff clerk at Lever Brothers I was amazed to discover that, in fact, I had learnt something about chemistry after all. One day I had an urgent request for the import tariff rate on a sodium compound into Germany. Unfortunately, the German import tariff book that I had was in German, and I couldn't identify the correct section. Then, from some dark recess in my mind, I remembered that the chemical symbol for sodium was 'Na', for

Natrium, the heading under which sodium was classified in that tariff. My boss was very impressed, on that occasion at least.

CHILDHOOD
One reads so much nowadays about how all the bad people - murderers, rapists, swindlers, crooks, and, probably, politicians - were the result of unhappy childhoods. The so-called experts and social workers will tell you that these unhappy childhoods came about because of strict or cruel parents, the break-up of the family home, poverty, bullying at school etc. If that were so, then how come I am not an axe-murderer at the very least? My father had a violent temper, mainly triggered by me it seemed, and I had a strict but not fanatical religious upbringing. He rarely praised my school work, and never understood my success at sport. (However, later my mother told me that he would often boast about me to friends and family, but not when I was there). However, to be fair, he was rarely negative about things I did. Also I can remember that we often played together at the park. While not poverty-stricken, we were certainly among the poorer classes. At a crucial age, the war took me away from my parents for long periods over the 5½ years, and I suffered very badly from bullying and often quite violent anti-semitism for most of my young life. Nevertheless, I find that I look back on my childhood with some nostalgia and pleasure. As far as I know - and I have the sort of friends who would tell me I am sure - I have not developed too many anti-social habits. To the best of my memory, I have never stolen anything, if you discount scrumping apples, swindled anybody - not even the Inland Revenue - nor ever hit a woman. I have a bad temper, probably inherited, but, knowing that it is there, I have kept in under strict control for 99.9% of the time. For various reasons I do not practice my religion as assiduously as once I did, but my basic beliefs remain, and I have a strong sense of right and wrong. It could be, of course, that the psychological scars I acquired when I was young will reveal themselves soon, but they had better get a move on, or it will be too late.

CHILDREN

I am of the old-fashioned school, who consider that children should be loved, cared for, disciplined and taught - in that order of importance - and that is what I tried to do with my own children. While we had, and still have, strong differences of opinion, usually about fairly minor things, I don't believe that they dislike me any more than other children dislike their parents. Indeed, now that they are both in their fifties, I have reason to think that they have some respect for me, and don't hold too many grudges from their childhood. Interestingly, they have retained a number of the traits that my wife and I instilled in them as youngsters, and, generally speaking, have turned out to be the sort of children anyone would be proud of. My son, Keith, and I often have tremendous rows, as I did with my father, but then we didn't bring him up to be a 'yes man'.

Sometimes I envy my children, Karen and Keith. When they were young they thought they had the answers to everything - and now that they are older, they know they do. That aside, we have had mainly good times when I consider, not begrudge, but consider, the cost that was necessary to bring them up. Not just the cost in money terms, but in time, space and inconvenience. Of course, there have been times when I could have easily rung their necks, but when one hears the 'horror' stories told by acquaintances about the problems they have had with their offspring, I sit back and, metaphorically pat my kids' heads. It is interesting to note the differences between them. Karen has a bubbly personality, is quick-tempered, volatile, full of confidence, and makes a caring friend or an implacable enemy. Keith is quiet, introspective, quick-witted, but lacking in confidence. He is basically good-natured, but given to bouts of anger, has an artistic nature, and is a brilliant mimic.

Like everyone's young children, my own made comments which have gone into family folklore. Two of the best were by my daughter, Karen, when she began Hebrew classes, at about age five. One time she informed us that they had been told how Lot's wife had been turned into 'a packet of salt'. Another time she got us rather worried when she said that the teacher talked about Moses and the 'pills'. We were rather perturbed until we realised that to a modern child pills and tablets were the same thing, and what she had been told about was Moses being given the two tablets of the law.

A Christian friend told me of when his daughter had returned from Sunday School and asked him what it meant when the Bible said that Lot had known his daughters. "Of course he knew his daughters, Daddy" she said. His life flew before him as he explained as straight as it is possible to do to a 12 year old. His explanation was taken in thoughtful silence, and the subject never came up again.

CHUTZPAH

It is often defined as "gall", "brazen nerve", insolence", but none of those definitions really catches the true meaning. The nearest that English comes to it would be the word "effrontery", but even that is not right. The classic definition is enshrined in the story of a man who, having killed his mother and his father, throws himself on the mercy of the court because he is an orphan. I don't like this story, but it goes some way towards explaining the meaning.

One of the best illustrations I can think of involved my old friend, Stan Davis. One evening at work he was sitting at his cleared desk at about five minutes to 5pm, our leaving time. He had a date with a girl and he didn't want to be late. At that moment one of the senior managers came out of his room into the main office, noticed Stan sitting there in his raincoat, and, in a most sarcastic manner, said " Davis, I don't think it's raining in here". Quick as a flash, Stan stretched out his upturned hand, and with mock surprise in his voice, replied, "Oh, it's stopped". The manager stood there a moment, speechless, then with a shake of his head, acknowledged defeat, and walked back into his room.

My own finest example came in 1964, when I was working at

TIMED TO PERFECTION
Stan Greenberg

Lever Brothers at their head office in London. The Olympic Games was being held in Tokyo in October, and I had been engaged by ITV to help at their London studio at night after work. Japan was 9 hours ahead of GMT and so quite a bit of TV coverage here was shown mid-morning. Nothing ventured, nothing gained. So, although I was little more than a clerk at the time, I asked one of the senior secretaries on the top management floor, who I had got to know some time before, if it would be possible to sit in the Company Boardroom, if it wasn't in use of course, to watch the television set there. I explained that my immediate boss would not mind as I would work overtime to make up the lost time. After she got over the initial shock of the request, she smiled to herself, and said she would ask one of the directors. Grinning, she came back and said that it would be okay. So for a week I spent every late morning in front of the Boardroom TV set – much to the astonishment of the odd director who happened to pop in. By the end of the week, the directors were sending their secretaries, or coming themselves, to see how Britain was doing at the

Games. Additionally, the secretaries took pity on me and when they made tea for their bosses I got a cup and a biscuit as well

CINEMA

It may seem strange that, despite only going to the cinema about a dozen times in the last five years, I still claim to be one of the great cinemagoers of all time. That claim is based on my 'exploits' in the 1940s and 1950s, when I regularly went to the 'pictures' four times a week, and often twice on Saturdays and/or Sundays. I remember on one occasion being introduced to an American, who had an entry in the *Guinness Book of Records* for having seen a record number of feature films in one year. I calculated that I had seen many more than he had in at least three different years, due primarily to the British fashion of having two feature films per programme - in the United States they only ever had one. As I think I was a little bit ashamed of how often I attended the cinema - and the implication therein that I had virtually no social life at all - I did nothing about it, and didn't contact the McWhirter twins. When I went to work for the Guinness book many years later, I did mention the above to Norris, but, as he pointed out, I had not kept detailed records, ticket stubs etc, so there was no way I could prove my claim anyway. However, I know it was true, and really that is all that matters in such cases.

Incidentally, perhaps one of the reasons that I don't frequent the cinema so often nowadays, is that I can well remember, in my youth, going to see a programme of two films for as little as 5p (new money), while I recently went to watch a single film in a local Emporium, for £9.80, nearly 200 times more. So that's what is meant by inflation!

CIRCUMVENTION

This word can mean 'to outwit', and I am sure that we have all circumvented rules, regulations and laws, at one time or another. However, I am using the word in its other sense, 'to go round', in this case, specifically, to circumvent the world. The first time I did this was in 1974, when I went out to New Zealand for the Commonwealth Games. It was my first long trip, and really it couldn't have got very much longer.

Firstly, I flew from Heathrow to Abu Dhabi in the Persian Gulf. From there the plane went to Singapore, and then on to Sydney. After a short stop, my journey continued to Christchurch in New Zealand. After the Games, I flew to Pago Pago, on Tutuila Island in American Samoa, a true South Seas venue if there ever was one, where we re-fuelled. From there my journey continued to Honolulu in Hawaii. A few days later I carried on to change planes at Los Angeles, before flying to Mexico City. After a brief stay I changed my booking from British Airways to Lufthansa and flew back to London via Frankfurt. To say that I was jet lagged by the end of it may be the biggest understatement of my life. I was totally whacked, and it took a long time for me to get back 'in gear'.

Since then I have circumvented the globe another three times; in 1982 when I went to Brisbane in Australia for another Commonwealth Games, 1985 after a trip to Canberra, Australia for the athletics World Cup, and 1991 when I visited Tokyo for the World Championships. This latter trip, when I was aged 60, took a lot out of me, and I fear that world circumvention, for me, is a thing of the past.

CLUBS
As Groucho Marx once said, "I would never join a club that would have me as a member". Despite all my contemporaries joining youth clubs, I only visited one once. Strangely, I think I can even pinpoint the date, as I remember listening to a broadcast of Freddie Mills fighting the American boxer Joe Baksi on someone's radio at the club, and that was in 1946. Probably due to my shyness, or perhaps I was just unsocial, but I could never get into the club scene, and never went again. Similarly, I have never joined a lodge or suchlike, despite many requests to do so. In fact, other than belonging to a charity committee, set up after the death of a close friend, the only 'gathering' that I have joined is my school's Old Boys Club, and I only joined that some 50 years after I had left school. I was probably worried that my old chemistry master was a member.

COLD WAR
In the 1950s, at the height of the Cold War, I subscribed to a Soviet sports paper. My sole aim was to get results from one of the world's top athletics nations, and perhaps also improve the faint knowledge of the Russian language which I had learnt from one year at evening classes. As I half jokingly noted at the time, I could say 'Don't shoot!', if little else. I had learnt enough of the Cyrillic script to make out athletes' names. I received my copy regularly by post, and I often wondered what the postman thought about it. However, I have reason to believe that for a time, I, or rather my home, was under observation from some organisation or other. For many weeks we noticed that there were a series of raincoat-

TIMED TO PERFECTION
Stan Greenberg

wearing men 'loitering' in the vicinity of a shop opposite our house, showing more than normal attention to us. After some considerable time this attention ceased, but when one reads John Le Carré novels it does make one think. Soon afterwards I stopped my subscription anyway.

Because of the hysteria induced, mainly in others, by a visit to the Soviet Union, one was probably more readily open to spy mania than usual. You tended to search your room for bugging devices - sadly I never found one - and you looked suspiciously at the old baboushka who sat at the end of the hotel corridor guarding the keys (and supposedly reporting your movements to higher authority). I tended to go along with this paranoia with tongue in cheek, so that, when in Moscow, I used to lean over and wish the breakfast table daffodils, with the implied hidden microphone, "Good morning".

There are numerous stories of people's reaction to their first visit to Moscow. The best that I have heard, supposedly true, is about the British sports team that was among the first to go there in the 1960s. Included in the team were a couple of servicemen who were warned not to discuss anything of importance since they would certainly be bugged. On arrival in the room that they shared on the first floor of their hotel, they set about searching for the 'devices'. Finally they noticed a bump in the carpet under a small table in the centre of the room. To their glee they discovered that it was caused by a large screw-like object set in the floor. "That's it", they thought and proceeded to unscrew it - and down in the foyer the main chandelier crashed to the floor.

On a BBC trip to the Soviet Union, to Kiev, in 1976, a number of people warned me not to tell anyone of my antecedents. We had a 'minder' (probably KGB) allocated from Soviet TV, who went everywhere with us, ostensibly to smooth things out. He was a big bear of a man, very pleasant, and at one point I did mention that my father had come from Berdichev, a small town not far from Kiev. Far from causing any problem, he was delighted to learn this, and took a special interest in me, giving me a private tour around Kiev. Learning of my fondness for Russian music, and that one of my favourite pieces was *The Great Gate of Kiev* from Moussorgsky's *Pictures at an Exhibition*, he proceeded to take me to the impressive ruins of that very gate. No, it was no trouble he said, after all I was 'a landsmann'.

COMMENTATORS

I have been privileged to know many of the top sporting commentators on TV and radio, and, by and large, they are a great bunch. I have particular memories of two of them, Harry Carpenter and Barry Davies. On a trip to Minsk in 1973, Harry had come along with a view to perhaps becoming an athletics commentator - he knew quite a lot about the sport. On the internal flight from Moscow to Minsk, some Swiss TV men, who were also covering the USA v USSR match, kept swatting flies which were buzzing around inside the aircraft. When one of them killed a fly with a deft backhand, Harry promptly called out, "Game, Set and Mouche". On another occasion, Barry Davies was "trying out" at a GB v France match. Their female sprinters and ours at that time were of a high standard, and it had been decided that the traditional 4 x 100m relay would be replaced by a 4 x 200m race, in an attempt on the world record. Barry was designated to try this as a test, happily recorded and not live. Concentrating on the data cards that I had given him, which had details about the members of the teams, he forgot that it was a longer race, and, only looking up at the track occasionally, read it as the shorter race. I will never forget how his commentary trailed off when he talked of the final runner passing the winning post, only to see her pass the baton on to yet another runner on what was actually the second takeover. One final memory is of Frank Bough linking our commentary from the Moscow Olympics with the words, "And now, the pole vault, over the satellite".

The commentator I knew best was Ron Pickering, who was almost like a big brother to me - a very big brother. Basically, we had very similar backgrounds, and liked many of the same things - especially films, music and certain comedy acts. I don't think we ever had a falling out, although I did one or two things in our joint work for the BBC over a period of some 23 years, quite unintentionally, which must have upset him. We had many good laughs and memorable times together. There was one occasion when I thought we might well leave this world together. During the 1972 Olympic Games in Munich, Ron was invited to give a talk one evening to about a thousand American supporters on the *Track & Field News* tour. We went to an enormous hall, where they were having a late meal, and Ron was introduced on stage - I sat discreetly to one side. The American athletics team had suffered a series of reverses unmatched in history: amongst which were two of their best sprinters missing qualifying round races due to misinterpreting the 24 hour clock times on the schedule; their star middle distance man had fallen in his heat; and various other things had gone wrong. Ron started his talk with a withering attack on the American attitude to foreign travel, specifically pointing out that "You worry more about having iced water with your meal, than getting the start time right". There was a deathly silence, and a couple of massive shot putters in the front sat bolt upright in their seats. I started to look for the best way out, as I expected that we would be lynched before the evening was over. After a couple of more comments along the same lines - incidentally, comments which I fully agreed with - the tension was finally broken by a voice from the back calling out "That's it Ron, tell it like it is ". At that the audience went wild, including the shot putters, cheering and clapping, and yelling "Right on". He was the hit of the evening, and we were feted royally.

COMMENTATOR PITFALLS
There are phrases which one uses in everyday conversation that can take on whole new concepts and meanings when used by commentators covering international sport. Thus, there has been the unfortunate reference to a triple jumper from a Central European country as "the bouncing Czech". Similarly, it is so easy to note that a runner from an Eastern Bloc neighbour took "the Pole position". With China's entry into top-class athletics, the problems have multiplied considerably. So it was that while reporting the

TIMED TO PERFECTION
Stan Greenberg

1984 Olympic high jump competition, and correctly noting the inconsistency of the Chinese world record holder, Stuart Storey referred to nerves being "the chink in his armour". On another occasion a competitor from China was described, again correctly but in the context unfortunately, as looking "rather fragile".

Catching out sports commentators is a national pastime. However, the public does not realise the pressures that affect even the best of them. Major problems, in the coverage of athletics particularly, are with the names of foreign competitors - where the rule seems to be that the longest names are prevalent in the shortest distances. Thus, in a heat of the 1972 Olympic 100m, the line-up included Vassilios Papageorgopoulos (Greece), Jean-Louis Ravelomanantsoa (Madagascar) and Jorge Luis Vizcarrondo (Puerto Rico). To the consternation of the commentators the first two got through as far as the semi-finals. Similarly, I remember that Sri Lanka (then Ceylon) had a high jumper who rejoiced in the name Nagalingam Ethirveerasingham. When faced with such mouthfuls, even the most experienced develops doubts. Yet another problem is with names that are no doubt innocuous in their own language but take on an entirely different, sometimes rude, often funny, aspect in English. One of the most recent was Korean runner Shim Duk-Sup. Any Marx Brothers fan will have trouble with that one.

There are some names that are obviously 'mind-blowing' to some. At a Great Britain v Spain indoor match it was pointed out to Ron Pickering that one of the Spanish sprinters was Juan Jones. Now the name is pronounced as 'Honesh' in Spanish, but as Ron had once been national coach for Wales it obviously played on his mind, so that when it came to announcing the line-up with that runner on the inside, concentrating his mind not to call him Jones, he allowed himself to 'wander' and said over the air "In lane Juan".

In their defence it should be noted that commentators do not have the luxury, as do those of us who watch sport from the comfort of our armchairs, of merely talking about the picture in front of them. They also have earphones through which all sorts of sounds and

TIMED TO PERFECTION
Stan Greenberg

messages are being transmitted, sometimes to them, but also to other people involved in the broadcast. It amazes me how they can think clearly enough to make the usually excellent commentaries that they do, with all that going on. The tension can build up horrendously during a live transmission when at the mercy of a foreign producer, often well-nigh useless at his job. At one meeting in Munich in 1971, the year prior to the Olympics, there were a host of virtually, or indeed totally, unknown athletes. Our task was complicated by the fact that there was a shortage of competitor numbers, and that these were often worn on their backs only. Identifying athletes became virtually impossible when the German producer insisted on giving a close-up of a competitor's face each time, so that one couldn't even be sure of which event - of the four currently taking place - he was showing. Somehow, we coped, luckily recognising, or wildly guessing at, athlete and event, but at great mental cost. At one point after a pole vault attempt, Ron Pickering cried out "Who on earth is that?" The local producer had done a switch and gone to another event, and Ron, usually so cool and laid back, had 'lost it' as they say. Looking at the face on the screen I incredulously said "Its Lynn". It was indeed Lynn Davies, in the long jump, who Ron had coached to an Olympic gold medal, and who was a personal friend. As Ron told me later, he had reached the stage at which he wouldn't have recognised a picture of his own mother if it had come up on that screen.

At that same meeting there were a lot of African sprinters, whose names appeared to be unpronounceable. I rushed around trying to get help from any team managers that were available, and triumphantly returned to the commentary box with my new knowledge. Proudly, I read them out, including, to the best of my ability, the inclusion of the 'clicking sounds' that many Xhosa-type names require. The senior commentator, David Coleman, stared long and hard at me, then picked up the inter-com to the producer, and quietly informed him that we would not be covering the next few sprint races. Though somewhat disgruntled that my efforts had come to naught, I can't say that I blamed him really.

TIMED TO PERFECTION
Stan Greenberg

While on the subject of commentator's nightmares, I relish the story of the mythical football result said to be used to test announcers - East Fife 4, Forfar 5.

COMPUTERS
Sitting typing this item on a day when the London Stock Exchange computer system has failed, and no trading could be performed, I will merely preen, say, "I told you so", and wait for the upcoming computer Armageddon. However, aside from my overall dislike and distrust of the malevolent machines, I have one major aversion - who was the idiot who designed the standard computer keyboard? It may be very good for top-rate typists, but to a part-timer like me it is a veritable Nemesis. Why are the 'Ctrl', 'Alt' and the 'Windows' keys just to the left of the space bar, about the worst possible place for people like me to inadvertently hit - and wipe the screen of work just done. Surely, keys that can have such a dramatic effect should be put higher up the keyboard, out of harm's - and Stan's - way. The other lunacy of the computer world is the incompatibility of the various makes of machines, while even worse is the incompatibilty of different models by the same maker. I know that it is all to do with 'market forces' - that catch-all excuse for everything wrong today - but it is still stupid, and staggeringly wasteful.

CONSISTENCY
How I hate the word, and the way little minds use it to protect themselves when difficult decisions need to be made. People are not the same, nations are not the same, situations are not the same - so how can one be consistent in the treatment of them. Some of the greatest tragedies to individuals, groups and countries have occurred because of that word, and the attitude behind it. On a rather trivial level, I think it has been the bane of athletics selection in this country. To my way of thinking it is not possible, nor sensible, to compare the method of selection of, say, athletes in the sprints, events in which we are fairly strong, to that of, say, the hammer, an event in which we are weak. The criteria needed to

differentiate between a number of sprint contenders, some with medal chances, surely cannot be the same as that for the possible one, or, God willing, two contenders for another event. But, as those in control triumphantly say, we must be consistent. Can somebody please tell me why? Nobody has ever explained it to me, other than to indicate that it gets them "off the hook". In similar vein, but far more importantly, is the way countries deal with each other. By what right does a government deal with, say, Iran, in the same manner as it deals with, say, New Zealand. But they do, don't they. You know why? Their policies are consistent.

"Consistency is the last refuge of the unimaginative"
Oscar Wilde

CONTUMACIOUS

According to one of my dictionaries, it not only means 'obstinate' and 'stubborn', but also 'opposing lawful authority with contempt'. Yup, that's me - but only when I think I am right. (Yes, I know, I always think I am right). That latter definition certainly applies to me in my relations with the various governing bodies in my sport, athletics, over the years. I have been involved in some quite famous rows with representatives of those bodies, and, in the main, I believe sincerely that the sport has benefited. Particularly, the arguments in the late 1940s and early 1950s about poor judging decisions - illustrated most notably by the incompetence shown over the result of the 1948 Olympic 10,000m race, and later, the lack of timing athletes beyond the first three finishers in track races. To add to the 'insult', the timekeepers often added 'injury' by going home with the details so that nobody ever saw them. Even when they did do their job properly, there was often some doubt as to the accuracy of the times taken. I well remember one timekeeper whose eyesight was so bad that he had to show his watch to a colleague to read after he had timed a race. I take a certain amount of credit for creating a climate of criticism which resulted in batteries of unofficial timekeepers standing behind the official ones, checking their accuracy. My colleagues, (members of the NUTS, a statistical organisation), and I, also brought pressure to bear on the ludicrous record categories which existed in Britain at that time, based primarily on outmoded nationalistic attitudes. As we, as a body, tended to provide the record sections of many programmes and magazines, we were able to force officialdom's hand by just ignoring the record categories we disagreed with, and listing new, more relevant, categories. Again, I believe the sport greatly benefited from this action. One last area of argument was to do with selection processes. Here, it was not so much that the selection processes were wrong, but that they were not using the most up-to-date information about athletes. By compiling regular ranking lists, and making other data available, we were able to greatly improve the quality of the selection process - later, with some of us co-opted onto various selection committees, it became even better.

CRAWLIES
There is one major downside to what I believe is otherwise a perfect marriage between my wife and I. Whenever there is a spider, beetle, or any other type of creepy-crawly about, I suddenly become acknowledged as the head of the household, and am expected to deal with it. What I can never convince my wife of is that I dislike the things even more than she does. Happily, my son is not as squeamish as we are, and, if he is around, he will deal with the problem - otherwise it is up to me. Sometimes, those damn spiders are so ruddy big. As I write this I am ashamed to note that I am taking nervous glances at the floor and walls - what am I, a man or a mouse? Anyone got any cheese?

CRITICS
One is given to understand that theatre, cinema, art, book and music critics serve a useful purpose, though, as people from Missouri say, "You gotta show me". Almost without exception, I find that things the critics dislike, I tend to enjoy, and the things that they rhapsodise over, I find rather boring. The fact that they are in a position to make or break a show or book is ridiculous. Sometimes,

TIMED TO PERFECTION
Stan Greenberg

I think that they just knock something to show how clever they are. There is a wonderful Peter Sellers/Irene Handl spoof of fatuous critics on the record, *Balham, Gateway to the South* - it comes to mind whenever critics refer to French or German literature in their pieces.

Another form of critic, I suppose, was the chap I used to see, when I was younger, at Royal Albert Hall concerts. He would sit in the audience, with a music score on his lap, and, every now and again, would jerk upright in an agitated manner, frowning and looking about him wildly. - I think it meant that someone had played a bum note. This would happen three or four times during a piece, much to the annoyance of people sitting near him. I can't believe that he enjoyed the music - so why did he go?

One piece of criticism that was directed at me, and, at the time, quite upset me, occurred when I was in my early twenties, and competing in a discus competition in the London Business Houses championships. I wasn't very good, but enjoyed doing the event, and I didn't come last. During the competition, the eventual winner, a well-known thrower and coach named Otto Feldmanis, came over to me and, to my great pride, complimented me on my style. Then, he added, in his fractured English, "But, you are so vee-ak!"

CRITIQUE
On Father's Day, not long before my 70th birthday, I received a card from my son, Keith, in which he had written the following message. "Sometimes you can be exasperating, sometimes you are funny, other days you can be really annoying. But, you are the only father I've ever known, and throughout all that you are irreplaceable, irascible, and incorrigible. In fact, you *are* you! And I wouldn't have it any other way!". Not exactly the ideal CV, but if I'm honest with myself, and look at things from his point of view, I guess I can go along with those sentiments. Not all children would be so kind.

TIMED TO PERFECTION
Stan Greenberg

CRUMPETS

I have not behaved often in a way that I am ashamed of, but one occasion does come back to shame me. Soon after we were married, Carole and I were walking around the local Co-op. As we passed the bakery section, she turned to ask me if we should get some crumpets, but, unfortunately, as she uttered that word she hiccuped loudly and violently. To my undying remorse, I reacted with remarkable alacrity, and by the time that the hiccup had drawn the humorous attention of other shoppers, I was at the other end of the store deeply interested in the vegetables. I don't think Carole has ever fully forgiven me for that lapse, but we still have a laugh, and puzzle other people, by crying out the word 'crumpets' whenever we hear a hiccup.

CRYING

When I was in Montreal for the 1976 Olympic Games, I checked in the telephone directory for someone I used to know in London. Muriel Silverman (neé Pater) had been my first girlfriend - when I was five years old. Our families shared the same house soon after I was born - we were upstairs and they were down. The Paters had four daughters, all very attractive, and the youngest, Muriel, was a month older than me. As the only boy in the house I should have been spoiled rotten, but I wasn't, unfortunately. The older girls probably thought I was a nuisance, and I must admit to being something of a crybaby. As we got older Muriel and I remained friends, but there was nothing more - at least not on her side. Like her sisters she grew into a beauty, with brains, and the boys
flocked around, while I tended to worship from afar. At the end of the War, two of the sisters married Canadian soldiers, and the whole family emigrated. Eventually our families lost touch, but we heard that Muriel had married and lived in Montreal.

When I rang up that day 28 years later, the phone was answered by a man with a deep voice, who I assumed was her husband - to my shock it was her grown-up son. Explaining, with some difficulty, that I was an old boyfriend of his mother, I left my name and number. She rang back that evening, very surprised but intrigued, and invited me to visit the following evening. She worked in a hospital as a psychologist - I told you she had brains - and also had a grown-up daughter. When I arrived at the ranch-style house I noticed a massive chain and collar on the veranda. Inside, I met her husband, son and daughter, - and the dog. It was the largest dog I had ever seen - a great slobbering, hairy thing, which remarkably took an instant liking to me. Perhaps it hadn't been fed yet. As I sat down and we started to reminisce about the old days, the dog virtually laid on top of me - and it was heavy. At this point, Muriel was mentioning that one of the things that she remembered about me was the fact that I cried a lot when I was young. I explained that it had been a long time ago, but noted that if they didn't get that blasted dog off me, I was very likely to cry again. Nevertheless, we had a marvelous evening, swapping stories and catching up on family news, and parted vowing to keep in touch. Needless to say, except for a couple of cards, we never did.

As a man, I have only cried on two occasions. The first time was when my father died in 1964, and then only when I was alone. The next time was at my mother's funeral service, when I just broke up in front of everyone. I was very embarrassed afterwards, but, as a cousin, usually very critical of most things I do, said "It only shows that you are human." Also, I was pleasantly surprised at how supportive my son was at the time.

CULTURE

Elsewhere I have expressed my feelings about Michelangelo's stupendous statue of *David* in Florence, but there is another sculptor whose work I admire.   He is the Norwegian, Gustav Vigeland, whose remarkable statues and scuptures dominate Frogner Park in Oslo. I have a particular fondness for him, as he was instrumental in getting me a rise at work. In 1956 I first visited Oslo, and was especially struck by the centrepiece of his *tour de force*. It is a monolithic column made up of interwined, writhing bodies climbing up over each other, and at the very top a hand reaches for the sky, while a surrounding series of impassive figures look on. I sent a postcard of this group to the Unilever shipping department, where I then worked, suggesting that it looked like the department's end-of-year promotion interviews, with the impassive managers looking on. My boss liked it so much that he pushed my promotion through six months earlier than anyone else's.

Another cultural visit resulted in a slightly less edifying result. When I went to Bangkok, on the way to the 1991 World Athletics Championships in Tokyo, I spent an enjoyable couple of days seeing the sights. Perhaps they were not the 'sights' that most tourists go to see in Bangkok, but they were the ones I wanted to visit - and they were wonderful. However, for many months afterwards, my BBC colleague, Stuart Storey, used to introduce me to people as the chap who went to Bangkok, "and saw all the temples".

CURRANTS

I have spent quite a lot of time in my life, and have been ridiculed for, taking currants out of biscuits, cakes and apple pies, which, I consider, have been 'contaminated' by them. I believe my dislike of currants, and their close relatives, raisins and sultanas, came from a documentary film I saw when I was young – and impressionable. Now, we have all heard people call them dead flies, which, of course, is ridiculous. However...... The film showed a place in California where vast plastic sheets were spread on the ground containing thousands, perhaps even millions, of grapes drying in the blazing sun until they turned into currants. It was very noticeable, to me anyway, that there were hordes of flies buzzing around. It seemed fairly obvious that if any of those flies were to land on the sheets and expire, or were otherwise incapacitated, no one could tell, and thus there was a very strong possibility that they would be eaten. Also, of course, all sorts of other things could easily have crawled onto those vast sheets of fruit. So perhaps now you will not think my dislike of currants etc is quite so odd after all.

TIMED TO PERFECTION
Stan Greenberg

CUSTARD

Some foods and meals have forever remained in my subconscious. One of these is custard, or rather the smell of custard when it is burnt. The problem is I love custard. When I was evacuated to Norfolk our school dinners were made (it is difficult to use the word cooked) at nearby Gaywood school. They supplied other schools in the area, and I wonder how many other young minds, and indeed bodies, were scarred by the memories of those dinners. Suffice it to say that in that region, any bad fog, muddy football pitch, or the banks of the River Ouse at low tide, was referred to as Gaywood stew. However, my memory is forever tainted by that smell of burnt custard. Why or how it was always burnt is a mystery. I suppose that it had to be reheated after it was delivered and perhaps that's where and when the dastardly deed was perpetrated. But one never forgets the smell and taste of burnt custard - it stays with you till the end. Perhaps in Purgatory, one of the horrors is that you have to eat burnt custard forever.

Perhaps foolhardily, I asked my new wife to make custard soon after being married. What resulted was terrifying. Using a tin of custard powder and milk, she must have mixed them in the wrong proportions. At her first try all that lay in the saucepan was a thin powdery liquid. Then with the addition of more powder, and an increase in heat, she became a veritable Professor Quatermass as she presided over a quivering, heaving, lumpy mass, which bubbled over the pan and onto the floor. The addition of more milk caused even more violent reaction from what now appeared to be some form of living creature. After a threat to pour the whole unholy mess over my mickey-taking head, it was decided to eat our apple pie untainted, and custard was not to darken our doorstep, or floor, for many a month.

CYNICISM

Oscar Wilde's definition of a cynic as "A man who knows the price of everything, and the value of nothing" is one I like very much. Nowadays, there seem to be so many people like this. Also, there is so much cynicism about politics, religion, health care, relationships, etc etc - you name it. I try not to take a pessimistic view of people's motives and actions, unless they actually affect me personally. The fact that others are suspicious and contemptuous of people's attitudes, does not automatically mean that I will view them in the same mean-minded manner. At least, I do try.

DANCING

I am not exactly a 'Fred Astaire' now, but when I was young I could not dance at all - at least not under the formalised rules of ballroom dancing then in force. Not having a sister, nor any close young female friends or relatives, I never learnt the necessary steps. Even if I had, I would have been much too shy to ask anyone to dance. At family weddings and the like, I sometimes got coerced onto the floor by my mother, but as she was an excellent dancer, she would try and lead, and I would usually make a fool of myself. In fact, the only time I ever danced with a 'stranger' was once when on holiday at Butlins. I think I must have been drunk - although that seems highly unlikely as I never drank at all in those days - but I asked a girl that my friends and I had met at the camp. As I recall she led, and I slipped, tripped and bumped all around the rather large arena, and thoroughly enjoyed it - even more remarkable, I think she did too. However, I never repeated the experiment, dancing that is, until my wedding day, when I knew I would have to lead off the dancing. It says a lot about Carole, who loved to dance, that she stayed with me even though we never went to a dance throughout our courtship. Anyway, at our wedding reception Carole and I were led onto the floor by the M.C. and the band struck up. We did no more than about five or six hesitant steps, just enough to stimulate the other guests to copy, when he took us off to see the photographer - I had primed the man beforehand to help me out.

The silly thing is that I always had a good sense of rhythm and movement, and in the privacy of my bedroom I would often create some terrific dancing moves. Quite possibly, if today's styles had been prevalent when I was young, I might have been a veritable John Travolta, but I just could not grasp the formal steps of my day.

However, there was one occasion, in a restaurant in Italy, about a year after we were married, when we fought our way onto the incredibly small, crowded, dance floor, to dance the only way possible in the circumstances - shuffling around squashed up against each other in the most intimate way. I must say that I really enjoyed that - and obviously still remember it. Since then I often frequent the dance floor at functions, and, according to Carole, I don't do too badly.

DEAFNESS

As I get older I must admit to becoming a little hard of hearing, so that I have the television sound up rather louder than my wife likes. However, there was a time, thankfully a very short time, when I went completely deaf. It was while I was working for Unilever, in the City, when I was in my middle thirties. One afternoon, working at my desk, I experienced the weirdest feeling, and suddenly realised that I could not hear anything. Not a thing, no background noise, no telephones - a constant irritant in the office - no talking, in fact I couldn't hear my own breathing. Horrified, it dawned on me that I was deaf. Apparently speaking very loudly, I told those around me what was wrong, and one of them helped me down to the excellent medical department which the firm had on another floor. Walking along the corridors and down the steps was quite frightening, and I realised for the first time how much we rely on sound to judge our progress and position. People would suddenly appear in front of me, without any warning, and were bemused by my startled reaction. The doctor diagnosed that it was only a build-up of wax, unusually in both ears at the same time, and the nurse used a sort of hosepipe which forced soapy water in them to cleanse them out. As I left the surgery, I was assailed on all sides by the most tremendous din. This continued when I got back to the office, and reached hurtful and almost unbearable proportions as I walked up a main road on the way to the station. It took a few days before that built-in baffle, which apparently we all develop, kicked in, and sound was relegated back to the level I had been used to prior to this incident.

DEBT

I find it difficult to sympathise with people who get into horrendous debt. I can understand the desire to have things that other people have – it seems that envy may be the basis of all debt – but I don't understand how they can spend money that they don't have, and surely must realise that they won't be able to acquire in the future. For this reason I abhor credit cards, and for years refused to have one, paying for anything I wanted in cash, or not getting it if the cash wasn't available. The only reason I use a credit card today is that I am able to accumulate airline miles, very useful for getting upgrades for frequent travellers like my wife and I. However, I am proud of the fact that I have never paid a penny of interest on any such card. Early in my life, my family, while not poor, had to 'watch the pennies' somewhat, and my parents taught me that if you couldn't afford something then you didn't have it. Therefore, I grew up being careful with what money I had – an attitude which remains to this day, and which I and Carole refer to as my I.S (innate stinginess).

I can remember, at school, being very impressed by the pronouncement of Mr Micawber in Charles Dickens' *David Copperfeld,* to the effect "Annual income twenty pounds, annual expenditure nineteen pounds, nineteen and six, result happiness. Annual income twenty pounds, annual expenditure twenty pounds, ought and six, result misery". It completely reflects my attitude towards debt.

DENTISTS

I am not particularly proud of the fact, but I rarely attend, indeed have rarely attended, a dentist. Unfortunately, I have always been a dental coward. It is not necessarily all my fault. When I was about 11 years of age, my local dentist decided that I had most of my milk teeth still in place, and that they should be taken out. An appointment with the dentist was made by my mother, with an attendant anaesthetist to give me gas. I remember that they spent an inordinate amount of time looking at some new piece of large,

TIMED TO PERFECTION
Stan Greenberg

threatening, diabolical equipment that apparently the dentist had just received. I sat waiting nearby in a positive trauma. By the time they got around to me I was wound taut, and as they attempted to put the mask over my face to administer the gas I kicked out, getting one of them in the stomach and the other on the arm. Whether or not it was in revenge, they removed all of those milk teeth in one foul swoop - and left a poor 11 year old boy to face his schoolmates with barely any teeth at all. I hardly saw a dentist again for another 34 years.

My next meeting with a 'Disciple of Beelzebub' came when I began working at Guinness, and I found that I had a bad abscess - a rare occurrence for me. I discovered that an acquaintance of mine had a practice nearby, and I went to see him. He dealt with the problem painlessly, and then expressed a horror at the lack of dentistry in my mouth. Now, it seems that in one respect I have been lucky, in that I have what is called ' a clean mouth', and that as teeth have gone bad they have broken up and fallen out. In fact, they were often pulled out by me in my room at night, sometimes with excruciating pain - such was my fear of the profession. I had no fillings at all at that time. My friend
insisted that I should have some, which he did most proficiently, but then started talking about my bite. It seems that my top jaw did not come down correctly on my lower jaw, which was not good he said, and that to put it right it would be necessary to break the lower jaw, and reset the bite. Yet again, friend or no, another 24 years went by virtually without seeing a dentist.

Then, I must admit to one deviation from the norm. It occurred in Switzerland, while with the BBC TV on a tour to a number of athletics meetings. The day we arrived in Zurich I developed a terrible toothache, which, surprisingly you might think, was very unusual for me. We were staying at a magnificent hotel just outside the city, and the concierge rang up someone in town to arrange an urgent appointment for me next morning, a Sunday and the day of the broadcast. When I arrived I found it was in a building in the centre of the financial district, and looked exceedingly expensive from the outside. It was even more expensive inside, and I recollect that everything seemed to be covered with plush. The dentist was a most pleasant, urbane man who spoke perfect English, and I almost forgot my pain and fear when I saw his assistant. She was straight out of a Bond film - a real knockout. Initially he said that he would give me an emergency filling, which should be attended to in a day or so back home. When I explained that I would not be returning to London for about a week he said that was too long, and that he would deal with it properly. Whether it was his technique, or the closeness of his assistant, but I didn't suffer any discomfort at all - at least not from my tooth. When he had finished, I expected that his bill would be enormous, and wondered if I had enough cash with me. To my amazement, given the emergency call, the plushness of the office, and the assistant, the amount on the invoice was remarkably low. I think he was something of a sports fan, and seemed genuinely interested in what I was doing. Happily, it had not been anything like as bad an experience as I had been expecting. But I have never been able to find another dentist with a 'Bond-girl' like that, so my dental phobia remains.

DEPRIVATION

When I was young I never thought of myself as being deprived. My parents were not well-to-do, but my father worked very hard and earned enough to keep food on the table. We went on holiday, albeit usually to Margate, every year, and, while never fashionable, I was always warmly dressed in bad weather. However, on reflection, there was one area in which I was very badly deprived, although it was nothing to do with my parents. It was not being able to take part in a couple of major sports – those of golf and tennis. In my youth, if not now, they were always considered to be 'rich' sports, as the cost of courts/courses was quite high, and one needed specific equipment and clothing to play. These things I could not afford. Even more limiting, there was a problem regarding my background, as invariably the clubs which hosted those sports were 'restricted' – i.e. they did not allow Jews to join. It is no coincidence that there are very, very few top-class Jewish golf and tennis players in this country, and what few there are, or were, came from clubs that groups of Jews had formed themselves in order to avoid the 'blacklisting'. Without being too immodest, I really believe that I would have done well in both sports had I had the opportunities when I was younger. Far too late in life I made some attempts at both, and did surprisingly well, probably because I have always had the eye and timing for ball games. But I began much too late (a) to get really into the games, and (b) to have the amount of spare time necessary to radically improve. Also, as I got older I begrudged the amount of time and money I would have to spend on sports which, for no reason of their own I suppose, had, as it were, turned their respective backs on me.

DIPPY CON
This has nothing to do with prison or the law, but with learning. In my life I have spent a lot of time regretting that I never acquired any "official" qualifications. Therefore, going through some old files, I was gratified to come across an imposing piece of paper (in fact a certificate) which states that I had been awarded a Diploma in Economics from the extra-mural department of the University of London. I had totally forgotten that I had earned the aforesaid document and "qualification" after three years of quite tough studying at evening classes between 1958 and 1961. The classes were not that tough per se – I seemed to have a penchant for economic theories – but they coincided with the period of my private life which included meeting, courting (now, there's a lovely word), and marrying Carole, and acquiring a house which required a lot of work done to it. It seems that I coped with everything, and now, as Carole has noted, can call myself a Dippy Con (Dip Econ – get it!).

DO IT YOURSELF
I have never been very good with my hands in such areas as drawing or making things. Prior to getting married and a house of my own, I had rarely used tools. When I had my own house, some six months before I got married, I realised that there were a lot of

things that needed doing - and I certainly couldn't afford to hire anyone. So, day after day, week after week, I went to the house after work, miles away from where I then lived - I didn't have a car - and I did it myself. Stripping wallpaper and paint, and replacing them, was not too difficult, and after a while I even enjoyed it, getting a certain creative pleasure from the end product. My next door neighbours, father and son, highly competent themselves, secretly had many a laugh over my efforts, but were very helpful.

On one occasion I decided to remove the picture rail from one of the downstairs rooms. I thought that the rail was just tacked onto the wall, and loosening one end I tugged heartily at the rest of it. To my horror great chunks of brick and plaster came away, as the rail was attached to large lumps of wood imbedded in the brickwork. There were piles of rubble and a channel about three inches high and deep around the top of the wall. I also then noted that the wall above the gap was not level with that beneath it. It was now very late, and I was truly close to tears. Dejectedly, I went next door to leave the key (they kept an eye on the place for us) and told them what had happened.

That was on a Thursday, and I did not visit the place again till the Monday evening. Opening the door of the room with much trepidation, I found that the room was clean and tidy, the gap around the room had been filled in and plastered, and everything looked marvellous. Again, I was close to tears for what my neighbours had done. They made light of it when I confronted them, but I never forgot that act of kindness. For the 25 years that we remained neighbours we never had a cross word, nor as far as I can remember or ascertain, an unkind thought. That is equally true of our relations with the people on the other side. After some of the horror stories I have heard from other friends, I now realise what a blessing it is to have nice neighbours. However, the thought does occur that we must be nice too.

DOCKS
A few years of my early working life were spent at Tooley Street docks, next to London Bridge station in London. They no longer

TIMED TO PERFECTION
Stan Greenberg

exist, partly due to industrial changes, but primarily due to the infamous work practices of the work force - or more likely their union. The early supplies of Birds Eye fish fingers used to come from Denmark, and one of my duties, when working for Unilever shipping department, was to be there when the ships were unloaded, and tally the number of cases delivered. As a member of the 'upper classes' i.e. anyone who wore a suit and tie, I had to run a gauntlet of hostile and crude comments, not least related to my perceived wealth as compared to these 'poor souls' labouring for a pittance. I found it very enlightening to note on a Friday, when I could compare my pay packet, which held a real pittance, with the wad of notes that even the youngest of the Dockers apparently received in theirs. In fact, I actually made enquiries to find out if I could get a job among them - I was still young and healthy then - only to be told, gleefully it seemed, that only family could work there. If you didn't have a family member already working there you didn't have a prayer.

After that 'revelation' - the money difference I mean - things got a bit easier for me, as they looked on me as a needy case Thus, when a box of frozen fish was dropped and burst open - a very regular happening, surprisingly(sic) - I was also given one of the packets, along with the rest of the work group. Another incident really put me in even better standing with them. When the lorries were fully laden with the boxes, packets of dry ice had to be thrown into the gap at the top of the container to help keep them refrigerated. These packets were quite heavy, and covered with a rather thin packaging of brown paper. For reasons I never understood at the time, the Dockers would not be involved in this part of the job, leaving it to the vehicle driver, who usually asked me to help him. It required a little strength, and timing, to heave these packets of ice up over the stacked fish boxes, and one would have to swing them back and forth a few times to build up the necessary momentum. On this occasion, as I was swinging back, the brown paper covering tore, and I could feel the dry ice against my bare hands. Now, I had been told that if bare skin rests against dry ice for very long it burns quite badly. I panicked, and, with a loud yell, I threw the packet as hard as I could towards the lorry. I missed it completely, and the now open packet of ice, impressively steaming from contact with the air, slid wildly down the road, to the accompaniment of great cheers, and a few expletives, from the watching Dockers. From then on most nasty comments stopped, as they took the 'nitwit' under their wing, so to speak.

However, I did almost cause a strike. One morning, apparently on a day when labour relations down there were more fraught than usual, I was passing a lorry from which a small package had just fallen, and lay near the rear wheel. As I went by I bent and picked it up and put it on the lorry. Immediately, I was approached by a solemn chap, who, quite politely, asked me to replace it on the ground. I said that I thought it had fallen off that lorry, a sentiment he agreed with, but still asked that I should replace it on the ground. I thought he was pulling my leg and told him not to be silly, or words to that effect, and walked on. His tone became quite threatening as he again asked me to replace the package. I was just going to ignore him, when one of the docks office staff came running up and practically pleaded with me to do as I was being asked. With very bad grace, I took the item off the lorry and placed it back on the ground. The shop steward, for that was what he was, then signalled to an old chap in the corner, who shuffled over and put it back on the vehicle. As I walked off with the office type, he told me that if I hadn't done as the chap had asked, he would have called the whole docks out on strike. I was extremely careful after that, but I found it very difficult to relate my own left-wing leanings in politics to the general attitude and behaviour of these working men.

DOCTORS
When I was 61 I discovered that I had high blood pressure. At last I realised why I had suffered for so many years with sudden drastic nose bleeds and far too many headaches, something that my old doctor never seemed to diagnose. My new doctor - an attractive middle-aged Cypriot lady - put me on a beta-blocker called Atenolol. Having always been wary of drugs of any sort, I asked her

if it had any side effects. She noted that there was a possibility of becoming drowsy, and then prevaricated somewhat and muttered something about impotency. At my expression of shock she looked me in the eye and said that it shouldn't worry someone of my age. I told her that I was merely old - not dead. Up to that time I had rarely seen a doctor other than for colds and sneezes - nothing major. Bye the bye, that feared side effect does not seem to have affected me so far, praise be.

DOGGED INITIATIVE

When we first moved into our house, some 52 years ago, the electrical system, installed in the 1930s, was way past its sell-by date. We made various enquiries about getting it seen to, and finally decided that our next door neighbour would do it for us. He was an engineer with the Post Office, but moonlighted with his father as an electrician, and as I had seen what he had done in his own house, I was quite happy for him to do ours. They did an excellent job. We soon realised that they employed one unique working method. His wife owned a little dachshund, named "Chippy", who was an integral part of the firm. When they needed to re-wire under the floorboards, they would first raise a couple at one end of a room, and another couple at the other end. Then they tied the wire to Chippy's collar, and put the dog under the floorboards. The wife then went to the other end of the room and called the dog. Without any trouble Chippy would squeeze his way over and around beams under the boards and gleefully greet his mistress at the other opening. In this way they did the re-wiring in double-quick time, with little mess and trouble. It was also great fun, not least, it appeared, for Chippy.

DONNER AND BLITZEN

Though they are the names of the best known of Santa Claus's reindeer, I use them here in their literal sense of thunder and lightning. One of the things I would look forward to in early Hollywood talkies was the point where the angry German – and there was always an angry German in those films – would swear

"Donner and Blitzen". (Oh, what pleased little minds in those far off days). On a recent winter trip to Bournemouth, we were subjected to a terrific snowstorm, during the middle of which there was also thunder and lightning - something that I have never experienced before during a snowstorm. Even I was moved to utter the famous phrase.

DOORS

I once read that on the door of Plato's room, the ancient Greek philosopher, whose teachings expounded the ideas of order and form, had placed a notice to the effect "Let no one enter who does not know geometry". It got me thinking about what notice I should put up on the door of my study. Other than "Keep out", I couldn't think of anything of particular relevance to my own philosophy – if any – and decided that if I ever do put such a notice on my door, it will read, "Let no one enter who does not know the winner of the 1936 Olympic 100m gold medal". (If you don't already know, it was Jesse Owens).

DRINKING

Nobody I knew when I was young – family, friends, or neighbours – ever seemed to drink too much. On the very rare occasion that my father went over his limit, at a party or a wedding, the only effect it had on him was to send him to sleep. The first time I can remember seeing someone I knew in a drunken state was, perhaps surprisingly, at my school during WWII. Our geography teacher was a Mr Prosser-Thomas, known affectionately as 'Tosser', and he was regularly "under the influence". However, when it was learned that his drinking was due to the fact that his wife and child had both been killed during a bombing raid, he was never taken advantage of. In fact, newcomers to the school were warned of the situation by the senior boys, and threatened with dire consequences for any misbehaviour. Despite his 'problem' he was an excellent teacher, and instilled in me a love of geography and, eventually, travel.

When I went to work, and played football with the company team, I began to see many cases of over-indulgence. However, to my knowledge, I have never been drunk. To a certain extent, I owe that status to something that my father told me when I first 'went out in the world'. He said that if I went to a pub with a group of people – and he pointed out that there was no reason that I should not go – I should always make it a rule to buy the first round of drinks. That way, I could leave at any time that I wanted to, without being a welsher. I always followed this advice, and I recommend it to everyone else.

I suppose my attitude to drinking has been shaped by that of my father. The best illustration of this is the fact that in the over 20 years that I lived in his house, prior to getting married myself, I never saw him drink to excess at home. In fact, except for the odd 'drop of schnapps' with a visitor, and the necessary wine drunk during the Passover service, I never saw him drink liquor at all. During that period we lived opposite a very popular public house, but, except for once when an uncle virtually forced him to go in to celebrate something, neither he nor I ever went into the place. Indeed, to this day I can probably count on two hands the number of pubs I have ever visited. I do like a good wine, but I don't like the taste of most real alcoholic drinks. How or why anybody can drink beer, whisky or gin is totally beyond me – I think they taste awful, especially the first time you try any of them. So why do people persevere? To act grown-up?

DRIVING ABROAD

The first time I drove a car outside Britain was when we were in Tenerife in 1978. The vehicle was a Seat, and, though I didn't realise it when I picked it up, its brakes were defective. At one point we, myself, Carole and the two kids, were parked very near the edge of a rather sheer drop, when the car began moving forward. I suddenly found that the foot brake was useless, but had the sense to grab at the handbrake, and just sat there for some little while, shaking. It was the closest we have ever been to meeting our maker. Eventually, I was able to reverse and gingerly make our way

TIMED TO PERFECTION
Stan Greenberg

to safer ground. Prior to that, I had nearly got us killed anyway, when I looked to my RIGHT as I began to move out of slow traffic into the fast lane. Almost too late I realised my mistake, and looking correctly to my LEFT, I narrowly avoided a large truck which was coming up at full speed in the fast lane. It was another ten years before I attempted to drive abroad again.

That time was in the United States, where I must say I have always found driving comparatively easy, although I have never tried to hire a car in a major town. What driving I have done there has been in Florida, and, other than the drive to and from the airport, mainly has consisted of going from our hotel to nearby malls or restaurants. The only 'long distance' I have done was from Orlando to Miami (about 200 miles) on the Florida Turnpike, which was one of the most awful trips I have ever undertaken. Not a hill, not a tree, not even a bush, for mile upon mile. It must be the most boring scenery on earth, as even deserts have dunes or some other physical features to catch the eye. But on this road, just nothing. Where were all the unsightly hoardings one had read about? I would have given almost anything to see one. It was ghastly, and I turned off onto the coast road about halfway down. This was much better, but one hits traffic lights at virtually every block, and thus the journey took much, much longer than we had expected – but at least I didn't fall asleep. The only thing about driving in the States that did catch me out at first, was the regulation that "right hand lane must turn right". Initially, I always stuck in the right hand lane because it was the slow one, and thus got caught out quite often. However, I did learn, eventually.

DRIVING TEST
It took me two tries to pass my driving test. Although I was very tense for the first one, I still think I was good enough to be passed, but I really believe that the examiner was getting his revenge. The reason that I say this was that I badly caught him out when it came to the emergency stop segment of the test. Having been especially good at sprint starting when I used to run, I had very fast reactions,

which as I got older, I retained. Add to that the fact that I was wound up as tight as a the proverbial 'drum', and you can imagine that when he suddenly smacked the dashboard with his clipboard, I reacted like lightning, and we stopped very sharply. Unprepared for my quickness, his head swung forward and crashed against the front window with some force. It was an excellent manouevre, achieved with full control, mine, but I don't think he forgave me.

I nearly blew the second test as well. Leaving the examiner's offices - a different chap this time - he gave me a sight test. As we crossed a minor road on the way to the car, he casually indicated a parked car and asked me to read the licence plate. I strained my eyes, and hesitantly, but correctly, read the number. He looked puzzled and asked which car I was looking at. When I pointed to a red car about 100m down the road, he said that he meant the blue car only about 20m away, and gave me the sort of look that said he thought I was trying to be a smart aleck. I had honestly thought he had indicated the distant car, and thought, but didn't say, that the one he did mean was ridiculously close for an eye test. At least, he knew I had good eyesight.

DRUMS
I have a good sense of rhythm, which I think stems from something in my early schooling. One of my earliest memories of infant's school is of music lessons. They took the form of being directed by a teacher in the use of various 'bangers', 'shakers' and 'tooters', ideally in time with her as she played some rousing music on the piano. These items were tambourines, bells, rattles, penny whistles etc, and, above all, small drums. All the boys would rush for these, as you were considered a sissy if you ended up with one of the other instruments. I think that this was the start of a lifelong love affair with drums, although I never got to play them again. However, as a teenager the jazz and swing band drummers, such as Gene Krupa, Buddy Rich et al, fascinated me. My wife often has to stop me unconsciously drumming my fingers on the table, chair-arm, supermarket check-out desk, or car driving wheel. In later life, I

particularly recall the pleasure I got from a documentary on BBC about African 'talking drums', and the sound (or should one call it the feeling in the pit of one's stomach) of the Korean Dragon drums during the opening ceremony of the 1988 Olympic Games at Seoul.

EARTHQUAKES & OTHER NATURAL PHENOMENA

In 1944, on school Xmas vacation in Manchester, I was awakened during the night by a strange sensation that I realised was the room moving, quite violently. I rushed outside, along with everyone else in the family, to find that most of our neighbours were in the street as well. The rumour went round that the Germans had dropped a land mine nearby. However, the morning newspaper reported that there had been a severe earth tremor throughout the north of England. It happened on a Saturday morning, 30th December, at 1.36am, lasted for about two minutes, and was centred between Manchester and Darlington. A really weird experience.

While working at Guinness in 1979, I went with the MD to the Jerusalem Book Fair, where we manned a stand on a shift basis. One afternoon, after the morning shift, I returned to the Hilton, and went to my room on the 12th floor to have a wash and brush up. While cleaning my teeth I was about to rinse my mouth from a full glass of water, when the water sloshed over the rim. I clearly remember thinking, "You're getting old Stan", i.e. my hand must have been trembling. Then the whole room swayed and shook. My first thought was that the nearby lift had made a very bumpy stop. It was only later that I found out that there had been an earth tremor. Happily there were no serious injuries anywhere.

On my very first trip abroad I had to cross the Baltic Sea by boat at night, and had the strange experience of watching the sun go down to the horizon and immediately begin to rise again - the Midnight Sun. It was very odd to read a newspaper on deck, without artificial light, at 12.30am. Needless to say I didn't sleep that night. The boat passed through the Aland Islands, and not surprisingly there were hundreds of people about on shore. It must be very difficult for people in that region to go to sleep, but since the condition lasts for months, sooner or later they must have to.

One of the most wonderful sights, and sounds, that I have experienced is that of the Horseshoe Falls, at Niagara. To descend into the tunnels beneath, and come out on a gallery within feet of the thundering water was fantastic, matched only by a trip on the *Maid of the Mist*, which takes tourists to the base of the falls. While attending the 1990 Commonwealth Games in Auckland, I visited the hot springs and geyser centre of Rotorua. My first impression of the city was one of smell - an all-pervading stench of sulphur - but all negative thoughts were swept away when I came to the thermal areas. The pools of boiling mud, as well as those of fiercely hot water, were quite remarkable, but my favourite item was Pohutu, New Zealand's largest geyser, which played to a height of nearly 30 metres.

I finally made it to the Grand Canyon in 1996. Flying from Las Vegas, the trip first took Carole and I over part of the Canyon. After landing, a coach took us to three vantage points along the South Rim. It was breathtaking - the sheer size, width, depth and length, let alone the wonderful rock colours, shapes and formations. Truly, it lived up to, and beyond, all my expectations. Writing the preliminary draft of this manuscript coincided with the appearance of the comet, Hale-Bopp, in early 1997. On a series of cold, clear nights, one was able to fully appreciate the phenomenon, even in a built-up area. It reminded me that although I had been unfortunate not to have seen Halley's Comet when it 'came back' in 1986, I had been very impressed by Arend-Roland in 1957.

EATING TO EXCESS

One of the greatest scandals of our time is the amount of food wasted in the western world, and particularly in the United States. On our visits to America, Carole and I have been initially overwhelmed by the sheer quantity and size of portions, and then become angry at the gross waste that results from these outrageous servings. We have learnt to order one sandwich, or 'wedge' of apple pie, between us, but we notice that other diners just tend to leave enormous amounts on their plates. On a recent trip, the first to the USA by my son Keith, the situation was highlighted by him when the waiter brought his drink of Coca-Cola. On seeing the size of the glass he told the bemused waiter that "we put flowers in that at home" – indeed the glass was as large as one of our flower pots. One of the restaurants we visited proudly boasted that their salt beef sandwich (there they call it corned beef) contained 1½lbs of meat. We watched extremely large men and women attack their meal, not one we noted was capable of eating more than half the sandwich, the rest being left for waste. A so-called individual pizza would feed three in the UK, and the tuna in my salade niçoise seemed to be the whole fish. Value for money is one thing, but this sort of extravagance is obscene in a world with so much poverty and starvation.

EMBARRASSMENT

In 1957 I went to Rimini, in Italy, with four friends. They were all much more outward-going towards the opposite sex than I was, and I realised that I was going to have to come out of my shell a little bit. During the holiday they met up with a party of five girls, so, whether I liked it or not, everyone paired up. The girl I ended up with was very nice and we got on quite well I thought, considering my total inability to function sensibly in her presence. Finally, I got around to doing more than just stammering stupidly, and while sitting on the beach one day tentatively I put my arm around her shoulders. Suddenly, a deep voice boomed out "Hello, young Greenberg. Enjoying yourself?" I turned to find, sitting just behind me, the barber whose shop was about 50 yards from where I lived at home, and whose clients included my father and most of our friends. The earth-shattering news that young Greenberg had had his arm around a girl would be all over the neighbourhood within weeks. That was probably the catalyst which led to me finally 'growing-up'.

TIMED TO PERFECTION
Stan Greenberg

EMOTION

I have always been saddened by a certain class of Englishman to whom showing emotion, at least outwardly, is in the same category of behaviour as sitting during the National Anthem, kicking the cat, or playing baseball. It may be that nowadays, with the widespread Gay culture, a man showing his softer feelings would be the subject of whispers. While in no way advocating the cheap, rather offensive, affections displayed by today's younger generation in public, the occasional public display, with good taste, can be pleasing to all. Surely everyone is warmed by a young person running to hug parents or grandparents, or a couple walking arm in arm in the park. But so many people seem unable to bring themselves to show such affection, even to their nearest and dearest.

I am a tactile person - I like touching. Now I don't mean that in a coarse way, merely that, for instance, if I am walking with my wife I like to hold her hand or put my arm around her. If we sit on a sofa I am liable to rest my hand on her knee or put it about her waist. This has sometimes apparently caused 'dismay' to others in the room. It reminds me of when I was young, and on greeting my elderly grandfather I would kiss him. My English friends often seemed to be most uncomfortable at this. But it seemed quite ludicrous to me to merely shake hands - in a manly fashion - with someone I held in such great affection and admiration. Some of my friends would rarely kiss or hug their female relations, let alone the male ones, and as they grew older so the prohibitions grew stronger. Englishmen, of any class, disdain the sight of grown men showing their feelings - except perhaps at a football match. In fact that is about the only place one sees two Englishmen kissing and hugging without anyone taking offence. The Italian or Greek male, as macho as they come, would not think twice about embracing a relation or good friend. It is certainly not considered effeminate for a son to embrace his father, or vice versa, in most places in the world, so why is it so in England.

TIMED TO PERFECTION
Stan Greenberg

END OF SCHOOL

During the 'phoney' period between taking the Matriculation exam and leaving school there were virtually no lessons as such. For a number of otherwise boring weeks we spent most of the school day playing battleships, draughts and chess. However, one day our form master turned up with some racquets, shuttles, and a mass of white linen tape, and asked if anybody would like to learn to play badminton. A few of us showed willing, and we helped him lay out and pin the tape to the wooden floor of the gymnasium, outlining a court. He found uprights and a net, and then instructed us on the basics of the game. From the start I seemed to have an affinity to it, and became reasonably proficient.

Later, when I was working for Lever Brothers, I joined the company badminton club, and became one of its best players, regularly competing in the London Business Houses league for the next twelve years or so. A very fast game – the shuttle moves faster than a squash ball – I would highly recommend it both for the exercise and entertainment.

ENGLISH

I am told that English is a difficult language to learn. When you consider the various, quite odd, pronunciations we use, it is not surprising. Just think of words which end in 'ough'. There is a joke about a foreigner visiting London. Walking with his English host, he attempted to show how well he had mastered the language. "The bird is on the boff", he said. No, he was corrected, it should be bough. His next attempt produced "You have a nasty cow". Again he was corrected, he meant cough. "Ah, that wall is very roff" - but his friend corrected him to rough. Despairingly, he noted that "the baker is using duff", only to be told it was dough. Thoroughly fed up, he was totally demoralised by a sign outside the Palladium which read, "Liberace - pronounced success!"

ENTENTE CORDIALE?

Like so many other British people I have had a love/hate

relationship with France and the French. As far as the country is concerned, I take great pleasure in visiting Paris, and I always enjoy my trips to Nice, but I sometimes think they would be such better places if the populace weren't there. Now I hope that remark won't get me into trouble with a number of French people that I call friends - but I won't insult them by using the phrase that I learnt from English friends who would be rude about my co-religionists and then say "But of course you're different". I often wonder if my prejudice has anything to do with the fact that my French language teacher in school was a swine, and perhaps my attitude to him has been extended to a whole people.

"What I gained by being in France was, learning to be better satisfied with my own country". While sometimes acknowledging what Dr Samuel Johnson was getting at, I cannot go along wholeheartedly with his implication. In fact, especially I remember a certain piece of learning that, at the time, I don't think I could have acquired anywhere else. I refer to my initial acquaintance, on my first visit to Paris, with that odd, low-level, sink, that I discovered next to the toilet in the bathroom of my accommodation. I must admit that, to start with, I thought it was a foot-bath, and was very impressed with the amenities and comforts provided, by my somewhat modest hotel, for their guests who did a great amount of walking around the city. I was quite surprised, in fact even shocked, when I learnt exactly what a *bidet* was for. On reflection I realised that it was quite a good idea really, but found it difficult to describe and to talk about when I got home.

When Carole and I were in Egypt in 1981, naturally we visited the pyramids outside Cairo. We had a very interesting and informative guide, who held forth at great length on the Great Pyramid. He told us that most of the early measurements had been made by Napoleon's engineers, and that they had estimated that if they took all the enormous stones that had been used in its construction, a wall some ten metres high could be built all the way around France. He was interrupted by a very English voice from the rear of the group, who called out "Why don't they then?".

TIMED TO PERFECTION
Stan Greenberg

When the Olympic Games were held in Montreal in 1976, foreign visitors had problems with many of the local shopkeepers, no doubt supporters of the Separatist Québécois movement, who refused to talk to, and often to serve, anyone speaking English in their shops. One doubts that they had ever read that American book "How to Make Friends, and Influence People". Funny how your memory plays tricks - I always thought I was taught in history that Britain beat the French in North America!

ENTHUSIASM

The American essayist/poet/philosopher, Ralph Waldo Emerson noted that "Nothing great was ever achieved without enthusiasm". Apparently the word 'enthusiast' means, literally, one who is possessed or inspired by a god – it comes from the Greek *en theos*. Whether or not that has anything to do with it, I have always found that I have done my best work when I have had some enthusiasm for it.

ETIQUETTE

This story is not about me for a change, but about a friend. In the 1960s Charlie Elliott was a good athletics coach. One of his athletes was a promising 400m runner named Martin Winbolt Lewis, whose family were quite wealthy. When Martin was first selected for a British team, his parents, to thank Charles for his efforts, invited him to their home for dinner. As Charlie said, he was no hick, but was rather overwhelmed by the dining table, which was laid out for a full formal meal. Each place setting had numerous knives, forks and spoons around the place mat, and he told me afterwards that he was somewhat worried about using the correct utensils for the right dish. The first course was grapefruit, and he waited to note what cutlery the other people used. At that point, with his attention distracted, the hostess suggested that he take some sugar - from a large silver bowl in the middle of the table. It had a silver spoon sticking out of it, and, as he noted later, he had enough manners to know that you should bring the bowl nearer to you to take the sugar. However, he was so flustered about the cutlery that he didn't think, and stretching out his arm, he dipped the spoon in the sugar and brought it back across the table to his grapefruit dish. Of course, it was a proper sugar spoon, with holes in it, and he thereby left a trail of sugar all over the table. He said it all seemed to happen in slow motion, and he was incapable of doing anything about it. The family made light of it, but he had never felt so stupid in his life. Incidentally, Martin went on to run in the Olympic Games.

<u>EVACUATION</u>

The day before World War II started, 3 September 1939, my primary school was evacuated to Peterborough. I can remember, quite clearly, waving goodbye to my parents, my mother crying, as coaches took the schoolchildren to the railway station. Another clear memory is of counting the wagons of an incredibly long goods train as it passed through Peterborough station. We were then taken to a hall where we waited for local residents to come and take us home with them. I am not quite sure how the selection process worked, but I fear that I was not too lucky with the people who took me. To be fair, they probably didn't want anybody in the first place, and, as no bombing of London had taken place yet, they didn't think it was necessary anyway. My parents told me later that I was very unhappy there, and they soon brought me back home. Years later I learnt that we, and other London schoolchildren, were billeted all around one of the largest ball-bearing works in Europe. Great planning by someone in authority - it would be a prime target when the 'hot war' began.

Over the next few years I was constantly evacuated again - to Buntingford in Hertfordshire (1941), Luton (1942), Manchester (1944), and Kings Lynn in Norfolk 1944-5) - in between times, returning home for a while. The worst part was the effect on my education, as it involved my joining and leaving about a dozen schools during a three-year period. By extreme good fortune I didn't suffer too much educationally, and except for a complete lack of understanding (to this day) of the concept of 'pi' in maths, I made quite good progress in my school work.

TIMED TO PERFECTION
Stan Greenberg

The family I stayed with in Buntingford (actually a nearby village named Hare Street) had an older son and daughter, and while the boy was quite horrible to me, the girl was much nicer and tended to 'mother' me. A few years ago, some 50 years after I had last seen or heard of them, the daughter, a grandmother now, wrote to me. She had seen my name on TV and wondered if I was her 'little Stanley'.

The last place that I was evacuated to during the war was at King's Lynn, in Norfolk. I was billeted, with a friend, Alan, on a middle-aged couple who had no children of their own, May and Ted Barnaby. She was a large, indeed fat, lady, while he was a hard-as-nails builder, and they were marvellous to us, kind, but firm when needed. Having spent some time in London during the raids, I was still a little nervous at night when I heard the droning of bombers - and did we hear the droning of bombers. Happily, they were ours, but there were literally hundreds of them, as towards the end of the war, the thousand-bomber raids on Germany used to rendezvous over the Wash, the large bay indented into the Norfolk and Lincolnshire coasts. The sound of those engines stayed in my mind for many years afterwards.

On a lighter note, May and Ted greatly influenced my drinking habits. Every weekend they would visit with friends at the local working man's club, and as it wasn't a pub as such, but more of a clubroom with a makeshift bar, they were able to take us with them. During an evening it wasn't unusual for Ted and his friends to knock back as many as eight or nine beers - but I cannot recall ever noticing him drunk in any way or form. The problem was that whenever anyone at the table bought a round, which was fairly often, they would also buy Alan and me a lemonade. I don't know if you have ever tried to drink eight or nine lemonades in an evening, but I can assure you that it has a very definite effect. We were with them until the war was over. Happily, we kept in touch for years after, and they visited us in London, and also attended my wedding.

TIMED TO PERFECTION
Stan Greenberg

EXTREMES

As a person immersed for most of my life in records of one sort or another, I constantly keep a check on my own excursions into the realms of measurable achievements. Not counting flying, the greatest height I have reached on land is 3900m *12790 ft*, just outside the village of Chinchero in Peru, while the lowest point was in the Dead Sea in Israel, which is 394m *1292 ft* below sea level (the lowest point on Earth). Of course, in an aeroplane I have been over 12,497m *41,000ft* but somehow I don't really count that. On a trip to the Taj Mahal, at Agra in India, the outside temperature was 108 degrees fahrenheit *42 degrees centigrade*, but I entered a below-floor-level room which was many degreees hotter than that. The temperature in Doha, Qatar, when I went there for an athletics meeting in 2001, was reported to be 110 degrees F *43 degrees C*, but it didn't seem anything like as humid or oppressive as at Agra. However, those figures were well beaten in June 2013, when we were in Las Vegas for my daughter's 50th birthday, and the temperature reached a local record of 116 degrees – we only stayed out in it for about ten minutes. At the other end of the scale, I have never been in ultra-freezing conditions, other than a British winter, as neither I nor my wife would ever go, of our own free will, to anywhere that had an exceptionally cold climate. However, the coldest occasion I can remember was at the National Cross-Country Championships in March, 1986, on Town Moor, Newcastle, which that day was perhaps one of the bleakest spots on earth. I was as cold as I have ever been, despite wearing thermal long johns, thick socks, even thicker shirt and pullover, a scarf, woollen hat, gloves and a padded anorak. The wind chill factor must have been near record levels.

The greatest speed that I have travelled at is 1232 km/h *766 mph* in a British Airways Boeing 747, on a tourist flight in April 2012, Las Vegas to Heathrow - there was a remarkable tailwind of 354km/h *220mph*. I can pinpoint the slowest speed with some accuracy, as I once was on a local train in Spain, which stopped continually, and even when the train was moving it was very slow. After that trip British Railways seemed to be the epitome of speed, organisation, and efficiency - mind you it was a long time ago.

EYESIGHT

I used to have what I believed was perfect sight, and it was particularly good over long distances. I can remember when I was younger, and in a bus queue, I took a show-off's delight in noting the number of an approaching bus way before anyone else appeared to see it. However, as I have got older there is no question that my sight has deteriorated. I suspect that the years of poring over statistics handbooks, with hundreds of footnotes in minute lettering, and staring for long periods of time at a computer screen, has definitely affected my sight, especially near at hand, so that I now need glasses for close work. Strangely, or so it seems to me, my long sight has retained a good deal of its clarity. This has resulted in an unlooked for comic turn between my friend, Mel Watman, and myself at athletic meetings. During the competitions I have no need of glasses, whereas he has to wear his. However, when the type-written result sheets come round, I have to put my glasses on to read them, while he takes his off.

FAIRNESS

As I have always taught my children, nobody ever promised that life would be fair. However, I have found it especially unfair at times. Social status is so often the criterion, particularly in this country. Thus, if you are well-off and somewhat strange in your behaviour, you will be called "eccentric". If you are poor, you will be "crazy". Then again, a rich person with a pronounced proboscis has a "Roman nose", whereas a poorer person with the same feature has a "hooked nose". If you talk a lot, but are liked, you will be called "ebullient", while if you are not popular you will referred to as someone "who talks too much". A well-to-do lady who is overdressed will be called "fashionable", while someone else, similarly dressed, will be called "tarty". And so it goes.

FAIR PLAY

My foreign-born father, who never played a game or took part in a sport in his life, nevertheless brought me up with the ideas of honesty and fair play. This has been a tremendous handicap to me in a country traditionally the home of 'play the game', but in which the implementation of those concepts are few and far between. In all things, whether it be sport, business, love or friendship, I have always 'played by the rules', and as far as I know I have never cheated or hurt anyone deliberately. But I have been 'done' so many times I have lost count, often by business acquaintances, sometimes by colleagues, and even by friends, but most commonly by shopkeepers and the like.

In sport, dirty play has become the norm. That horrifying concept, the 'professional foul' in football, has totally ruined the game for me. Why such surprise is shown when it is suggested that matches have been deliberately thrown, shows an unbelievable lack of insight into the current state of human nature. Rugby games are plagued by stamping, while in cricket, tampering with the ball is much more common than previously thought. In my sport, athletics, some coaches obviously train their athletes to try and beat the starting gun. And so it goes on. A lot has to do with the imported credo, from America, that 'winning is the only thing'. Personally, I always thought that attitude to be stupid, usually promoted by people who are themselves lacking. Any good sportsman knows that to play well, to the best of their ability, is the only really important thing. But, then, I am overlooking the current level of monetary rewards, aren't I. And I haven't even mentioned drugs.

Unfortunately, people today, and especially the youngsters, only seem to be interested in themselves, with rarely a thought for the old, the weak, or the very young. The new commandments seem to be: Take as much as one can and give back nothing; Expect help from everyone, but give help to none; Win whatever the cost, but win - never mind the rules; Under no circumstances 'play the game'. I suppose playing fair is an outmoded idea, but I appear to be stuck with it.

FAITH

"Faith can move mountains", so I have read. I don't know about that, but it can certainly build them. There are various massive structures around the world, many of which I have been lucky enough to visit, which leave me overwhelmed - undoubtedly the intention of their builders in the first place. The Pyramids of Egypt, Stonehenge, the Temples of Bangkok, the Dome of the Rock in Jerusalem, the Basilica of St Peter's in Rome, Angkor Wat in Cambodia, Teotihuacan outside Mexico City, all these, and more, testify to the incredible achievements of people in the furtherance of faith. However, I must admit to a terrible negative feeling about these awe-inspiring edifices. If the same devotion, skill, money and effort had been directed to bettering the lot of mankind in general, and the local populace in particular, what might have been accomplished. Of course, it is improbable that anything like the effort needed could have been generated 'just' for humanity. That is why I think that the major religions, throughout history, have failed. They glorify themselves as well as their deities, while doing little or nothing for the welfare of their followers. But then, what do I know!

At school I could never understand why some famous missionaries and explorers, who brought the questionable benefits of Western religion to the so-called heathen, could be lauded as great men, when, in many cases, they had left their families destitute at home. How could they be praised for 'saving souls' in some dark corner of the globe, while their own children were starving in some equally dark corner of London, Glasgow or Liverpool. Happily, my own religion does not actively proselytize - it has been said that it is because we think we are 'on to a good thing' and don't want to share it.

FAME

Andy Warhol implied that in the television age everyone will be famous for fifteen minutes. I believe that I have had my 15 minutes worth, in a fairly small way, and in the most unlikely place. While

TIMED TO PERFECTION
Stan Greenberg

visiting Israel in 1980, my family took a ride from Jerusalem to the Dead Sea, through the Judean desert. The vehicle was a medium size tour bus, and we were about halfway to our destination when a young boy passenger made his way to where I was sitting, and quite loudly asked for my autograph. I should explain that at the time I had been Sports Editor of the popular *Guinness Book of Records* for about five years. Apparently, he was an avid reader of the book, must have noticed some sporting stickers on my shoulder bag, and put two and two together. It caused not a little consternation as people craned their necks to see who the 'celebrity' was.

However, it continues to amaze me how often people recognise my name from credits shown after BBC sports programmes, and when I have done questions for *Mastermind*. Strangely, some people have insisted that they have actually seen me on TV, and are surprised when I tell them that I am never seen on those broadcasts. Actually, I have been on the box on a few other occasions, albeit briefly. Twice, while at Guinness, I was asked to adjudicate record attempts on *The Record Breakers*, and another time I was on a quiz programme that was used to introduce a Russian language course. On a different occasion I was interviewed by Mick Robertson about the Olympics, on the Children's Channel. During the 1996 Olympics, I appeared on Channel 4, being asked about the perceived lack of British success. During the same week I also appeared on Sky News to give my thoughts about the suggestion that ballroom dancing become an Olympic sport. After my answer, I fear I may not be asked again.

I have rarely been heard on TV athletics programmes, although David Coleman often complained that because I tended to speak too loudly, when passing information to the commentators, I was probably heard more often than him. However, at the 1989 World Cross-Country Championships, held in Stavanger, Norway, I was the only BBC representative present, the commentary being done, off tube, from the London studios, using data that I sent over a telephone link. The British runner Tim Hutchings ran superbly to win the silver medal behind John Ngugi of Kenya. It was decided that Hutchings should be interviewed, and as I was the only one there, I was to do it. With great assistance from Jim Rosenthal of ITV, I arranged for the Unilateral, as it is called, and then did my first ever interview. The camera, quite correctly, was never on me, and at the end Tim finished with the words "Thanks MEL." My moment of glory had passed - not for the first time I had been confused with my friend Mel Watman. I think that my attitude to fame is summed up in a quote from the comedian Woody Allen, when he said, "I don't want to achieve immortality through my work. I want to achieve it by not dying".

There are a number of good jokes which end with the punch-line "You don't look Jewish". Though not of the same calibre, a recent occurrence along those lines had Carole and I in fits of laughter, much to the puzzlement of the other people involved. We had taken a day trip from Las Vegas to Yosemite National Park. This involved flying initially over the Sierra Nevada mountains (some of them reach heights of over 13,000ft) to the small airport of Merced in California. As we came out of the miniscule terminal building, our 'tour' mini-bus driver was awaiting us, and greeted us with "Hiya, Carole and Stan". We were very surprised that he knew who we were, until we realised that there were only two other people on this tour – and they were a Japanese couple. I suppose we did look like the obvious ones named Greenberg.

FAMILIES
When I notice the close-knit extended familes of one's Italian, Greek and Indian neighbours, I get a little jealous and nostalgic. As an only child, married to another only child, such a scenario cannot be ours. I have wonderful memories of my mother's (two brothers and a sister) and father's (three brothers and a sister) families, and their get-togethers. Of course, a large family inevitably brings more opportunity for discord and strife, and, indeed, tragedy, but also for much love, companionship and support. I still think back with great affection on the regular gatherings on weekend evenings at my

maternal grandmother's house, when there would be about eight adults and four children on hand. Such things are rare today, as, generally, family members no longer live as close to each other as they used to, and often live in different towns, or even different countries. However, it seems that today friends have taken the place of family. Carole and I have far more friends - and I do mean friends, not just acquaintances - than my parents had, and we often have quite large parties at our home.

FASHION

I have never been particularly interested in fashion, and especially not when applied to men. Why someone would wear something that did not suit them, just because it was the 'in' thing to do is totally beyond my comprehension. A perfect example of what I mean can be seen at any banquet, wedding or smart dinner within the last few years. Whereas the women, though not as uniformly smart as they used to be on such occasions, still usually look pretty good, the men, on the whole, look incongruous. The main reason is the ridiculous fad of the winged collar dress shirt. I defy any man to look anything other than stupid, and uncomfortable, in one. Yet because it is said to be the 'fashion' everybody, or at least those with no mind of their own, wears one. When my daughter, Karen, was at 'that' age I asked her why she didn't set a fashion of her own, instead of slavishly following whatever someone else decided. Her answer was along the lines of "Dad, what do you know?", and my reply was that in that respect I knew as much as whatever idiot was coming up with whatever the current fashion then was.

Then we come to button-down collars on shirts, and trousers with turnups - both of which I recall I abhorred in the 1950s and still do. I am totally convinced that one of the primary reasons for the decline in Marks and Spencer sales in the 1990s was their insistence in stocking such items almost to the exclusion of garments which did not have these monstrosities. However, I should give the reader the one really crucial fact with which to judge my remarks - in those 1950s I was known as the 'sartorial blot' of the Unilever Shipping

TIMED TO PERFECTION
Stan Greenberg

Department. In mitigation I must state that, in those days, I had little money to spend on anything, let alone smart clothes. Also, such things just did not bother me at all then, and so it remained until I got involved with the other sex, when I began to think a little more about my appearance.

As always, my own man, if not clever, I never went along with other fads, such as pop music and coffee bars. When I first started taking Carole out, she and her friends were well into the coffee bar scene. As I dislike coffee, I upset a few bar owners by first asking for tea, and raised many a laugh by then innocently asking for a 'cup of chino', not realising, not caring very much, that the drink involved - which was ridiculously expensive at the time - was a cappuccino.

The lunacies of modern fashion were brought home to me a few years ago when Carole and I were in Paris. One afternoon we were strolling down the Champs Élyseés (as one does, doesn't one), when we were approached by a young Japanese couple (It seems that Japanese couples play an important part in our lives, doesn't it?) It transpired that they wanted us to go into the nearby Louis Vuitton emporium and buy some small women's purses – at about £200 a throw! The problem was that they wanted to take home three or four of these purses, apparently very prized in Japan, but that the shop had only allowed them to buy one. The man gave me 900 euros (about £640) and asked that we get as many items as possible. It was very bizarre to be offered so much money by a complete stranger, and I assumed that I looked too decrepit to have run off with it. It seemed a bit of a lark, so Carole and I entered the shop on our mission. Trying not to look like a couple, I going to one counter and Carole going to another, our ruse was soon discovered by the grim-looking woman in charge, and she pointedly told us that we could have one item only. Even then there were all sorts of identity checks made – presumably to see if we had obtained an item in the last few months – and, although I was paying by cash, they insisted on obtaining my name, address and telephone number (which they appeared to check on a computer), before they finally gave us the purse. So there I was, willing to spend another £300-£400, and they wouldn't let me.

What a way to run a business, even if they do want to keep the brand exclusive. I made a mental note never to buy any Louis Vuitton shares. When we returned to the Japanese couple we were very apologetic that we only had one purse, but they were quite philosophical about it. I returned the remainder of the money, although the chap wanted to reward us for our trouble. I said that the experience had been something of a reward in itself, and we left them to try and get someone else to go into the shop for them.

FATHER

With hindsight, I now realise that my father was quite a remarkable man. Born in the Ukraine, he had what appears to have been a Fiddler *on the Roof* existence, until he left, with his mother, a young sister and two brothers, just before the outbreak of WWI. At a young age, about 12, he was the man of the family as they travelled across Europe, since my grandfather was already in Britain setting up a home. Dad never went to school here, starting work immediately, aged 13 to help the family income. An insatiable reader, he taught himself English, and became fascinated by historical subjects. When I was at primary school he seemed to know more about history than most of my teachers, and it is no coincidence that it became my best subject too. At one time we had a very old set of the *Encyclopaedia Britannica*, and Dad read them like other people read novels. He had finished at least four volumes by the time we gave them up to the wartime waste paper drive. By the time he had his own business, as a small-time furrier, he had learned enough about accounts to be complimented by the tax man on his books.

Dad had a real temper. Usually it was me on the receiving end, and I must admit that most of the time I deserved it. During one argument, we came to grips, and Mum, in her peacemaking role, tried to separate us. Aiming a clout at me, Dad accidentally hit her -

TIMED TO PERFECTION
Stan Greenberg

something that had never happened before. Taking advantage of the consternation thus caused I ran out into the garden - a euphemism for our very small backyard - and locked myself behind the big heavy door of the outside lavatory. Having made sure Mum was not badly hurt, Dad sought me out and literally tore that massive door off its hinges. Boy, did I get it that time. Over the years we had many arguments, and often I got clouted. Many was the night I went to my room and plotted ways to kill him, such as cutting away the stairs so he would fall through, or dropping something heavy from a window. Nevertheless, when he died at age 64yr, after a short illness, during which I went to the hospital as often as I could, I cried my eyes out. Probably the previous time that I had cried was about 20 years before when he had last clouted me. When I read the tripe spouted by so-called child experts about the harm caused by (deserved) corporal punishment to adolescents, I really have to smile. What a pity my father could not have brought up some of the spoilt, pampered, vicious, whining brats that prevail in society today. One thing he never believed in was the 'long-term threat' - the habit that parents have of threatening a misbehaving child with dire consequences when they get home. With my father you got your punishment then and there, no matter where it was, in the street, Marks & Spencers, Lyons tea rooms, or my grandmother's house.

One of my uncles used to recall regular Sunday 'matinees' at the latter, when Dad and I had words. My grandmother's place was on the lower level of a large house. The floor above had a corridor leading from a front door, reached by steps from the street, to a back door from which more steps lead down into the garden. There were stairs up from my grandmother's to the middle of the upstairs corridor, and she also had her own back exit to the garden. Thus, to all intents and purposes, there was a 'freeway' through the house. When we had an argument there, at the first twitch of a muscle from my father, I was off up the stairs to the corridor, with him in hot pursuit, along the corridor to the back door, down the stairs, in the downstairs back door, through grandma's kitchen and living room and back up the stairs again. My uncle reminisced that the family would be sitting there with their conversation periodically interrupted by doors opening and slamming and figures running through the room. They would follow the course of events with their eyes raised to the ceiling, as they followed the footsteps upstairs and along the corridor, time and time again, until either my father stopped exhausted, or a shrill scream signalled that I had made an error.

I don't think it unfair to say that my father was not a particularly brave man. He avoided trouble whenever possible, but, nevertheless, became a fire warden in London at the beginning of the war. Thus, when the family went to live in Luton in 1941/42 he volunteered to become one of the wardens in our street. He did this primarily because he felt that being the only Jew, the usual remarks would be made if he didn't. On the first occasion that the sirens sounded, he dressed hurriedly and rushed out to the street so as not to be last. He waited, and waited, and waited, and then went looking for his new colleagues, who had been so gung-ho about their involvement when they approached him to join. He eventually found the head warden, a prominent member of the local Council, safely ensconced in his garden dugout shelter. On that occasion, with a certain grim satisfaction, but without a word, Dad went back to bed.

"It is impossible to please the entire world, and one's father" - so said the French poet Jean de la Fontaine in the 17th century. Not for the first time I have found that a famous saying seems to have been formulated just for me. While, generally speaking, I got on well with my father, I was always aware that he wasn't all that impressed with what I was doing, educationally, sportwise, and work related. He never actually criticised my efforts as such – other than repeatedly commenting on the amount of time I *was wasting* on my sporting interests - but seemed to me to imply that I hadn't done as well at school as I should, and that my career at work could have been better. In fact, according to my mother, he often praised me to family and friends, but never if I was there. I hope that I have been more open with my own children.

TIMED TO PERFECTION
Stan Greenberg

FAWLTY TOWERS
One of the *Fawlty Towers* episodes on television included two famous situations, one concerning a fire alarm drill, and the other involving the visit of some German tourists and the phrase "Don't mention the War". On the day after a repeat of that programme I was discussing it with a colleague at Guinness, as we were about to go to lunch. Just at that moment an office fire alarm test went off, and sent us into uncontrolled laughter. Then, incredibly, as we walked down the corridor, the door of the Managing Director's office opened and out walked two representatives of the company's German publshers, whom I knew quite well. As they recognised me and came forward to shake hands, my colleague whispered in my ear 'Don't mention the War', and I nearly lost control. Somehow, I spluttered greetings, excusing myself as best I could, until I could get away and out of the front door to dissolve in hysterics.

FEAR
The ultimate fear, I suppose, is death. It is not something that I think about very much, although I do get the occasional morbid thought now and again, usually when I find sleep difficult. But the one time I really was terrified of dying was when I experienced my first air raid during World War II. I had been evacuated initially, but had returned home as the people on whom I had been billeted had made my life miserable. One night the sirens sounded, and my parents and I went into my father's workshop, a downstairs room with thick walls. Blankets and pillows were put under a trestle table in one corner and I tried to sleep. The very distinctive droning made by the German bombers woke me and then there was a tremendous barrage of gunfire. A mobile anti-aircraft battery used to be set up at the wide crossroads near our house, and it was mainly the noise of that which I heard. But I thought it was bombs, and although only about 10 years old, and not really understanding about life and death, I became very fearful that I was going to be killed. I cried and screamed uncontrollably until the raid was over, distressing my parents, who could not calm me. However, I must have gone right over the top that night, because after that I was

TIMED TO PERFECTION
Stan Greenberg

never really frightened again.

In fact, within a few days, despite bombs dropping nearby, often I went to a window to look through the blackout curtains to see the searchlights swinging about the sky. Later in the war, when the V1 flying bombs came over, it became almost a game. We would hear them, with their steady droning noise, then, when the engine cut out, we would duck down, in the street, or under a desk at school, and count to ten. If you reached ten then, as the current joke went, you were okay. It seems ridiculous now, but that is how it was for most of London's population. One just carried on normally with just this odd 'disturbance'.

Since those days I have rarely worried about death. If I am honest I must admit that I occasionally worry about being injured or seriously ill, and perhaps of the process of dying, but not of death itself. Sometimes, and again it seems to be in bed at night, I have thought how sad and annoying it will be to have the world carrying on without me. I think that such thoughts are more due to my innate sense of curiousity, or nosiness, than fear - the fact that things will be happening and I won't know about them. Now, that does seem to upset me. I used to have a lot of fears. Fear of the dark, fear of meeting new people, fear of being ridiculed, of being knocked about. Those fears normally took the form of worry. I would worry for weeks about the most silly things, like having to make a speech somewhere, or going to a party at a friend's house, where I knew he would introduce me to a girl. That would drive me to ludicrous lengths to get out of going - I once cycled 100 miles on a Saturday afternoon to avoid a friend's party that evening, ringing him from Norfolk to apologise for forgetting this previous engagement. Public speaking is something that I have still not got used to, and I regularly turn down things I would secretly love to do. As I got older I found that I was causing myself a lot of grief with such worries, and made a conscious effort to change my outlook.

TIMED TO PERFECTION
Stan Greenberg

Nowadays I only worry, if I do at all, about things that are within my power to do something about. So I completely disoriented a couple of Jehovah's Witnesses who turned up on my doorstep. Though I really have little or no interest in what they, and similar groups, have to 'sell', unlike some of my neighbours I would never shut the door in their faces. In fact I quite like to discuss ideas with them, sometimes to their acute discomfort, and sometimes to mine. As our basic parameters of religion not only differ radically, but often oppose, such discussions are rarely dull, and often quite interesting. On this particular occasion they started their 'pitch' by stating that "We are all worried about the state of the world today, with the threat of nuclear war etc". Their bibles have passages marked, which foresaw this situation and which purport to give guidance and hope.

Now I don't mock these people, for I acknowledge that they sincerely believe in what they are doing, and in what they have been taught. But, as I explained to them, I honestly do not worry about such things, things over which I have little or no control. As I told them, what I worry about are things which I can do something about, such as my family, my friends, the weeds in the garden, the state of my fence. That attitude seemed to upset them terribly, more so when they realised that I meant every word. I also said that if people spent less time trying to convert/coerce others to what they believe, and more time in putting right what was wrong, sometimes terribly wrong, in their own beliefs, perhaps the world wouldn't be in the state that was worrying them in the first place. Here endeth the first lesson.

FILING SYSTEMS
Because so much of my professional life, and much of my private life as well, has been involved with the use of various forms of filing, I tend to take an interest in other people's systems. So it was that while waiting to confirm an appointment with my doctor's receptionist, my attention was taken by the filing cabinet behind

her. Each drawer was identified by the first three letters of a patient's name, e.g. AAR - DAC. To my consternation I realised that my family's dockets were in a section marked GRA - HAM, surely a most unfortunate arrangement for people of our particular religious persuasion.

However, I came to realise that any system was better than none, a situation starkly brought home to me when I visited the office of the solicitor dealing with my late mother-in-law's will. Every possible surface, of floor, desk, chair, window-sill, even flower-pot stand, was covered with stacks of paper. Literally hundreds; perhaps thousands of them. How he ever found anything is totally beyond my understanding, and based on how long he had taken in dealing with our case, it seems he couldn't. My wife, who was with me, will never criticise the state of my study again.

FINANCE

I have always claimed to know a little about most things, but there is one particular area of life about which I am almost totally void of knowledge - indeed, there are those who would say even of common sense. That is about the subject of finance. This state of affairs developed in the first place, I am sure, because early on I didn't have any finance to worry about. Then, later, when I began to acquire some of the wherewithal, it always seemed to come and go quite smoothly, so I never bothered too much. It was only when I was married, and had children, that I realised the topic was quite important for our future. It was then that my G.A. (the guardian angel that I have referred to before) seemed to take a hand. When I left Unilever, instead of copying most of my friends, and taking out the money that I had been putting in their pension scheme, I left it in. It was not from any great insight or financial acumen - though that was what it was in fact - but more a case of not knowing what to do, and therefore taking the easy way out, and doing nothing. Similarly, I left my pension money in the GLC scheme when I left there, and also when I left the Guinness organization. Then, as a freelance writer, I put money into a couple of private schemes. So, from being financially inept, I appear to people, not in the know, to have been very astute in such matters.

FINANCIAL ADVICE

Soon after our first child was born Carole became friendly with a young woman who lived nearby. After a time we invited her and her husband around for a cup of coffee, and I met him for the first time. He was much younger than I, and a trifle pompous I thought. Asked about his job, he declared that he was a stockbroker, a title I thought a little ludicrous as he was still in his early 20s. Pushed a little further, he said he actually worked for a stockbroking firm, but that he had an important job telling their clients about Australian stocks and shares. Noting my look of doubt he said that only that morning, a Friday, he had been ringing round advising them to buy into a particular mining stock. I took it all with a pinch of salt, and thought no more about it until the following Monday morning, when the newspaper headlines were full of news of the incredible rise of the Australian mining stock, Poseidon – the one he had mentioned. Yet another chance at fortune lost!

When I became a freelance writer, I took out two private pension schemes, one with Equitable Life and the other with Standard Life. When it came time to convert to a pension, in my infinite financial wisdom, I assumed that I would just have to take whatever those two companies offered me. Luckily, my old friend, and accountant, Alf Wilkins, told me that, if I wanted to, I could move the 'funds' to a different company altogether, and he put me in touch with a Financial Advisor. He turned out to be my G.A. (Actually, as he was an Indian gentleman, I doubt that he was, but he may himself have been guided by mine). This gentleman was very efficient and soon came up with some alternatives. In the meantime I had been checking annuity tables in the Sunday newspapers. Finally, he advised a particular fund, and the yearly amount it would pay for the amount that I would invest. When I pointed out to him that that company was not quoted in the top six tables that were in my newspapers for the last month or so, he said he couldn't understand it but showed me the written offer from them. It was a very good sum, so I took his advice and accepted. The following week 'my' company was shown at the top of the tables in all three newspapers that I bought. Now, how do you account for that? Incidentally, the recent problems that have engulfed Equitable Life, causing their pensions to be cut viciously, would have put me in a serious situation if I had taken up their offer in the first place.

FIRST JOB

The exciting news of passing the Matriculation exam came during the summer holidays of 1947, just after my 16th birthday. I had thought of the possibility of university (it would have been Cambridge from my school) after another two years of study, but I knew that my family could do with some added income. My father had more or less left the decision to me, stating that he would support my decision. If I had known anyone - family or close friends - who had been to university I would have made the effort. But, in those days, it didn't seem very important and I opted for work. I now think it was a major error on my part, but we all have these crossroads in life, and who knows where the other path may have led. Without any idea of what I wanted to do - I did know that I did not want anything to do with accountancy or suchlike - I followed the example of a friend, Stan Davis, and went for an interview with the firm of Lever Brothers (later Unilever Limited) at Blackfriars. I was taken on for a wage of £2.12.6d per week (£2.62½p in today's money). To my delight, a few weeks later when I arrived to start the job, there had been a wage increase, and mine was increased by 2s 6d(12½p). I was so proud when I brought home my first wages.

A hundred or so young men comprised the Lever Brothers intake that year, and all of them with a minimum of Matriculation level. Initially, they were spread around the company as messengers and 'gofers', while they were indoctrinated into the mysteries of the organization by a programme of lectures and factory visits lasting several weeks. Some of this was quite interesting, but the majority

TIMED TO PERFECTION
Stan Greenberg

was rather boring. Unlike most of the others, I rarely took notes, relying on my memory if a query came up. Thus, I was shaken when, at the end of the course, it was announced that we had to provide an essay to show what we had learned. Most of the others wrote up a diary-like report of the day-by-day lectures, using their notes, so I was in trouble. My answer was to let my imagination run riot, and I wrote a sycophantic story of how my young mind had been stirred by the various lectures. I wrote that now when I deliver a shipping note for, say, perfumes destined for soap manufacture, my interest was stirred by the lecture of the gentleman from the perfume department who had listed (rather drily) the various items and where they came from. Visions of the Orient, Cathay and Samarkand, were conjured up, and the mere transfer of that piece of paper took on a quite different aspect. (Yes, it does make my stomach turn a bit now).

Similarly, I wrote that when I took something to this or that senior manager, I now saw him in a different light, as a man dealing with international trade in soaps and soap powders to exotic locations; (Remember this was 1947 and not many ordinary people had ever travelled abroad). Anyway, I wrote a long essay, mainly in the same vein, and with slight tongue in cheek. To my surprise, and the consternation of my colleagues, I won a prize (books of my choice), and the notice of some important people in the company. Years later, I was told by some of the judges that they were fully aware of my lack of notes (and implied lack of interest), but after reading the other essays, most of which were basically in the same boring format, they had been entertained by my piece, which they thought most original. I am sure that this story proves something profound - but I can't think what at the moment.

After the first ten years, most of which I spent in the Shipping Department among dozens of other clerks, I applied for a job in Economics and Statistics, a department run as a personal fiefdom by Ronald J Brech. That fine gentleman, related to the famed management guru of the same name, believed in interviewing personally anyone who was going to be under his direction. He refused to deal through Personnel, which made him very unpopular with them, but not with his staff, who took it, correctly, that he had chosen them himself. It was the first time that I had to endure an 'American' interview. Seated around a table were Mr Brech, his senior assistant, and Peter Towell, the head of the section which had the vacancy. I sat facing them, and was immediately harassed. That is the only way I can describe it. They 'attacked' me, verbally of course, throwing questions at me, one after the other, leaving me very little time to think about my answers. They also picked up on any comments that I made which appeared to contradict something I had said previously, leaving me bewildered, and not a little angry.

Suddenly the questions centred on the Common Market. Remember, this was in 1958 and the EEC was in its early days. I was asked what I knew about it, to which I answered that I didn't know much except what I had occasionally read. They pressed me on what I had read, and what views did I have about the whole project. I commented that from what little I knew it seemed that the concept was a good one for Europe as a whole, and for the member countries in particular, and that it was a shame that Britain was not involved, giving my reasons. This elicited knowing looks between them and I thought that perhaps I had said the wrong thing. It turned out that they were, in fact, all very much against British membership of the EEC at that time, indeed against the Treaty of Rome in toto, but they were quite impressed with the thoughts behind my opinions. Then Mr Brech's assistant, whom later I came to regard highly, incorrectly picked me up on an apparent contradiction, and I lost my temper. Pounding my hand on the table I wagged my finger at him and corrected him forcibly, but, I hope, not rudely. At this they looked taken aback, and brought the interview to a fairly quick conclusion. I thought that I had well and truly blown it, but to my great surprise, a day or so later, I was offered the position. Peter later told me that it was at that point I clinched it, because Mr Brech wanted people in his department who would stick up for themselves and their opinions (if they thought they were right) against anyone, irrespective of their status. It transpired that I was to concentrate on the EEC, in relation to the tariffs and trade measures which were being implemented, as far as they affected Lever Brothers trade and commodities.

As such I then had a number of stimulating years under a head of department who gave a person a job he thought they could do, and if they did it well, he would never interfere or question their competence. So it was that when the Chairman of the company, Lord Heyworth, wanted to know something about the Treaty of Rome, I, as the expert, was sent up to explain it to him. I was very nervous, clutching my rather dog-eared copy of the Treaty in my hands, when I was ushered into his office. Greeting me with "So that's the famous book is it", he held out his hand to receive it. In my haste to give it to him I let it slip, and it fell to the carpet, the flimsy binding pulling apart and the pages falling out and spreading all over the office. I was frozen with embarrassment and could not move, so that when his secretary came in, she saw me standing there, while the Chairman was scrabbling around on the floor at my feet picking up the bits of paper. Happily he did not take it badly, and I was able to recover and give a good account of the salient points of the Treaty. By lunchtime that same day the story was all over the building.

On reflection, I realise that I was very prone to incidents of a like nature, and became quite famous for them. There was a particular occasion when I was called to see Mr Brech. Entering his office I remembered that the previous time I had been there I had great difficulty shutting his very heavy door behind me due to the strength of the door springs. So this time I gave it a vicious shove behind me as I moved towards his desk. I was unaware that recently the springs had been disconnected for overhaul, so that the massive door slammed shut with a tremendous thud, causing Mr Brech, literally, to leap into the air, knocking over his equally heavy chair. That story too seemed to spread like the proverbial wildfire, and I had the impression that for many months after, he was distinctly nervous whenever I entered his office. Later, I heard he told someone that, whatever else, it was never dull when I was around.

Another time, I was doing some typing when Peter Towell came out of his office holding a cup of tea, and sat alongside me waiting to ask something. Accidently I happened to press the tab key, making the carriage extend to its full length. As though in slow motion, both he and I watched it as it slowly nudged his hand and tipped the contents of the cup into his lap. I never did find out what it was that he had come to ask me about, and it took a lot of fast talking to convince him that it was an accident.

The sports facilities at Lever Brothers in the late 1940s and early 1950s were first class, and I availed myself of a lot of them. In particular, I played football and badminton, but, as I wanted to continue running, I had to resurrect the pre-war athletics section myself. At one point, I actually had the captain of England in 'my' team. Ken Wilmshurst, five times AAA champion in the triple jump, joined the company in the 1950s. He was captain of the English athletics team at the 1954 Commonwealth Games, at which he won the long jump and triple jump, as well as reaching the final of the 440y hurdles. He could run a very fast flat 440y, and happily joined our medley relay squad, refusing the offered captaincy - much to my gratification. With him we were virtually unbeatable, even though I ran the last 220y leg. He would cause a stir at work by hopping up four or five steep flights of stairs every morning on the way to his office.

My last years in E & S were not happy I am afraid. I was upgraded, but, unfortunately, worked for a section head who nearly drove me crazy. Not personally unpleasant, but work-wise he was impossible. He had a photographic memory, and such people always need to reassure themselves that they are right. So, when reference was made to a report or letter, he had to prove that he had remembered it correctly. His staff would spend (waste) hours looking through the filing for the damned thing. After having spent 20 years with

TIMED TO PERFECTION
Stan Greenberg

Unilever, I decided I had to look elsewhere. Because I now had two children I was nervous about where to go - I was very much into job security, pension rights and that sort of thing. So I ended up at the GLC.

FLYING
I had always been fascinated by flying, and one of the greatest disappointments in my life was when I was discharged, honorably I might add, from the RAF in 1949, after only a few weeks, due to medical reasons. During the war I had become expert at plane-spotting, and in my bedroom there had been large posters of aeroplane silhouettes, Allied and enemy ones, most of which I knew. When I was called up for military service the first thought that came to mind was that I would get to fly. However, the first flight I made was not until 1961, in a Caravelle, a French plane which had a remarkable rate and angle of climb. I was travelling with my wife and her parents to Rimini, and I was really excited at the prospect, but I gasped out loud as the plane suddenly tilted upwards as it sped along the runway, and seemingly climbed vertically. It was a great flight, and it certainly gave me the taste for more of the same. I have since done a tremendous amount of flying, all over Europe, to all the continents, and around the world four times. I estimate that I have flown a total of over 1,000,000 miles *1.6 million km* since that first time.

Not all of my flights have been on large commercial planes. A couple of light planes left lasting impressions on me. The first was a four-seater taking Stu Storey and myself from an athletics meeting in Belfast to another one in Gateshead. It was the first such plane I had flown in and I was a little shaken at the way it was buffeted by the wind. I sat next to the pilot, and found it quite fascinating as he explained what he was doing, and how he 'followed' beacons to stay on the correct route. Another interesting outing came with a surprise helicopter flight I gave Carole over Disney World, at Orlando, Florida. I thought she might balk at the idea, but she

TIMED TO PERFECTION
Stan Greenberg

thoroughly enjoyed it, as did I, and we are now thinking of arranging a balloon flight somewhere. On my last BBC trip, to Victoria, Canada, for the 1994 Commonwealth Games, I took the opportunity of a small seaplane flight over the glacier in the Olympic Mountains, just over the water in the United States. It was really spectacular, not least the take-off and landing on the water. Then, just a few years ago, my wife, son and I took a Zeppelin balloon flight over London, which was really fascinating.

One other flying experience specifically sticks in my mind. In late 1966 Carole and I were part of a group of athletics fans who went to Paris for a GB v France match. We flew from Manston to Le Touquet, and the plane used was memorable. It held about 30 people, looked a little decrepit, and stood on the tarmac on its tricycle undercarriage (i.e. one wheel under the nose). The stewardess called out that we should fill the front seats first, so jokingly I asked her was that because the plane would tip up otherwise. "Oh yes" she said, to everybody's discomfort. As we climbed in it was noticed that one lady in the party was in a fairly late stage of pregnancy, and everyone shouted at her "To the front, to the front". Then when we landed, after a short, but bumpy, flight, we had to unload from the rear rows first. I think it is true to say that some of us were unusually quiet during the trip, and one of the group, a member of the RAF, seemed positively terrified. That did not have much of a calming effect on the rest of us.

FOGS
Not long ago my son commented that it was foggy, and I nearly laughed out loud. Young people today have no conception of what city fogs in Britain used to be like before the Clean Air Acts were introduced. I can remember real 'pea-soupers', in which you could not see more than a foot at most, and which were a serious hazard to your health. I recall the horrendous fog, or rather smog, of December 1962, which was the worst that I ever experienced in terms of the affect on one's health. Along with many of the

TIMED TO PERFECTION
Stan Greenberg

population of London, both Carole, who was then pregnant, and I wore surgical face masks when we went to work, and they were frighteningly filthy by the end of the day. It was reported later that some 4000 or more people of West Indian origin had died, as their respiratory systems had been unable to cope.

During WWII, in Manchester, I had gone to the cinema with my father one evening, in reasonably clear, albeit dark, conditions. When we came out, it was impossible to see your hand in front of your face, quite literally. My father's eyesight was not very good at the best of times, and in these conditions was useless. Holding firmly to his arm, I wasn't too worried, as I was pretty certain that I knew the way back to our house – it was merely a case of feeling the hedges on my right until a gap, i.e. a road, came up, and then turn down that road which would take us straight home. After a while I realised that something was very wrong when I scuffed my shoes on a tram line. Now, the only tram lines in that area meant that we had actually turned left at some point, and gone up an entirely different road - in the opposite direction. Although I considered this to be impossible, I worked on the basis that I had done just that, and was able to slowly retrace our steps, and eventually, about an hour and a half later (for a normal ten minute journey) got home. We passed council workers and police carrying large red storm lamps, but we didn't see them until they were level with us. Also, despite walking into a number of lampposts, I couldn't see the glow of the lamp above. It was a very disorienting and frightening experience.

On another occasion, at the Farnborough Air Show in Hampshire with friends who had a car, the fog came down suddenly towards the end of the show. It was a nightmare to get out of the car park. As far as I could tell, there was only one narrow exit open, and hundreds of cars were trying to get out of it in virtual pitch black conditions. I sat on the car's bonnet and directed my driver friend out as best I could in the ensuing chaos. Once out of the car park it was still pandemonium as the fog got thicker, if that were possible, and some cars slipped into ditches at the sides of the very narrow approach roads. It took about two hours to get clear of the Farnborough area. In those days fogs really were fogs.

FOOD

I am certainly no gourmet, indeed, mostly I merely eat to live, but certain meals have stuck in my memory. One year I stayed in Budapest at the Gellert Hotel, once a very fine establishment, but it had deteriorated somewhat. For breakfast on the first morning I had ordered a plain omelet, toast and jam, but had not received the latter, despite continued requests. The next morning I ordered the same items but stressed that the waiter should not forget the jam. When my order arrived, again it was missing. That is, until I cut open my omelet - there it was, in the omelet. The runny jam and the semi-cooked omelet resulted in an unappetising conglomeration which I left congealing on my plate. Then a friend, the late Jim Coote of the *Daily Telegraph,* came and sat at my table. Engrossed in the menu he looked down at my plate and asked what it was. I replied it was a jam omelet. It says a lot about his opinion of my eating habits that he didn't bat an eyelid, but merely remarked that he didn't think that he would have that.

Perhaps the most memorable meal I ever had was well before I could afford to frequent good restaurants. In 1949, I teamed up with a workmate to cycle down to Devon. I had never remotely cycled such a distance before, and my friend was a top class racing cyclist. Thus, most of the journey consisted of he shooting off at his own speed, reaching our destination hours ahead of me, while I made my weary, but happy, way through the then virtually traffic-free countryside. On the first Sunday we made the journey from Exeter to Bideford on the north coast of Devon. Eating was a problem as no shops or restaurants were open anywhere, and as evening drew on we were really hungry. By the time we arrived at the boarding house we had booked we were quite worried. The landlady said it was much too late for her to make anything. In desperation we went looking for a chocolate machine. To our delight we found a fish and chip shop open - on a Sunday evening, a mystery to this day. I still relish the meal we had then, of double fish and chips with a plateful of white bread and butter and a large mug of tea. I sometimes think that if my circumstances were unfortunate enough for me to be offered the proverbial last meal, I would order exactly that one.

The ordering of food in restaurants is another area of my life seriously affected, at times, by my interest in the cinema. In particular, an episode from a Marx Brothers film, *A Night at the Opera*, has caused me some embarrassment. It is the famous ship stateroom scene, in which a vast number of people end up in Groucho's miniscule cabin. He orders food, with his choices punctuated by Chico and Harpo asking for "Two hard-boiled eggs". Thus, every order has added to it "and two hard-boiled eggs". This situation has been a source of great fun in my family, but it got out of hand one day. When my children were quite young we took them to a good restaurant. As I gave the waiter our order, the kids in turn added, "and two hard-boiled eggs" to everything that I was saying. As the items were such that the addition of eggs would not be unduly unusual, the poor waiter kept writing these instructions down. I, of course, had to tell him to ignore the eggs business, but he got into a terrible state, and eventually got the whole order wrong. I didn't complain, and indeed gave him a decent tip to recompense him for all he had gone through. Outside the restaurant I enjoyed the joke as much as the children, but they got a serious warning about trying it again. However, Carole and I have sometimes succumbed and confused unsuspecting waiters with the routine.

FOOTBALL (PLAYING)
I first played soccer at school, continued later at work, and had a fairly successful career as an outside right. I was not particularly skillful with the ball, but I was fast, and this often proved decisive. The defense players I came up against were invariably carbon copies of the England defenders of the time - big, rough and ponderous. As when the Hungarians demolished England in 1953

TIMED TO PERFECTION
Stan Greenberg

with their speed as much as skill, I found that if a long ball was put in the right place I could easily outrun them. Often I missed many easy shots at goal, but eventually I would be lucky. Nevertheless, my scoring rate was quite high. Purists got very upset, but I enjoyed it. When I had friends playing at right back, right half and inside right, between us we could destroy a defence's confidence and defeat their pre-arranged plans to play the offside rule. It only took a long hard kick by one of my mates, and the cry 'Go, Stan'. In one memorable game against quite good opposition I scored 4 goals - and missed another four.

In 1989 I was invited to a reunion of the Unilever Football Club. I had left the company over 20 years before, and had finished playing for them about eight years prior to that, so I was going to meet men I had not seen for nearly thirty years. I was quite nervous when I entered the meeting-place, but when I joined the group I began to recall nearly all the faces, although names eluded me. Most of them remembered me, and soon we were reminiscing about old times and games. To my great surprise they all seemed to remember two things about me. One was my toe-punting, and the other was an article I had written for the club magazine. I was never able to kick with my instep, and so toe-punted the ball. As football boots then had reinforced toe pieces it never hurt my feet, and I developed a lot of force and accuracy with the style - which nevertheless was frowned upon and ridiculed by most of my teammates. However, I was able to use this punting to great effect, especially when taking corner kicks, as I had the ability to drop the ball onto my teammates' heads virtually at will, with many a goal thus scored. Additionally, on a number of occasions, I actually scored direct from the corner kick, usually the result of a slice which curled the ball neatly under the crossbar out of reach of the keeper. A very spectacular shot, I rarely let on that it was invariably caused by a bad kick. In fact, in pre-game plans it was suggested sometimes that I should try such a shot as a surprise. Little did they realise that I didn't have much say in the matter. Also, I often scored with direct shots at goal from a fair way out. Sure, lots of people do, but very few punt with their toe. The main characteristic

TIMED TO PERFECTION
Stan Greenberg

of a toe punt is that it causes the ball to rise in a gradual climb. Usually the ball would go way over the top. (I could have made my fortune at American Football with that sort of kicking). However, if I was a certain distance away from the goal when I punted, it would send the ball into the top of the net to the consternation of the goalie who would be expecting a nearer ground shot.

The magazine article was a sore point to all concerned. The club was having a period when too many players were pulling muscles during games. It was obvious to me that this was due primarily to the lack of warming up prior to games. When players have been sitting at desks all week, and then for a few hours indulge in violent exercise, it is not really surprising if the muscles rebel. Especially so when they are not tuned up first, by stretching exercises and running. I always spent about 10-15 minutes before a match, running around the field, interspersing sprints, while all my colleagues just practised shots at goal. This was patently a useless exercise since they rarely had the opportunity during the game, and even if they did they rarely scored. I made the socially bad error of writing this in my article which stressed the need for proper warming up. I also claimed, at the time correctly, that I had never pulled a muscle in my life, and rubbed in the point that as the fastest man in the club it was likely that the stress I was putting on my legs was generally greater than they put on theirs. The article caused a lot of comment, and quite a lot of bitterness. One of my pithier comments was about games held up while players rolled about on the floor with cramps or pulls. The Saturday following the publication of the piece I missed my train to the game, and arrived minutes before kick-off. Unable to warm-up I unfortunately got a long ball within the first few minutes. Dashing after it, you can guess what happened. Down I went in agony - and the game went on around and over me for about five minutes before the whistle was blown. To hoots of derision, from my own team, I left the field, and the article and I passed into the realms of myth and legend.

There was another 'infamous' occasion in my football career at Lever Brothers, which caused quite an uproar in the club, and in the

TIMED TO PERFECTION
Stan Greenberg

league in which we played. It was the only time that I ever deliberately fouled someone - and it was a player in my own team. Are you comfortable? Then I'll begin. We had an excellent centre-forward in the club, who had ball skills way beyond the rest of us. However, as with other players of the ilk, he was a selfish player, retaining the ball far too long, ruining quick breaks, and allowing the defence to regroup and steady itself. There he would be beating man after man, sometimes going back to beat the same man again, while the rest of us forwards seethed and yelled for a pass. On the rare occasion he did pass, it was always a perfect one, but usually too late for us ordinary mortals to make good use of it. Incidentally, besides being a tremendous ball player he was also a terrible cheat, and was quite proud of his skills of cunningly fouling people and slyly handballing. I abhorred this aspect of his game, not least because it made the opposing defence mad, and they would then take it out on me. Anyway, in one particular match I got thoroughly fed up with his shenanigans, and something snapped. I came roaring in from the wing as he feinted and elbowed and kicked his way through a group of players in the middle, and at full speed shoved him in the back, sending him flying, to land in a heap some distance away. Consternation reigned. The referee blew his whistle angrily - but then wondered what he should do. He had never had a case of someone deliberately fouling a teammate. My captain got between the player, now breathing fire and brimstone, and me, trying to pacify him. The other team stood by totally bemused, but from their remarks they obviously realised why I had done it. Indeed, so did my captain and most of my team. I refused to apologise, and the match was continued with dire threats coming my way from the centre. However, it seemed that for the rest of the game my 'friend' was much less selfish with the ball. He also developed a nervous twitch, glancing over his shoulder as though expecting something. I can't remember what happened after the final whistle, but we were put in different teams for a long time after that.

In 1976 I had missed an opportunity which would have crowned my soccer 'career'. The family were on holiday in Spain, at

Torremolinos, and one of the other hotel guests was Malcolm MacDonald, top goal scorer in Division I in 1974-75 for Newcastle. Just transferred to Arsenal, he had made headlines on all the sports pages in Britain. The waiters at our hotel had a soccer team, and they challenged the British tourists to a game. I added my name to the list, which included MacDonald, and was selected to play at outside right to his centre-forward. The great day arrived and we set off for the pitch, a rough cinder and dirt one, in the town. Just as we arrived a torrential storm burst and destroyed any possibilty of a match. We were unable to rearrange it. So my only chance to play with a top-class player was missed. Perhaps it was just as well.

FOOTBALL MEMORIES (WATCHING)

I own up to the heresy of all heresies, and admit to supporting both Spurs (my first love) and Arsenal, at the same time, in the 1940s. This "aberration" came about because during World War II the Arsenal ground was used by a barrage balloon unit, and the team shared the Spurs ground at White Hart Lane. Thus, when I wasn't able to travel to Spurs' away games, I would watch Arsenal instead. However, I have not been to a live match in Britain since 1948, and only one abroad.

FOREIGN TRAVEL

About a week after leaving hospital with her baby son, my mother went to Margate to recuperate from what was, I am told, a difficult birth. A holiday at such an early age probably gave me my taste for travel and I have been lucky to have travelled extensively. Rarely have I been anywhere that I found dull or uninteresting, though that may say more about me as an inveterate tourist, than for the places I visited. When I was 12 years old I saw a film about American sailors in Hawaii, and it set me dreaming of strange, exotic places. Later, I listened regularly to radio's *Armchair Traveller,* which consisted of travel talks interspersed with appropriate music. It has recently occurred to me that another stimulant was a famous series

TIMED TO PERFECTION
Stan Greenberg

of cinema travelogues, made in the late 1930s and 1940s, introduced by Lowell Thomas.

These things definitely stimulated my imagination, and I made a list of places I wanted to visit, never dreaming I would ever see any of them. Happily, now I have been to all of them. Hawaii, New York, Monte Carlo, Paris, Rome, Florence, Venice, Jerusalem, Berlin, Prague, Moscow, San Francisco, Istanbul, Athens, Hollywood, The Leaning Tower of Pisa, the Taj Mahal, The Pyramids, The Grand Canyon, and The Great Wall of China. In 2003 I made it to the last one, Machu Picchu.

Despite this insatiable urge to travel abroad, I did not make my first foreign trip until 1952, to Finland, when I was 21. After that, for quite a while, I was able to travel only irregularly, mainly on holiday, and only to Europe. However, in 1972 I made my first trip further afield, to New York. Then two years later, after the Commonwealth Games in New Zealand, I spread my wings even farther, and stopped off in Honolulu and Mexico City on the way back. By the 1980s, mainly courtesy of the BBC, I was visiting about a dozen places worldwide per year. My peak year was 1985 when I went to: Paris, Athens, Lisbon, Erfurt, Oslo (twice|), Bremen, Helsinki, Nice, Budapest, Moscow, Zurich, Berlin, Cologne, Koblenz, Brussels, Rome, Canberra and Florida. Currently, I have been to, and stayed for a period of time in, 50 separate countries on every continent. I take some pride in noting that I always made time for sight-seeing in whatever place I was - and experienced some wonderful moments relating to structures, natural wonders, or art. God willing, I haven't finished yet.

Most of my travelling was on work-related, usually on a very tight schedule, but I always managed some sightseeing. My 'quickie tours' became quite famous. Assuming I might never return to whatever place it was, I tried to see everything possible. Once, in Rome, when much younger, I left my hotel at 6am and returned at 7pm, having done a well-planned walking tour of all major, and quite a few minor, historical sites.

TIMED TO PERFECTION
Stan Greenberg

It was some years before I visited the Soviet Union. The first time was to Minsk, but due to the vagaries of internal travel in that country we flew to Moscow first, and then 640km *400 miles* back towards London. The internal plane journey was on a modern jet, but it had some 'odd' features, not least the chintz covered lamp-shades, and a lump of solid ice on a screw-head *inside* the plane.

When abroad, I find that the intricacies of foreign currency can be easily overcome if you take a little time to acquaint yourself with the exchange rate. Often being in three different countries within a week, I rarely experienced any trouble. However, I got my come-uppance on a weekend trip to Istanbul with my wife in July, 1993. I had noted that the exchange rate was a very high figure, but hadn't taken it in fully, and was startled when my four-night hotel bill totalled over 1 million Turkish lira. After the initial shock I realised that it was only about £300 or so.

My mother never travelled abroad until she was 68, when she accompanied us to Italy. We were quite anxious that she might react badly to her first flight, but we needn't have worried, as she took to flying like the proverbial duck to water. Indeed, she soon became something of an authority on the nuances of foreign travel and flying when talking to family and friends. She then had a trip to Israel, with her sister when she was 73, and as she was now older and it was to be a much longer flight, we were on edge, but all went well. Her last flight was when she was in her 80s, to Tenerife with us. However that seemed to satisfy her wanderlust as, though she lived for another 13 or so years, she didn't deign to accompany us on any of our later trips.

FRIENDS
I have many acquaintances, from work, play and everyday life, but, comparatively, few friends. I don't think that means that I am an unfriendly person - indeed I think I am quite gregarious, although basically shy - but to my mind a real friend is a rare individual.

Usually, such a person is someone I have known well for a long time, in some cases for almost a lifetime, and though it is possible we haven't met up for a number of years, we can practically pick up the conversation from the last time. On the whole, we tend to share many of the same interests and passions, and therefore we are on the same 'wavelength' about things. These people would be among the first I would turn to in times of sadness, and of gladness, knowing that I will get the sympathetic and sensible response that I need. They would be someone with whom I could discuss, and know it would be in confidence, my troubles, my successes, my fears and my joys, my health and, sometimes, my finances. Similarly, they would seek my help on the same matters. Such people are virtually family, and are treated as such.

FRISKED

When Carole and I went to Madrid for a few days in 1996, we were warned to be very careful of pickpockets, and especially of gypsies. While out for a walk one day, we noticed three very attractive young gypsy women coming towards us. Even though my wife and I were arm-in-arm, as they drew level one of them deliberately bumped into me. She leaned against me and I felt her hands all over my body, and pockets - which under different circumstances would have been quite interesting, or perhaps stimulating might be a better word. In the course of this frisking, my glass case came out, or was pulled out, of my shirt pocket, and fell to the ground. The woman made a big thing about picking it up for me, apologising and returning it. After they had gone on their way, we marvelled at the brashness of it, but we had a good laugh, because I had taken the precaution of putting all my paper money and credit cards into that glass case for safety, and she hadn't realised what she was holding.

FRUSTRATION

One of the most frustrating things that have happened to me in my life occurred in early 2006. It concerned a piece written about me in an athletics magazine. Over the years I have had quite a number of paragraphs which mentioned me in various newspapers and magazines, and usually most of them have been quite flattering. A number of them have been in foreign publications, including American, French, German, Italian and even Israeli ones, and I have not encountered too many problems in understanding them. I should state that I had no reason to think that this new piece contained anything denigrating or offensive, as it had been written by a good friend who lived in California. However, the problem was that his name was Ken Nakamura, and he had written it for a Japanese athletics magazine, a copy of which he sent me, AND I COULDN'T READ A WORD. You cannot imagine how frustrating it is to see a whole page of print, with your photo at the top, all of it obviously about you, and you can't understand any of it. Happily, after some pleading e-mails, Ken made time to send me an English translation of his article, which, unusually for the genre, was factually correct and in context.

GAMBLING

Gambling has never played an important part in my life. However, there has been the occasion when the results of a gamble have provided some good moments. The first that I can remember was when my father won the football pools just after the war. Now, he didn't actually win the pools, as such, but won something on the pools. In fact, it wasn't very much. After years of trying, he got a correct line of the 'Easy Six', and received the princely sum of £17 15s. It was as though he had won thousands. He gave the odd 15s to me, £5 each to my mother and his old father, and then with his £7 he took us out for a meal and to the cinema. At the end of the day he had nothing to show for it except a pleased grin - he had beaten 'the system', and that was what mattered. He never won again.

When the Government issued Premium Bonds dad duly bought a few hundred - the economists where I worked at that time thought it was very foolish and provided studies to show that it was not a

TIMED TO PERFECTION
Stan Greenberg

particularly good investment. However, what appealed to dad was the fact that he couldn't lose the money - the fact that inflation eroded it was a concept as difficult for him to understand as the laws of cricket. Over the next few years he won prizes to a value of a third of his total stake. When he died the bonds were transferred to me and, at a time when we badly needed money, up came a £1000 windfall. I must contact those economists one day!

In 1996 we visited Las Vegas for the first time, and Carole discovered that she had a magic touch with the slot machines. However, neither Carole nor I would ever take chances with money that we cannot afford to lose. Nevertheless, a number of our friends think that we have got a gambling 'bug' because of the number of times we have visited Las Vegas in the last few years. Well, I will admit to an element of excitement when we go there, but we have rarely 'gambled' in the true sense. Invariably, we play on 1 cent and 5 cent machines, or very occasionally a 25 cent one, and can, and have, spent long periods of time having a lot of fun. We used to play on the 'one-armed bandits', but now stick, almost exclusively, to the new generation of computerised pictorial machines. They have wonderful 'features' which open if one gets a certain combination of characters, and these often lead into other 'features', which, as well as adding to one's winnings, provide a lot of entertainment and laughter as you play them.

On the last ten occasions, I have used a two-wallet system that I have developed. I have found that if I stick strictly to the system I will always come away with at least 80% of my initial stake, but, quite often, I have broken nearly even at the end of each of my stays. Much of this is due to the fact that in Las Vegas the casinos claim, and I believe, that they repay 94-96% of bets to their customers. They still make obscene profits on the other 4-6%, as they know that most dyed-in-the-wool gamblers will continue playing until they have lost all of their original stake.

My system is as follows. I start with an amount I have decided I can afford, or am willing, to lose. This I put in the first wallet,

TIMED TO PERFECTION
Stan Greenberg

literally. When I play, I use a $5 bill at a time. Now, in a 25 cent machine that gives you 20 credits. If, and usually when, this figure goes over 40 I take it out immediately – nowadays payments from machines are done by paper vouchers, not coins. (This is a pity, as it was always so much more thrilling to hear the sound of coins dropping into the payout tray – especially if it was a biggish win – although one's hands did get filthy picking up large numbers of coins). Since I still want to play, I then put in another $5 bill and so on, until I have used up all the money that I intended using that session. Under no circumstances do I play with the winnings, all of which goes into the second wallet. That wallet and contents eventually goes home with me, untouched. There is another little wrinkle which works in our favour. Staying at the Mirage or Luxor hotels, we belong to the MGM Group's Player's Club, which is a loyalty scheme. Most casinos have them. By means of a card, which is inserted into a machine prior to playing, points are racked up according to the amount played with. This data is recorded on the Club's computer, and at the end of the holiday one gets a cash 'dividend' and/or money taken off one's food bill at the hotel. More importantly, if one visits the hotel again, you can get a substantial amount off the cost of the room rate, based on how much you have played with on previous visits.

Note, I have said how much you played with, not how much you lost. The real 'high rollers' get fabulously luxurious rooms completely free, plus all sorts of perks. We have found that although the sums we have played with are not excessive, we have been able to benefit from the 'casino rate' instead of the normal hotel rate. Thus, on my last visit, I paid only $60 a night, for a room which in London would cost about six times as much. Over a period of eight nights that made a considerable saving – and I count that saving as part of my winnings for the trip, as we would not have got that lower rate if we hadn't played the time before. Even without that 'bonus' we have had a week's worth of great entertainment at a very reasonable cost. There are not many places you can do that these days.

TIMED TO PERFECTION
Stan Greenberg

GAMESMANSHIP

In the late 1940s Stephen Potter wrote his books, *Gamesmanship -The Art of Winning Without Actually Cheating,* and *Oneupmanship - How to make the Other Fellow Feel That Something Has Gone Wrong.* Instantly, I became a devotee, his methods ideal in helping overcome my chronic shyness. Initially, I used them playing billiards. Against mediocre players I became almost unbeatable. My success came from the mistaken attitude that it wasn't 'done' to pot the other player's cue ball. In fact, it is very bad play, as you are taking one of the three balls off the table, leaving only one to play against. When I found that opponents got inordinately upset when it occurred, I did it all the more, and very blatantly. I also struck the balls exceedingly hard, in the belief, often realised, that if they went around the table often enough they might hit each other eventually. Allied to this was my ability to work out angles quite well. A combination of the two tactics would reduce poor players to incompetents in no time.

In tennis, I discovered, accidentally, that 'good' players, who use their first serve to get their length right, following with a second on target, would get apoplectic if I ran after the first ball while they were attempting that second serve. Of course, I was sternly told to keep still, but every now and again I would twitch as though to follow the misplaced ball, and then correct myself rather flamboyantly. This too seemed to distract them. Against players who were not as good as they thought they were, the tactic worked wonders. With quite a good service of my own, I was able to win a lot of matches.

In other areas of activity, Potter's teachings sometimes enabled me to 'go one up' as well. One time, at Lever Brothers, my boss, Peter Towell, was formally introducing yet another new whizkid round the office. This was usually a bit of an ordeal for both resident and newcomer alike, and it seemed to me that this chap was a bit snooty. Actually, I was quite wrong, and he was just very nervous. Anyway, as they approached my desk, Mr Towell, not looking at anyone in particular, said "and this is Stan Greenberg". I leapt to my feet, grabbed the new man's hand and said, "That's strange, that's my name as well". He jerked upright, coughed and stuttered, and protested that it wasn't his name at all, while Peter Towell shook his head in bewilderment. The poor chap later told me that at that moment he was totally disoriented, and truly hated me. Surprisingly, perhaps, later we became good friends.

GASTRONOMY

As I have stated previously, I am no gourmet. In fact, there are those who consider me a barbarian as far as food is concerned. Brought up on typically Jewish/East European foods - which were delicious, but not very good for one's long-term health - in later life I veered towards a more healthier diet. Thus, the amount of vegetables and fruit consumed in our household is frightening, from the cost point of view. My own preference for vegetables is to eat them in their raw state - no, not potatoes. Of course, if I am visiting people and am given cooked vegetables I will eat them, but, if I have a choice, I will always have them raw. A salad at our house will usually consist of two types of lettuce, red cabbage, carrots, radishes, spring onions, celery, tomatoes, green cucumber, broccoli and cauliflower. We gave up red meat totally when the BSE scare started, but Carole and I had been 'going off' it for some time anyway. It has re-entered our diet in a very small way, but we prefer chicken and turkey now. Personally, I enjoy a nice piece of fish anytime. Indeed, when we were the guests of Sir Eddie Kulukundis at *Comme Chez Soi* in Brussels, one of the top restaurants in Europe with a wonderful menu, we both had poached salmon - and excellent it was.

There is a lot of snobbery to eating out. I have been to a number of London restaurants which, apparently, are said to be very good, but I didn't think much of them. Especially those who seemed to specialise in 'nouvelle cuisine', which to my mind is just an excuse for putting very little on the plate and charging an excessive amount for it. Others seem to take the attitude that if you charge a lot for something, it must be good. What a fallacy, and not only about food.

GENES
One hears a lot today about the influence of genes on one's life. Practically everything that one achieves, or indeed doesn't, is blamed on the genes passed on by your immediate family and other predecessors. Frankly, I am not so sure about that. In my own case I can find no interest in sport, either watching or playing, in the backgrounds of either of my parents, or grandparents, and yet my life has been dominated by such an interest. Where did that come from? Perhaps it is based on my ancestor's abilities to outrun or outfox various bullies and other oppressors - abilities that they must have had or it is unlikely that I would be here today. The fact that most of my immediate ancestors were very religious people, and that the Jewish Sabbath is on a Saturday - the traditional sporting day in Britain - no doubt had a lot to do with it. Also they were very hard-studying, and hard-working people, and probably begrudged time spent on 'frivolities'. I know that my father had done no sport at all, until I introduced him to it, and to his last days he could never understand my obsession with it. He truly thought that it was a total waste of time and effort. Undoubtedly, he would have changed his mind if he had lived long enough to see what it all lead me to eventually.

GENIUS
On a recent trip to Florence I was struck by what that city produced in the 15th century in terms of men we now consider geniuses in their respective fields. In alphabetical order there was: Filippo Brunelleschi, architect of the Pitti Palace and the Duomo; the painter Sandro Botticelli; the sculptor Donatello; the incredible Leonardo da Vinci, who cannot be categorized; painter and cleric Fra Angelico; another sculptor Lorenzo Ghiberti; painter Domenico Ghirlandaio; Filippo and Filippino Lippi, father and son painters; the politician and writer Niccolo Machiavelli; the painter Masaccio;

another immortal, Michelangelo; religious reformer Girolamo Savonarola; painter Paolo Uccello. It is perhaps true that many of the above would not have achieved their exalted status without the patronage of the de Medici family, especially Cosimo and Lorenzo, themselves, perhaps, geniuses for the way they appreciated and encouraged great talents.

GERMAN

Although I took a year of German at evening classes after I left school in 1947, I had actually 'learnt' some rather earlier. During the war, before I joined my grammar school, Hackney Downs, which had been evacuated to King's Lynn in Norfolk, I attended Parmiter's School in east London for a time. During the first week, which was an induction period, the form master, who also taught German, decided to give us the rudiments of the language. The first thing he taught us was how to count, and he duly enunciated, Ein, Zwei, Drei, Vier, Funf, Sechs etc. I quickly found out which of my new school-mates were of my faith, as, without exception, they all said the fifth figure as "Finiff", which is five in Yiddish. Like me, they had probably learnt it from their grandparents, and found it very difficult to stop using. The German master nearly blew a gasket every time one of us did it – so needless to say we kept on doing it.

GOBBLEDEGOOK

My dictionary defines this as pretentious or unintelligible language, and one comes across it more and more today. It is particularly rife in the legal profession, but is spreading into other areas of life. The Marx Brothers were the first to bring it to my attention with the contract cameo between Groucho and Chico in *A Night at the Opera*. Groucho reads the initial line of the contract, "The party of the first part shall henceforth be known as the party of the first part". The supposedly uneducated Chico doesn't like the sound of it, "particularly the first part", so that clause is torn out, along with most of the following ones. Today, things are far worse. I am aware that many people are against the European Union for various, often spurious, reasons. Personally, knowing a bit more about the Common Market than most, I am not. However, in favour or no, everyone must have the same reaction as mine to the statement by a US expert, that the EU is "a postmodern polity with a multilevel governance system".

The following comes from a travel brochure of a well-known company, which presumably wants people to travel with them. However, they note that "Compensation will not be payable if we are forced to cancel or in any way change your holiday due to war, threat of war, riot, civil strife, industrial dispute, terrorist activity, natural or nuclear disaster, fire, adverse weather conditions, rising or falling water levels or closure of locks, perils and dangers of the sea, technical or maintenance problems to transport, closure of airports or seaports, or other circumstances amounting to force majeure". Nevertheless, having given you all that to mull over, I am sure that they wish you a happy holiday - if you still want to go.

GHOST TRAIN
The plot of a 1941 British movie concerned a gang of smugglers who used a small rural railway in their operations. To keep anyone from getting too interested in their activities they spread the story of a 'ghost train'. At one point in the film, the local stationmaster eerily asks some travellers the rhetorical questions, "Where do it come from? Where do it go?" As with so many other bits from movies, this has gone into Greenberg family folklore, and the phrases can often be heard repeated in the house when we are looking for some elusive object.

GOING BACK
They, whoever 'they' are, say that you should never go back. Well, I don't know about the wisdom of that or not, but I have found that if you have lived a fairly long time, there is nothing much to go back to. The nursing home I was born in has disappeared in the mists of time. The house I used to live in, my parents' house, no longer

exists, and, of all things, is part of the grounds of a mosque. The synagogue in which I was taught my faith is now the aforesaid mosque. My old secondary school, the one I spent my formative years in, a wonderful powerhouse of education, has gone – destroyed by a vindictive local education department. The resort of Margate, where I went with my parents for our annual holiday for many years, is a mere shadow of what it was. The Greater London Council, for which I can honestly say I enjoyed working for seven years, no longer exists, while the *Guinness Book of Records*, without the late Norris McWhirter, has, from my point of view, changed for the worst. When I re-visited the Norfolk town of King's Lynn, where I was evacuated towards the end of WWII, I found that the house, and indeed the street, where I resided have disappeared under a bus station. The White City, the wonderful old athletics stadium where I spent so many happy, albeit at times frustrating, hours for over 30 years, is no more, with a BBC building over the site. My local cinema is now a massive block of flats and shops, and the Unilever football ground, where I spent many a happy and energetic hour, is now Charlton Athletic's training quarters. Even one of my recent popular holiday destinations, Las Vegas, has changed almost beyond recognition from the first time I went, with grand hotels demolished and even grander ones built in their place.

Happily, old friends have tended to remain the same, in outlook if not appearance, although, of course, some of them are sadly no longer around. While I don't believe in spending one's old age always looking back to 'better times', it would be nice, now and again, to revisit places which one once enjoyed. However, the modern world and its inhabitants seem to preclude that possibility.

GONE
In moments of contemplation, I sometimes think about the things, places and institutions which formed much of the framework of my early life - all are long gone. Among them were Lyons tea rooms, Gamage's store, the removal firm Carter Paterson, and Walls Ice Cream 'Stop me and buy one' tricycles. Other things I find missing from modern life are manners and courtesy, and good, intelligible,

popular music. And while I am at it, let me be forthright and say that I also miss seeing young women's legs - they never seem to wear dresses or skirts anymore. Similarly, one rarely sees young men in smart clothes - that doesn't mean expensive, but smart, neat, clean. I do not subscribe to the maxim that anything new must be better. In fact, I almost take the opposite view, and expect that anything new will be ugly, coarse, difficult to use, and probably not even necessary. Unfortunately, all too often I am proved right. Upsetting, isn't it?

GREATDAY
Not counting my wedding day, or the births of my children, my greatest day was 31 July 1948. The day before, my friend, Stan Davis, had asked me if I would like to see the Olympic Games at Wembley. I had always been interested in running, but had never actually been to watch a major athletics occasion. He had two tickets for the first Saturday of the XIVth Games and I agreed to accompany him. They were standing area tickets, on a first come first served basis, so we arrived very early in the morning and got to the front, at the beginning of the back straight. There we stayed throughout the day, having brought food and drink with us, until about 6.00pm. The weather was perfect, at 80F *26C*, and the colour and excitement really got to me. I specify colour, as an outstanding memory is of the track suits worn by the Puerto Rican pole vaulters, Barbosa and Vincente. They were bright yellow and purple, and to someone only used to the black or dark blue sort worn in Britain at the time, they were eye-catching. Five gold medals were decided that day, including a thrilling 100m for men, and the hammer. This latter was won by a Hungarian, Imre Nemeth. I was to meet him in later years in the Nepstadion, Budapest, where he became manager, and also see his son Miklos match his father, winning the 1976 Olympic javelin title.

I was totally fascinated by it all. Previously, I had been a soccer fan, but this athletics, in which I had always enjoyed competing, was something else. Overnight I became an athletics fanatic, and it changed my life forever. I didn't know it at the time, but only 50 yards to my left that day was another young chap, Alf Wilkins, who I met at the next Games, and who became one of my best friends. However, my 'Great Day' was not over yet. Immediately after the last event at Wembley I hurried to meet other friends at the London Palladium, to see the last night of the Jack Benny Show. The Palladium at that time had bi-weekly changes of variety programmes, and we had booked for the whole season. Probably, that is why I could not afford to see more of the Olympic Games. That night was a superb finish to a wonderful day. In the first half of the bill was a fairly new English comedian, Ted Ray, but the whole of the second half consisted of the Jack Benny group, including singer Dennis Day, comedian Phil Harris, Eddie "Rochester" Anderson, Jack Benny and his wife, Mary Livingstone. As a capper to the evening, film star Alice Faye, the newly married wife of Phil Harris, who was sitting in the audience, was cajoled onto the stage to sing. What a finish. What a show. What a day. Four years later, prior to the 1952 Olympics which I attended, Eddie Anderson's son, Billy, just failed to qualify for the US team in the 110m hurdles.

GREATER LONDON COUNCIL
Having been at Lever Brothers for 20 years I was very nervous of looking for another job. I didn't think that I had any special "saleable" skills, although I had reason to believe that I was bright and well-organised, but how do you prove that to a potential employer. One day when I was having a particularly bad time, at work, an advert for the GLC (Greater London Council) caught my eye. It was for traffic counters, and I certainly thought I could do that. Also a giant organisation, like Lever Brothers, I assumed it would be equally secure. Having to keep my possible defection secret, I went to the interview one lunchtime. I spoke to a very pleasant man, Dr Tony Ridley, Chief Research Officer, Highways and Transportation. Before we had gone very far he said that he thought I might be better suited for something else they had in mind. So he arranged for me to see Brian Martin, his superior, then and there, and once more my life took a different turn. This

interview went like a dream, even though I wasn't exactly sure what it was he was after. All my answers, and questions, seemed to be the right onesong like the proverbial "house on fire". I was offered the job they had in mind, which was   to set up an information room for the Transportation Department, working on my own and answerable straight to Mr Martin. The money, holiday entitlement etc, was better than I was already getting, so that was that.

Interestingly, the job had never been officially formulated or put forward to Personnel Department, and no concrete decision about it had been taken, until I suddenly turned upwith the hoped for qualifications and   attitude. So I believe I was the only person to ever get a job at the GLC which had never been advertised. My first day at County Hall caused kerfuffle in the Personnel Department. However, as Peter Stott, The Traffic Commissioner and head of my department, was somewhat like Mr Brech had been at Lever Brothers, I was quickly "processed". I spent a very happy, fulfilling, eight years at the GLC, watching "my child" grow into a library/information section of some 20 people. I grew too, but more in the eyes of my customers than in status terms, as eventually, and understandably, more senior people were brought in over me. I made many good friends and (with all modesty) gained the respect of some brilliant planners and engineers for whom I did research. Also I was on excellent terms with then head of the library, who often sought and acted on my advice. I realise how much I owed Dr Ridley fir being a first class interviewer (i.e. keeping a larger picture in view), and I was delighted when he went on to mastermind mass-transit systems in Hong Kong and Newcastle. Sadly, later as head of the London Underground, he felt it necessary to resign from that position in the aftermath of the disastrous 1987 King Cross fire.

GREENBERGS
When my father went into business in the 1920s he always said that his was the only name of Greenberg in the Greater London telephone book. Now I note that in the Barnet book alone, there are

some 16 entries with that name. As a young boy, I found that the only Greenberg of note was the famous American baseball player, Hank Greenberg. Nowadays, there seem to be Greenbergs all over the place, and not only that, but there are some well placed Stanley Greenbergs too. One of them was a top adviser to the US President, and later came to Britain to advise our politicians. Another was a script writer for a number of top US TV shows. With regard to the latter, my stock went very high with an elderly relative who knew that I was doing something with television, and then saw this credit on one of his favourite shows, and put two and two together to make five.

Recently I have been notified of a reference to a member of 'the tribe' in a book, *The Day The Laughter Stopped* by David Yallop (1976). Writing about the silent screen's obsession with custard pies, the author notes that the baker who supplied the Keystone comedies with their pies was a chap named Greenberg, who concocted a creation of blackberries and whipped cream to get the desired effects. (You will realise that I find this highly significant if you have read my previous item regarding my liking of custard). I also wonder if the screen writer mentioned above, Stanley R Greenberg, is related to that baker. (Who cares, I hear you say - well I do, for obvious reasons). Then, of course, there is our Italian branch. I well remember that on my first visit to Italy, back in 1957, the hotel clerk looked at the name I had just written on the registration form, and immediately called me Signor Monteverdi - and continued to do so, boringly, for the whole two weeks. Incidentally, the works of 17th century Claudio of that ilk, are usually considered to be the predecessors of modern opera.

GROWLING
In the summer of 1959 I went with my then girlfriend Carole and her parents to Alassio, in Italy. The trip was especially memorable because it was there, on the beach, that I asked her father for her hand in marriage. (Ah, how quaint!). Also it has stuck in my memory because of an incident which annoyed me, but was thoroughly

enjoyed by Carole. One morning, as we made our way to the sea through the narrow streets, we passed two young Italian boys partially blocking our way. As Carole, looking very fetching in her swimming costume, pushed by, the boys made a low, undoubtedly appreciative, growling noise. Walking just behind her, I shoved my face directly into one of theirs and made a very loud growling noise, which shook them rigid, and made them flatten themselves against the wall. I trust that the shock of it taught them some sort of lesson, but it certainly boosted me in Carole's eyes, as well as doing her ego no harm at all.

Come forward about 30 years. We were at an athletics match and were watching the women's long jump. In the competition was a world class East German named Susen Tiedtke, who just happened to look as good, perhaps even better, than she jumped. At one point Carole commented that I seemed to be very taken with Tiedtke. When I asked her why she said that, she replied that every time the German got ready to jump, I, apparently, made the same sort of growling noise that the boys in Alassio had made.

GUINNESS BOOK OF RECORDS
At the end of 1975, I was at my desk in the GLC Transportation library when the telephone rang. This happened, on average, about 50 times a day, but that call was to change my life, yet again. It was from Ross McWhirter (one of the twins, the other was Norris, who had started the *Book of Records* in 1954), who wanted me to be the Sports Editor of the book. I had known them from my athletics interests, had helped them occasionally with their newspaper columns, and had worked with Norris on BBC TV. This invitation was so 'out of the blue' that I couldn't think straight. Apparently, my face drained of colour, for when I replaced the telephone, my office colleague looked very concerned and asked if someone had died. He said I looked as if I had received a tremendous shock. Well, indeed I had.

To someone with my interest in sport and statistics, there was no better job to have. Even so, I was unsure whether I could put my family in jeopardy by leaving the security (that old bugbear again) of the GLC. Ironically, if I had stayed at County Hall I would have been made redundant a few years later when the GLC was eliminated by the Government. Of course, I agreed to talk to the McWhirters, and meanwhile sought the advice of friends and relatives. Financially, I would be better off, although I would have to become self-employed, something I had always vowed never to do. Nevertheless, I couldn't turn down such a prestigious post, which not only would be interesting beyond belief, but also great fun. Everybody said I would regret it if I did not accept, and even my mother-in-law agreed, although she insisted that I should confirm the salary as soon as possible. Oddly, in my first two meetings with Norris, money was never mentioned, other than a promise that I would not lose out by the move. Neither Norris nor I liked discussing money matters, and the subject didn't come up during our more detailed talks about how, what, where and when. Thus, I sent my resignation to the GLC's Personnel Dept before I knew exactly how much I would get.

That letter was sent on a Thursday, and I had the following day off to go to Gateshead for a cross-country race for the BBC. On that Thursday evening Carole and I were at Ron Pickering's house. He and his wife, Jean, had kindly invited us to cheer up my wife, who had lost her mother very suddenly the previous week, and was having a hard time coping with the loss. We were watching TV when we learnt of the murder of Ross McWhirter earlier that evening. The news came as a terrible shock. We knew that Ross was very outspoken about Irish terrorists but found it difficult to believe they would react in such a way. The evening broke up and I took Carole, again very upset, home, and packed for my trip up north. Ron and I did not have our minds fully on the race on Saturday, but it was only on the train back that it occurred to me that my own position, work-wise, was uncertain now. Would the Guinness book still continue? Would Norris want to carry on alone? Could the enterprise survive such a loss? I had resigned from the GLC with nothing in writing about the new job. What would I/could I do if it no longer existed? That Sunday was one of the most miserable and worrysome of my life.

When I arrived at work on Monday, Don Kennington, the head of the Library, called me to his office. He had already spoken to the Personnel department, and they had agreed to put a stop on my resignation until such time that things became clearer, and if I wanted to stay they would be only too pleased. I was amazed that such a monolithic organisation like the GLC could react in such a thoughtful way. It was three or four weeks before I could contact the Guinness publishing office, but Norris now needed me more than ever, and in the early days of 1976 I joined the *Guinness Book of Records* as the Sports Editor. I had re-activated my resignation from the GLC to take effect at Christmas, and the library and other colleagues gave me a send-off the like of which had never been seen there for a person of my 'lowly' status. I am not ashamed to say that I was close to tears at my leaving presentation.

I spent the next six years of my life with the *Book of Records*, and, I believe, greatly improved the sport section. Personally, it was one of the happiest periods of my working life, but it was very hectic as I was doing ever more BBC work in my "spare" time. In 1981, when I reached 50, I felt I couldn't cope with both occupations, and only leant towards the BBC work due to the tremendous amount of travelling which was entailed. As I have noted elsewhere, I am an inveterate tourist.

HAIR

While rarely worried about my appearance, especially when I was young, I have always had a thing about my hair. Not that I have spent much time or money on its look, but more a worry that I could keep it as long as possible. My father began losing his when quite young, and had a decided 'skating rink' by middle age, and my mother's very fine quality hair was thinning badly at the end of her life – mind you she was in her nineties. My own hair was starting to go in my sixties but seems to have had a new burst of life as I reached my seventies, and definitely appears to be getting thicker in my eighties.

One 'good' thing about my hair it is that as I get older it gets greyer, or, in fact, whiter. Recently, Carole and I were at a function where a number of the men and women, about the same sort of ages as us, had obviously dyed their hair – often in not particularly attractive nor complimentary shades. When one woman happened to comment that my hair was very white, I quickly said, "Yes, it is, but then I dye it instead of leaving it at its natural dark brown". I got a very sharp look, and the conversation ended there and then.

HAMMERED
Many years ago, when I was fairly young, and reasonably fit, I went to Enfield athletics track to watch a coach, Don Vanhegan, imparting skills to some novice hammer throwers. After a time he invited me, actually he virtually shamed me, into having a go myself. Now the athletics hammer is a 16lb *7.26kg* iron ball attached to a strip of wire and a handle, the whole being some 4ft *1.22m* in length. It is thrown from a 7ft *2.13m* circle, which during competition is enclosed by a metal or rope 'cage', with a fairly small gap left in the front through which the hammer is meant to be propelled. The approved method is to twirl the implement around your body a number of times and then throw it to land within a marked out sector of the ground. Having watched the event many times, I was quite au fait with what I had to do - the problem came when trying to do it.

There is a very funny hammer throwing sequence in the Buster Keaton movie *College*, in which he tries various athletic events in order to impress his girl. In this he twirls the hammer around his head, but cannot throw it, or, because of centrifugal force, let go of it. As it takes control of him he staggers around the field sending other athletes fleeing in terror. Well, I now realised just how dangerous that stunt was for the star. I too could not throw it nor let go - it was a case of the force being with me, in this case the

TIMED TO PERFECTION
Stan Greenberg

centrifugal force which had control of it and me. The other throwers were yelling at me to "ground it", but I could do nothing other than twist around at the end of this deadly twirling ball and chain. My life flashed before me as I began to get tired, and realised that my arms would fail and the chain would wrap itself around me, prior to the ball killing me. However, that guardian angel was with me, and having had his fun, he edged me towards the net until the hammer entangled itself and fell to the ground. I was truly shaking with fear and exhaustion, but the others convinced me to try once more, and I finally learnt to let go. I must say that it was a marvellous feeling when I actually threw the thing ' correctly' and it went about 69ft *21.00m*. Needless to say, I never repeated the experiment, but it left me with a much greater appreciation of the event, and the throwers.

Throwing the hammer can be a very absorbing and exciting event to watch at an athletics meeting, but unfortunately there have also been some very serious, even fatal, accidents around the world. One incident that I witnessed was particularly scary, especially as it was so unexpected. I was at an international meeting in Germany in 1971, which featured some top flight throwers. The protective cage had not been set up properly it seems, and at one point the hammer flew askew. and headed for the running track. This track was one of the new all-weather rubberised types which were then coming into vogue, and, to everyone's surprise, the hammer bounced on it like a child's ball. Landing from quite a height, it bounced high into the air and, amid wild cries of alarm, flew straight towards the packed stand. Luckily, the front wall of the stand was just tall enough to interrupt its flight, and no one was hurt, but the sight of that deadly ball and chain bouncing back up into the air stayed with me for a long time.

On another occasion, at a meeting in Edinburgh's Meadowbank stadium, a rogue hammer tore right through the protective netting of the cage, and flew straight at my BBC colleague, Ken Norris, the former international runner, who was standing near the start line of the 200m. It missed him by the proverbial whisker, the wire and handle of the implement tearing the coat of a nearby BBC cameraman. It landed on the track just as the 10,000m runners were passing, breaking the leg of one of them.

HANDWRITING

My handwriting is lousy. Even at school, under constant criticism, it was never very good. In my defence I think that my mind works, or perhaps worked, quite fast, and therefore I found that my writing had to be fast as well. To achieve neatness meant writing slowly, and that took up even more time for homework, which could be better spent kicking a ball about. Somehow I got away with it at school - perhaps the brilliance of what I wrote diverted teachers - but I had problems in my business career. Much of my early work was involved with documents, which had to be legible, and often I had to do things all over again. Then I discovered the typewriter, and although I never learnt to type properly, I do very well using three or four fingers. Using a typewriter didn't improve my handwriting, and it got worse, but it wasn't a problem until I began the statistical work for the BBC TV commentary team.

That involved producing cards on which I wrote various data about athletes in all the events which the team covered. Despite my best efforts, they often had trouble deciphering some of my items. The best comment on my stuff came from David Coleman, the senior commentator. The previous evening I had been working in my hotel room when an enormous spider - I hate the things - crawled across the floor. It took all my courage to get rid of it. The following day I recounted the story to my companions. David immediately asked what I had done with it, and I replied that somehow I had thrown it out of the window. "Shame", he said, "you should have got it to write the cards for you".

HATE

I think that Dr Johnson's comment about someone that "He hated a fool, and he hated a rogue", could well apply to me. I do not hate

TIMED TO PERFECTION
Stan Greenberg

people for their nationality, their colour, their wealth, nor their religion, but I do dislike people for their ignorance, their stupidity, or their lack of humanity. I hate the lazy idiots who leave supermarket trolleys behind your car in the car park; the cretins who drive on motorways and round corners while talking on their hand-held mobile phones; probably the same people who throw litter from their car windows; the children, possibly of those same people, who drop litter indiscriminately in the street on their way to or from school; dog owners who allow their pets to foul pavements; the 'rights-protesters' who deliberately smoke in designated no-smoking zones; the drunken louts and loutesses who reel out of pubs screaming obscenities; the lowest forms of life who savagely attack little old ladies to steal their pension money; and so on and so on. Unfortunately, in this day and age, the list seems endless.

Years ago, I worked with a man who had been captured and interned by the Japanese in WWII, and had suffered terribly under their 'care'. Because of this, and its subsequent effect on his digestion process, he could never eat a large meal, but had to munch non-stop, virtually all day. Needless to say, he really hated his captors, and would have nothing to do with anything related to Japan or the Japanese. Thus, although he worked in the shipping section of the company, it was tacitly understood, and accepted by the top brass, that he would never deal with documents related to Japanese cargo ships - which was quite a problem as such vessels were in great use by shippers of bulk cargoes at the time. Also, his wife was under strict instructions never to buy anything made in Japan. At a firm 'do' she recounted that on the rare occasions when she hadn't checked properly, and he noted that a plastic washing-up bowl, or whatever, came from there, his immediate reaction was to throw the offending article straight out of the window of their flat. This worried her terribly, not because she wanted the article, but because their flat was quite high up in a tower block, and you never knew who was walking below/

On a somewhat lower level of my 'hate' list are: the length of commercials on television; people wearing Bermuda shorts;

unshaven men in TV ads and playing in football matches; open-toed sandals; dim-witted journalists who call football 'the beautiful game'; women who wear deliberately-torn jeans, presumably because they think it's 'fashionable'; and those awful wing-collared dress shirts that young 'celebrities' – some of them still unshaven - wear at functions.

HEALTH

The Roman poet, Juvenal, made a good point when he wrote, in the 1st century AD, *mens sana in corpore sano – a sound mind in a sound body.* I remember seeing the saying in a friend's Latin schoolbook, and being very impressed with it. On reflection, I think that when I was young I had a very sound body, but that my mind could have been somewhat sounder. The problem was that I spent so much time on sport, i.e. working on the body, that I tended to overlook the mind, and didn't study as much as I should have. Later in life, as I think I tended to develop my mind more, I fear that I have overlooked the body, and have allowed myself to get more and more unfit. Thus, now, at a rather advanced stage of life, none of that wonderful saying really applies to me anymore.

HEAR, HEAR

The 1964 Olympic Games were held in Tokyo, and because of the time difference many of the important finals were happening live, early in the morning in Britain. The 10,000m final began at breakfast, and I listened to the radio commentary on a transistor set. On the way to the railway station, so as not to disturb anyone, I put the set in my pocket and ran the lead of the earpiece under my coat and up through my collar. As I reached the platform, the race reached an exciting stage with a few laps to go. Reception was not good and I moved to the back of the platform, and leaned against a wall, concentrating, and holding the earpiece tight against my ear. At this point, and with the runners into the final lap, I noticed a gentleman making his way towards me, obviously intent on talking. I didn't want to be rude, so I tried to avoid his eye as he approached.

However, he stopped directly in front of me and said, quite loudly, "You know this type is much better", and opened his coat and shirt to reveal a large square hearing aid held to his chest. As I gazed at him open-mouthed, desperately trying to hear the commentary, he said, even louder, "I would recommend this type, you know. Excellent, really, and never any problems with it". At that I tried, unsuccessfully, to pull the radio out of my pocket to show him that I wasn't using a hearing aid. Of course, it got stuck, and as I wrestled with it, still trying to listen to the tremendously exciting finish, I must have seemed like a lunatic - and a deaf and dumb one too as I had not said anything yet. The poor, kind, chap, gave me a pitying look and thankfully moved away, muttering about how useless it was to try and help people who wouldn't be helped. By now, practically everyone on the platform was staring at me, hopelessly entangled with the wires, and nearly choking myself in my anxiety to reveal the radio - which was caught in the cloth of my pocket. When the train arrived, people actually moved away from this nut case, which made it possible to get a seat for a change.

HELICOPTERS

My first flight in a helicopter was over Disneyworld in Florida. Since then I have taken a few more trips by this exciting mode of transport. Carole and I have flown down into the Grand Canyon – an enthralling experience - in one, and also flown over Las Vegas at night. About a year ago I took my son, Keith, for a helicopter flight over London. Actually, taking off from Essex, it flew down to the Millennium Dome, and thence along the Thames to the London Eye and back, and provided a marvellous view of the city. I must say that when they bank it is quite nerve-wracking, and for a moment you feel you are going to fall through the glass-walled cockpit.

TIMED TO PERFECTION
Stan Greenberg

HEROES

Most of us have heroes at some period of our lives. I have had quite a number reflecting my interests in sport, cinema and literature, as well as some in 'real life'. My first heroes were fictional ones, such as Wilson of the *Wizard*, Tarzan, and, as I grew older, Mr D'Arcy, from Jane Austen's *Pride and Prejudice*. My sporting involvement gave me Jesse Owens, Sydney Wooderson, Stanley Matthews, McDonald Bailey and Emil Zatopek, and they remain in my thoughts today. As a frustrated dancer, Fred Astaire still holds a place in the list, not least because he made some excellent films with Rita Hayworth and Cyd Charisse.- what more can one seek to attain. The ability of Groucho Marx to demolish the pompous with a few well-chosen words placed him high in my pantheon, while Oscar Wilde, despite his other proclivities, could do the same with the written word. The writer, Stephen Potter, and his Lifemanship stories, had a profound effect on my early life.

At various times I have been particularly impressed by one of my school-teachers, or a religious leader, and now and again a relative or friend has caused me briefly to take him as a model, but, all too often, such role models seem to have a serious failing, or 'feet of clay'. Thus, I am saddened that in recent years I have not added to my heroes, either real or fictional. Perhaps that is the reason that so many older people appear to live in the past. Maybe it is just that they can find so little to stimulate their imagination today - technology or no.

HIRE CARS

I am not in the habit of hiring cars. The odd mini-cab or taxi, yes, but hire cars were usually out of my price bracket. However, there are always exceptions. One such occasion was on a trip to New York with my wife, who had never been there before. I wanted to make it memorable, and so I decided not to take a cab into the city from Kennedy Airport, but book a Limo, as our American friends call it. I was expecting it to be a small van-type vehicle, but it was

TIMED TO PERFECTION
Stan Greenberg

one of the longest, smartest cars I have ever seen. The inside was vast, and as there were only five passengers on this trip, we could really stretch out. The facilities included a bar, telephone, radio and TV - and there was probably a swimming pool in the boot. It was a very grand feeling to be driven up to our hotel in it. Surprisingly, it was not that expensive, cheaper I recall than a cab would have been, and without the hassle.

Another experience was on a trip to Malta. It was a long weekend break, for which I was using Air Miles to pay for the flight, so I thought I would splurge somewhat on the hotel, booking us into a top-class establishment. On arrival at this truly excellent place, I enquired about a possible excursion for the next day. Of course, I expected a coach tour, but the following morning, on the way to breakfast, the concierge informed me that our limousine was waiting. It was the latest model, large, Mercedes, complete with driver/guide, and it was ours for the day. We now know how the traditional 'Lady Muck' feels. It was terrific, being chauffeured all over the island, with people staring to see who was in the posh car. The driver was a young (and handsome according to Carole) man who spoke very good English, and knew all the best places to go. It cost 'an arm and a leg', but we agreed it was worth it. However, I don't think we will do anything like it again, at least not until I win big in Las Vegas.

HOLIDAYS
In our 55 years of married life, holidays have always been a priority with both Carole and myself, and in nearly every one of those years we have been away at least once. When I was doing a lot of travelling with the BBC, I felt I owed it to Carole and the family, and would make special efforts to arrange something at the end of the season. If possible it would be to a venue abroad. I have always been a great believer in the maxim, 'Travel broadens the mind', and I have encouraged the concept in my family. Not that Carole needed much encouragement, nor my daughter Karen. Even my son, Keith, who is less adventurous than his sister, has

been to Tenerife, Spain, Italy, Israel, Australia and China. I have always stressed that it is not just the visiting of these places that matter, but that one should be receptive to what one sees, hears and experiences on the trips. So many people go to wonderful places, but 'see' nothing. Karen, with her husband Paul, regularly goes abroad, and, I notice, still learns things, as she did when she was younger. I remember that on her first trip abroad to Majorca, when she was only four, she had picked up more Spanish than I had.

HONEYMOON

I wanted to prove to Carole's family that she meant more to me than athletics, so I arranged our wedding at the time of the 1960 Olympic Games in Rome. Originally I considered Estoril, Portugal, for our honeymoon, but thought it would be too expensive - and opted for Switzerland (which worked out far more expensive). Even Carole agrees we should have gone to Rome, as an Olympic city can be a marvellous place, and it would have been unforgettable then. Our honeymoon was great anyway. Staying overnight at the Grosvenor Hotel, Victoria, we caught the boat train the next morning, and travelled in a first class carriage through France. It was a most enjoyable trip, and my new wife surprised me. In our compartment were two other passengers. One was a former teacher, a very experienced traveller, from whom we learned a number of travel tips. The other was an elderly gentleman who was a well-known author. I knew that Carole was an avid reader, so I wasn't too surprised to find that she knew his work. What did surprise me, pleasantly, was that she, then not quite 20, could more than hold her own in the conversations that ensued about literature and books in general. For the first of many times I was very proud of my wife.

Strangely, I had picked Lucerne as a honeymoon site some six years previously, well before I had ever thought seriously of marriage at all. I first discovered it in 1954, and had been struck by its charm. We spent a most happy time getting to know the place, as well as each other. The town is overlooked by Mount Pilatus,

TIMED TO PERFECTION
Stan Greenberg

about which there is a legend that it is the profile of Pontius Pilate who came there and died. If one looks at the mountain top sideways one sees the undoubted outline of a man's face, with a beard when mist is about. Our hotel room overlooked the river and had a magnificent view of the mountain, and we got cricks in our necks looking at it. From the top of Pilatus itself, there is a superb panorama of the mountains and Lake Lucerne, a scenic masterpiece. Another day we took a romantic boat trip to the far end of the lake, to Altdorf, the centre of the William Tell legend. Things were very expensive, and it was good that we didn't want to go out much in the evenings - make of that what you will. I feel sorry for today's youngsters who know each other (in the Biblical sense) only too well before they get married. They lose the excitement, the mystery, of an old-fashioned honeymoon.

When we returned from our honeymoon, we stayed overnight at my parent's house. The only bed available was my old single one. I had often fantasized about having someone in that bed with me, and in my adolescent dreams there had been no problems. However, a 3ft wide bed was not really made to accommodate two people, no matter how friendly or loving. My parents were rather staid and old-fashioned, and I wonder what they made of all the noise that night. Being a restless sleeper at the best of times - that night was impossible. Twice I almost knocked Carole out of bed by turning over unthinkingly, and the ensuing thuds, cries and hysterical laughter emanating from our room, throughout the night, must have given me an entirely different status with my parents. Naturally, they never said a word at breakfast, which made us giggle even more.

For our 25th anniversary, I intended to take Carole back to our hotel in Lucerne, but it no longer existed. Instead we went to Florida, and I am happy to say that we didn't go out much in the evenings there either. Ten years later, for our 35th anniversary, we did go back to Lucerne, to a nearby hotel with the same view, and did many of the same things we had done so many years ago - and you can take that in any way you want as well.

HORROR

The horror genre in films and books has become a massive money-earner in recent years. Unlike the mildly scary movie productions when I was young, which left more to your imagination than anything else, today's offerings are truly horrifying. Nevertheless, I see no reason why this booklet should not jump on the bandwagon. My son-in-law, Paul, is a serious collector of those garish American comics, and one day, to the great delight of the rest of the family, he produced one entitled, *Greenberg, The Vampire*. Subtitled "A tale of the healing power of chicken soup", it is a grisly story about a Jewish man who becomes a vampire after being bitten by one, but is saved by his mother - who else?

HOSPITAL

So far, I have been very lucky that I have rarely been in hospital. In fact, since I had my tonsils out at the age of about 6 I have only been in a hospital, for treatment as opposed to visiting, on one other occasion. That was in the summer of 1999, and a wart had developed on the inside of my nose. It was decided that it should be removed, and I was told it could be done quite simply at a local hospital's day surgery. Needless to say, I was somewhat on edge when I turned up at the required 7am, to find about a dozen other people waiting for various types of simple surgery. Because I was the only one that was not going to need a general anaesthetic, I had to wait until the end. So I sat around in one of those hospital 'shrouds' - the ones with the open backs - for about five hours, getting more and more nervous. Finally, it was my turn, and the surgeon explained what he was going to do, and that it would only require a local anaesthetic. However, first he put a cotton bud up my nostril which had a weak solution of cocaine on it. This was followed by an injection, which I must say I did not feel at all. Then, after asking me if I suffered from claustrophobia - actually I do, but I didn't tell him - he placed towels and things over most of my face and eyes, just leaving my nose sticking out. It must have looked like the Matterhorn on a cloudy day. I was also hooked up, via my thumb, to a machine which measured vital signs. Suddenly, one of the nurses urgently nudged me and asked if I was okay. When I replied, I could hear sounds of relief, as it seems that I was so tense, and holding my breath, that the proper vital signs were not registering. After what seemed like only a few minutes, I asked the surgeon when he was going to start, to be told that he had finished. I had felt nothing, not even any pressure as he cut or dug or whatever. By teatime I was home, feeling no ill effects at all. Now, if all hospital surgery was that easy, I might have it a lot more often - but then again, maybe not.

HOT AND COLD

Extremes of weather and temperatures are normally taken in their stride by the British. The variations that occur, even over a short period, are the stuff of legend. The comedian, Bob Hope, summed it up at the Palladium, when he told the audience how much he loved Britain. He commented that he had been fortunate to be in the country in all four seasons, winter, spring, summer and autumn - "It was last Thursday, I think". At least the London pea-souper fogs are gone, but the climate still plays its tricks.

My own unforgettable experience of bad weather was in March 1972, on the occasion of the National Cross-Country championships at Sutton Coldfield. What an appropriate name. I had driven up wearing only a suit and thin mackintosh, as London conditions were not bad for the time of year. During the day the weather worsened, the wind gained force and the temperature plummeted. The rain turned to sleet and ice, so that conditions for runners and spectators alike became treacherous. For the senior men's race it was Arctic-like. An icy wind blew, from which one could find no shelter, as there were few trees about. The sleet penetrated my clothing, and my legs and body were soaked and bitterly cold. Rather stupidly I held my ground and stayed until the race was over, amid gruesome scenes as distressed athletes collapsed at the finish. Some were taken to hospital. How none of the runners suffered permanent damage is a mystery, but

TIMED TO PERFECTION
Stan Greenberg

unfortunately it transpired that one of the officials collapsed and died on his way home. When I reached my car I was frozen, soaked through, and shivering uncontrollably. Seriously, I considered removing my trousers to dry them by the car heater on my way back down the M1. However, my natural pessimism prevailed - how would I explain my state of undress if I was involved in an accident. That was the most miserable journey I have ever made, and it took days to fully recover.

Another time, I was in a similar state due to totally opposite conditions. In January 1981 we were at Aswan in Egypt. I went on the Nile in a felucca, which tacked back and forth for an interminable time as the prevailing winds were against it. It was very pleasant and peaceful, with hardly a sound to disturb the tranquility. Kingfishers sunned themselves, and white egrets posed imperiously on rocks. All the while the sun beat down - and I had forgotten to wear a hat. Carole hadn't come on the boat ride, and so no one noticed that my forehead was getting very red. After some hours, the felucca docked near the hotel and I made my way to our room. I felt very odd and got into bed. I drifted off to sleep, but awoke about midnight, shivering and shaking, but sweating profusely, and waving my arms wildly. Carole had to call for help, and I was wrapped up in blankets which were then held firmly under the bedclothes, making a sort of strait-jacket to hold me still. I was in a delirious state throughout the night, with Carole putting wet towels on my head. Thankfully it had passed by morning. Strange that one can suffer the same symptoms from two opposite forms of weather.

HOTELS
Many years ago, Carole and I went to Paris for a weekend - yes, I think it turned out to be a dirty one - and stayed in rather cheap accommodation. The hotel was quite adequate, but it didn't have a lift. As it only had 10 rooms that shouldn't have mattered, except that our room was number 9 - and it was on the fifth floor! It was the narrowest hotel I have ever encountered. There was no lift because

TIMED TO PERFECTION
Stan Greenberg

there was no room for one. A tight spiral staircase, with chairs strategically placed on the upper reaches, was the only access to the rooms. You made very sure that you never left anything in the room that you were going to need for the rest of the day, because you sure weren't going back up for it.

Another hotel to make an impression on us was the Luxor at Las Vegas. Built in the shape of a pyramid, the rooms are reached by means of an 'inclinator', i.e. an elevator which moves partially sideways to fit the sloping sides of the structure. Like most of the other major hotels in that city it was outrageous, but fun. Since then, we have also stayed in the Mirage, an excellent establishment, but have recently returned to the Luxor, but now stay in the tower annexe.

During the 1986 Commonwealth Games the BBC installed its people in one of the better hotels in Edinburgh. It was well situated, ,just off Princes Street, within easy reach of the stadium. I had a lot of research work to do each evening, and went to bed very tired. As this was one of the few major championships held in Britain I had taken Carole with me. One night, about 3.00am, the fire alarm outside our door rang loudly, scaring us out of our wits. Ringing the reception desk, I was told it was a false alarm. About an hour later it rang again, and again I was told that it was a mistake. When it erupted once more at 5.00am I stalked down to the foyer to find a local fire brigade officer very apologetic. I suggested they should disconnect the alarm while the trouble was traced, but he said they couldn't do that in case there was a real fire. Pointing out that nobody in this hotel would take the slightest notice of a 'real' fire alarm that night, I stalked back to my room. Thoroughly awake, and annoyed, I decided to dress and do some more paperwork. To my disbelief, at about 6.30am, the Edinburgh Early Warning alarm siren sounded on a nearby roof. I clearly remember that when I heard it, bringing back nasty wartime memories, I said to Carole, "Good, I hope they bomb this bloody hotel". Happily, it was also a false alarm, apparently purely coincidental to those at the hotel. To cap the story, I was nearby the following night when David

TIMED TO PERFECTION
Stan Greenberg

Coleman collected his key. As he did so, with a disarming smile and not a trace of annoyance, he sweetly asked if they could tell him when the alarm was due to go off that evening as he was going to have a late bath.

In 1991, Carole and I stayed in Birmingham while attending the AAA Champs. As the first evening consisted mainly of preliminary rounds she stayed in the room while I attended the meeting. Returning late, and cold from the chilly evening, I went straight to bed, reading for a while. Suddenly, the radiator went berserk, sending clouds of steam into the room and boiling hot water on the floor. While Carole got towels to soak up the water I phoned the front desk, and within minutes the manager and an engineer had arrived. Then, another knock, and more people came in, followed soon after by even more. The room, now like a sauna from the steam, was beginning to fill up. The manager was apologising for the incident, when there was yet another knock. As Carole went to answer it she muttered "And two hard-boiled eggs", a reference to the famous Marx Brothers stateroom scene in *A Night at the Opera*, which, not surprisingly, had me falling onto the bed in hysterics. The manager thought I was having a heart attack, and pleaded with us to go to another room on the floor above. When I had recovered sufficiently, we packed and left the "stateroom", and went upstairs, to find ourselves in the most sumptuous suite we had ever seen. It had a beautifully furnished dining room-lounge, kitchenette, very attractive bedroom with tasteful four-poster, and a magnificent bathroom with a double-size jacuzzi. To make the most of it, we had breakfast in the room next morning.

I always travel with a selection of travel plugs. They have enabled me to convert various appliances, e.g. shavers, travel kettles, hair dryers, and computers, for use in the various countries I have been in. Over a period of 30 years I only had a problem once, in Russia, when the only place I could plug into was the electric light socket. So, on many occasions when I couldn't get room service, or was too busy to get out to eat, I was able to make myself a cup of tea, or, sometimes, some soup. Though never a boy scout, I have always believed in 'being prepared'.

HOTEL EXTREMES

The 1992 athletics World Cup was held in Havana, Cuba. Arriving late in the evening, my BBC colleagues and I made our way to the hotel to which the organisers had allocated us. My room was on the 10th floor, and was rather 'sparse'. It was not comfortable and I had great trouble relaxing, particularly noticing 'things' crawling on the walls and the floor. Having finally dropped off to sleep, I was awakened at 2.00am by the telephone. There was nobody on the other end. An hour later, it rang again, and this happened twice more. I was incensed, especially at the operator - who mumbled something and replaced the phone each time I complained. I decided to storm down to the reception desk, but found that there were hardly any lights in the corridor, and the lift didn't work - apparently they saved electricity at night. Next morning breakfast was inedible as far as I was concerned. I was in the depths of despair, with a lot of work to do, when Stuart Storey came in. He had been so appalled by the hotel that he had risen early and gone searching for a better place - and found it. He had booked us into the "Nacional", one of the better hotels I have ever been in. It was the complete antithesis of the other hotel, with delightful rooms, excellent restaurants, lifts that worked all day and night, polite staff and telephones which only rang when they should.

HOW ARE YOU FEELING

We all use the expression, but what does it mean really? For instance, I feel very well - or at least my wife says I do, and she ought to know. She says that I feel like I did when I was much younger - but I suppose that your hands and your fingers are the last things to go! In her favour is the fact that she also feels very well, but then she always did. It was probably one of the reasons that I married her.

TIMED TO PERFECTION
Stan Greenberg

HUGGING

I am a great believer in the power of a hug, and have enjoyed, and intend to continue to enjoy, hugging my wife and children. In fact, we have instituted a family hug, in which all four of us group together and hug everyone else, all at the same time. It is of particular significance at times of great stress, and lets the others know that everyone cares. It is very therapeutic, and great fun. I fully recommend the practice to all and sundry.

HUMOUR

I have a particular sense of the ridiculous, which some would, and do, consider very odd, but certain things really do get to me. Thus, I delighted in the report and picture in the newspaper of a fortune teller's tent on a pier which had a sign saying ' Not here today owing to unforeseen circumstances'. Similarly, I recall checking the pamphlet of instructions that were included with some sleeping pills which had been prescribed for us some time ago. Along with various warnings of overdosing etc, there was the bald statement that 'They may cause drowsiness'.

There is an American comedian, Steve Wright, whose 'way-out' humour strikes a chord with me. An example of his style is the story he tells of being born by Caesarean section - which has had no ill-effects except that he tends to leave a room by the window. He also tells of waking up to find that he has been burgled, and that everything had been replaced with exact replicas. Also that he likes skating, but on the other side of the ice.

When young, I had to visit various shipping offices in the City of London, and was amazed to find them the source of dozens of jokes/comments on the main news stories of the day. What was most surprising was that those news stories would only have been broken on the morning news, and yet when I arrived, at about 9.00am, the jokes etc were rife. I used to think that there must be an office somewhere, staffed by people whose only job was to invent funny items about whatever came to pass. Often, when I returned from my rounds, my departmental head would call me into his room just so that I could tell him the latest jokes that would make him the centre of attention at lunch.

A recent story on the internet, was about an elderly Jewish couple who were shipwrecked on a desert island. They were getting very upset at the thought of seeing out their days there, but then the husband perked up, and cheered his wife with the thought that "Our synagogue building fund subscription is due next week – don't worry, they'll find us!" If one looks for it, even in this rather grim world, one can find 'funnies' everywhere. The latest that I have seen was the sign in a shop window, "We trust in God. Everyone else pays cash".

HUSBANDCIDE

My wife, Carole, thinks that there should be a specific title for the crime of killing one's husband. She thinks that there are very good grounds for defence of such a heinous action. She would use as an argument: that he doesn't stop talking on the telephone when he has a sore throat; that he doesn't pay attention when his wife is talking to him; that he brings someone home for dinner without telling her; that he changes channels to watch sports coverage on the TV in the middle of her favourite programmes; that he never puts the seat down in the toilet. I would deny strenuously any of the foregoing, except, perhaps, the last. However, unfortunately, I believe she thinks that is the worst crime of all.

ICE

Normally, when one talks about ice, one is referring to the cubes put into drinks, or, perhaps, the freezing of small pools of water in a British winter. However, I always think of two occasions when I have been totally overawed by ice. Firstly, there was the Athabasca Glacier, part of the Columbia Icefield, in the Canadian Rockies. I shall always remember the exciting ride we had on a 'Snocoach', which took us onto the glacier itself, and then walking, very carefully I might add, on it. The effect was overwhelming. Secondly, on a recent trip to the United States, the part of the flight over southern Greenland, usually shrouded by cloud, was in clear sunlight. The view of the mass of ice stretching from the shoreline into the horizon was incredible, and has to be seen to be believed. I shall never again look at ice cubes in the same way.

IDIOCY
In the movie *Duck Soup*, Groucho Marx says of someone "He may talk like an idiot and look like an idiot, but don't let that fool you. He really is an idiot." There is no question that there are some incredibly idiotic people about and I am not necessarily referring to the so-called celebrities who are nightly on the TV, or the overrated, overpaid, oversexed soccer players who seem to abound today.

ILLEGAL
A sign in a dentist waiting room caught my eye recently. No, the appointment wasn't mine, as you would have realised if you have read my comments elsewhere about the profession. But, back to the sign. It stated clearly and succinctly that "Tickling and groping was an offence under the 1927 Salmon and Freshwater Fisheries Act". After the initial shock, it did occur to me that the statement probably only refers to fish, and that therefore I would not have to go on the run from the law.

ILLNESS
I seem to be very prone to catching colds. Unfortunately, I may be the world's worst patient - indeed, according to my loved ones, I am. Although I like to be left alone to suffer most of the time, perversely I also like to be fussed over, so that one way or another, I drive Carole crazy. If she doesn't visit me in 'my bed of pain' for any length of time, I throw paper messages down the stairs containing "Supplies Low", "Expedition in Trouble - Send Relief", "In

Need of Water" etc. It is noticeable that when I am not well interesting television programmes are non-existent, the radio has nothing I want to hear, and I have nothing left to read. In such circumstances, I can be, and, I believe, usually am, quite impossible. But as I point out to Carole, the clergyman did say *In sickness and in health*. On the plus side is the fact that when she is not well, I am totally at her beck and call, a veritable Florence (or, perhaps more appropriately, Fred) Nightingale.

IMAGINATION

I am blessed, I think, with a vivid imagination. It was useful at school, especially for essays, but in other ways I suffered badly. When I was six, that imagination, allied to a popular song of the time, seriously affected me. I was alone at my grandmother's house one Sunday evening - the adults were playing cards in another room - when the radio began playing a catchy tune. That wouldn't have caused any problems, except that then the vocalist sang the words. For the next five years or so I was unable to go to sleep until someone had checked - just to make sure. It was some fifty years before I heard the song again. It was by Nat Gonella's band and called *Skeleton in the Cupboard*.

An even more bizarre twist of mind came when I was much older. A chap named Andrew Huxtable, a pleasant enough individual, was a fellow member of an athletics organization. It struck me that he had an uncanny ability to appear and disappear at will. Let me explain. At the old White City stadium, our group congregated after meetings in a very open area. You would be talking to Andrew, and then, having turned briefly to someone else, you would turn back to find he had gone. Not just from nearby, but nowhere to be seen, although there was vast open space all around. No one else had seen him go. Similarly, with Andrew nowhere in sight, suddenly he was beside you. I discovered that other people had noticed the same odd behaviour. This was a great relief, as I was coming to the inescapable conclusion that Andrew was a figment of my imagination - although that worried me even more. I mean, why on earth would I want to conjure him up. A Rita Hayworth (for you older readers) or a Raquel Welch, I could understand, but an Andrew Huxtable? Happily, he does really exist.

INCOME TAX

The first time I ever earned anything from my interest in athletics was in the 1960s, when I wrote an occasional piece for a magazine, and sometimes helped a member of the press over the telephone. Now and again I would get a small, usually very small, cheque for these services, which tended to arrive a considerable time after the deed. Therefore, I often forgot that I had been paid these sums. One day I received a bewildering (to me at any rate) letter from the Income Tax people, implying that I owed them more tax than had been deducted via the PAYE at my workplace. I visited their Moorgate office one lunchtime, giving my name and tax number, and was seen by a clerk who carried a small folder with my name on it. I started to query their letter, but as he opened the file I noticed that there was a statement with the name of a national daily newspaper on it. Wisdom dawned. I explained that I sometimes received these small sums but that I hadn't realised that they were taxable. He pointed out that when those sums reached a particular total from the one source within a tax year, they had to be declared by that source. However, he explained that I could claim any expenses incurred to earn those sums. That evening, for the first time, I added up the amounts that I was spending on my athletics interests - books, magazines, entrance fees, journey costs, tickets etc - which I considered put me in a position to earn that money. The total shook me, and ruffled the Income Tax people too when I sent them a detailed list of items I claimed against those earnings. They stated that most of it was really expenses to do with a hobby, but they did accept a good proportion of what I claimed, and it was way above the trivial sums I had earned. From then on I began keeping proper records, and it was quite a number of years before I needed to pay any tax on those 'extra earnings'.

INTERVIEWS

On a number of occasions I have been lucky to be interviewed, mainly on radio, usually about books that I have written or been connected with. The first important one was on Essex Radio, when I was with *The Guinness Book of Records*. The interviewer was an attractive woman who was quite knowledgeable about sport, and made me feel comfortable with the experience. Years later I was introduced to her, now working on BBC TV, and to my amazement she remembered me and the occasion - her name was Helen Rollason. Other interviewers, have been John Dunn, John Inverdale, Mick Robertson (on a children's satellite TV channel) and Giles Brandreth. During the 1996 Olympic Games I was interviewed at home by one of the TV channels, and was asked what I thought about the possibility of ballroom dancing becoming an Olympic event. After my answer, I don't think I will be asked again!

INTOLERANCE

Having suffered so much from intolerance myself, I have always taken pride in my own tolerance of people, at least in respect of colour and creed. I have had, and still have, good relationships with all manner of people, and I hope that I only judge them, if at all, by their behaviour to me and other people, and not by what they look like or how they worship.

Having said that, and meant it, I also have quite strong feelings about mixed marriages of people from different cultures. This has nothing to do with one person being better or worse than the other. Lord knows, there are enough problems to be overcome in marriage, even between people of similar upbringing, without adding those caused by other influences. So it was that, initially, I was upset when my daughter, Karen, informed us that she wanted to marry Paul. Despite the fact that he was the son of old friends, Bob and Heather Sparks, had a decent job, and seemed nice enough, he wasn't what I had expected as a son-in-law. As I told him and his father at the time, it wasn't what he was - more a case of what he wasn't. I had always assumed that Karen would inevitably marry a Jewish boy, and had never contemplated anything else. It so happened that I had not been too impressed with some of them she had been out with, but had never considered the possibility of an alternative. In the event, and they have been married for 26 years now, Paul has turned out to be an excellent son-in-law, and, as far as a parent can tell, a good husband. He has taken part in, and contributed to, family occasions, and though he is Catholic by upbringing, though not practising, he has shown considerable interest in our Jewish festivals - especially those that involve good eating. When Carole and I note some of the problems that have beset others, whose children 'did the right thing', we are pleased that after our first protests we didn't take them any further. We have never had any qualms about introducing Paul as our son-in-law, in any company, and I trust that he feels the same way about his in-laws.

INVENTIONS

My maternal grandfather was a remarkable man. An immigrant from Eastern Europe, and a deeply religious one at that, he taught himself to read and write English so well that he became exceptionally adept at word and number puzzles. He had an inventive mind and a nimble pair of hands, so that any repairs around the house were always given to him to fix. Especially, I recall the automatic timer he made, well before any such thing was readily on the market. As I stated, he was a very religious man, and his religion forbids the turning on or off of electric lights during the Sabbath – the Jewish Sabbath begins at sunset on a Friday night and ends on the Saturday evening. During the short daylight hours of winter, this meant that you would have to leave the lights on for 24 hours – a safety hazard, as well as an unnecessary expense.

He devised an apparatus which I thought was wonderful. He fixed a small shelf to the 'lounge' wall just above the electric light switch. On it he fitted an old-fashioned, large-key, alarm clock, and attached a long length of cord to the barrel of the key. The other end he fitted around the lever arm of the switch. The alarm was set, prior to the onset of the Sabbath, to a time when he and my grandmother were prepared to go to bed, and they waited. At the set time the alarm would sound, and *voilà*, the key would turn, wind up the cord, which would flick the switch, and the lights, off. Later, he refined it by eliminating the ring of the alarm bell.

In the early days of WWII, all gas masks were carried in cumbersome square cardboard boxes. My grandfather designed a cut-down box, which matched the shape of a folded mask far better, and which would save much needed cardboard for the war effort. He took it along to the War Office, but apparently they didn't take much notice of his design. However, a few months later a similar type of box appeared in shops everywhere, and once again the British establishment had put one over on a poor immigrant.

IRISH
The first time I visited Ireland was for the 1979 IAAF Cross-Country Championships, held at Limerick, and one or two things happened which reinforced one's preconceived ideas (or indeed prejudices) of the country. I do not mean to denigrate the citizens of that lovely place, but one soon understands why there are so many Irish stories. For instance, on race day there was a notice in the Press room which stated that "It will be dry today, except for some rain". Then later in the afternoon there was an announcement made to the effect "Can anyone here open a locked door without a key?". Apparently the equipment room was locked, with the key missing. The spectators found the message hilarious, not so surprising as many of them certainly looked as though they had the required skills.

At the 1979 European Indoor Athletics Championships, the great Irish runner Eamonn Coghlan won the 1500m title in the last event of the meeting. The championships were in Vienna, but for reasons probably only known to 'the little people' the Irish TV commentator, an ex-athlete himself and truly a darling man, signed off his broadcast with the words, "And goodnight from Prague". As a member of a minority often the butt of cruel, not funny, remarks, I am not in favour of the Irish joke. However, one that I do enjoy, and have great empathy with, is the one about Murphy's Law. This states that "Anything that can go wrong, will go wrong". Recently I have been told of an addition to this, known as O'Brien's codicil to Murphy's Law. This states that "Murphy was an optimist". Indeed, he was.

ITALY

My first contact with anything Italian was in the food line. Not, as probably happens today, via pastas and soups, but in the form of 'Hokey-Pokey' ice cream. I have no idea why it was so-called, but the term used to be applied to the lemon water ice that was sold by street vendors when I was young. There was an Italian ice-cream seller who had a pitch down a side street, just opposite my parents' house. I vaguely remember that he was a jolly man, and nobody ever complained about him. That is except for my mother. In the winter he would switch his wares to hot chestnuts and jacket potatoes, and I don't think my mother ever forgave him for the fact that my father and I both preferred his potatoes to hers. There was a taste to his product that has never been matched in my memory. The local children would hang around his stall, and play little tricks on him, but I can't recall him ever losing his temper. At the beginning of WWII everyone was shocked to learn that he had been arrested and interned as an enemy alien. He never returned to the area after the war ended, but he gave me an interest in things Italian, and it is probably no coincidence that one of the first places I visited abroad was Italy. I have remained an aficionado of the country ever since.

That first visit was in 1957, when I went with five other chaps to the Adriatic coast resort of Rimini. The two weeks, in an excellent hotel, cost just under £50.00, travelling by train all the way from Calais. The one good thing about an otherwise awful journey was that we changed trains at Milan, and had an opportunity to take a taxi to the wonderful Cathedral there. Nearby is the opera house, La Scala, which looks quite dull on the outside, but is magnificent inside.

JELLYFISH

I have been the recipient of various 'stings' by unscrupulous builders and cab drivers, but by far the worse one was of the physical variety. Most people have stories about bee or wasp stings, but I had a terrible experience at the hands, or should I say tentacles, of a Portuguese Man-o'-War, in other words, a jellyfish. When I was about seven or eight years old, and I can still remember the occasion very clearly, I was paddling in the sea at Margate, in Kent. Suddenly, I was aware that the water was full of white, semi-transparent, floating objects. One of them wrapped itself around my leg, and it felt as though it was on fire. My screams attracted the attention of a grown-up, who picked me up, pushed the thing off my leg, and rushed me to the first-aid post at the back of the beach. My leg was bright red, and burning from the jellyfish stings, and it took a long time for my yells to stop. Apparently I was quite delirious for a time. Large weals were left on my leg for over a week, and the incident virtually ruined the holiday. It would have been a long time before I went back into the water, but soon after we returned home the Second World War began, and I was not to go on a beach for a number of years.

JERUSALEM

It is one of the most wonderful places in the world - certainly of the places that I have been lucky to have visited. There is an atmosphere about the place that I have never encountered anywhere else, and it is not dissipated by the constant problems which beset it. Sitting on the Mount of Olives, gazing at the magnificent panorama of the city, with its ancient walls and gates, the Dome of the Rock shining in the sunlight, the tower of David's Citadel in the distance, is a moving experience. I am sure that it will be so for anyone, no matter what their beliefs. I fulfilled a long-held wish when I uttered a quiet prayer at the West Wall (better known as the Wailing Wall) of Solomon's Temple, and, rather surprisingly, felt very uplifted afterwards. What a shame - indeed a blasphemy - that the city is rent by so many religious factions. Why does religion divide the world rather than bind it together? And if there is a Supreme Being, why does he allow it?

JOBSWORTH

My wife has a way of describing certain people as a jobsworth. She can pick them out the proverbial 'mile away'. They are the ones who will invariably deny you access, or information, or some other courtesy, with the phrase "It's more than my job's worth". At one time or another we have all come across them, particularly working for some authority, such as the local council or a utility company. Mind you, their tune will invariably change if some monetary reward is offered - presumably their job can't be worth that much. What a poor, sad, miserable lot they are - unfortunately, there are quite a lot of them about.

One of my last memories of the White City stadium was the annual Oxford v Cambridge meeting in 1969. Having been to every one since 1949 I dutifully made my way there, with Carole, to find that there were probably more people competing than watching. I had obtained some complimentary 'posh' seats on the home straight side, and looking around saw that the 40,000 capacity stadium was basically empty. I then noticed two people, just two, sitting over on the back straight, in 'T' block, who my binoculars helped me identify as friends Shirley and Les Crouch. So Carole and I wandered round, behind the stands, to the appropriate entrance. There we were met by a commissionaire - a dapper old soldier - who asked for our tickets. I showed him my 'posh' ones and told him we were coming over to sit with our friends - whose tickets were considerably cheaper. He refused us entrance pointing out that "all seats are numbered and reserved". Initially in good humour I pointed out that there were about 15,000 empty seats over this side, and that as we had dearer tickets "it didn't really matter did it". "Oh yes it did" he said, and barred our way. I am afraid that I then lost my temper, and if Carole had not intervened I may well have lashed out. I pushed my way past and told him I was going in. At this he stormed off, muttering about "numbered and reserved" and threatening all sorts of dire consequences. We entered and joined our friends - the four of us in a vast sea of empty seats. Happily we never saw the man again. However, I now realise why this country has been able to defy invasion over the centuries - people like him would never let them in.

JOGGING

I am afraid that even at my 'peak' as a runner, badminton player and footballer I did very little training, relying on my general fitness to keep me going. It was only as I got older that the idea of going for a jog even entered my head. For a time, in the evenings, I would go to our local park, Hackney Downs, and jog once around it - and then limp home. I soon discovered that running on the tree-lined pathways hurt my feet, so I was in the habit of running on the inside grass verge. Then one night, running quite smoothly, one might say running on air, I put my foot down.....onto nothingness, and crashed into a drainage ditch which the local council was having dug. Luckily I only bruised myself, but jogging was curtailed for a time, and never really restarted.

JURY SERVICE

Twice I have been called to jury service at my local Crown Court. Both times the call came at an inconvenient time as far as work was concerned, but one has to do it, and my employers of the time had to let me go. I cannot recall anything special about the first occasion, but the second time remains one of the most embarrassing times of my life. The very first case, which turned out to be the only case I was on that session, was about a purveyor of hard pornographic material, and the jury had to look at various, quite obscene and unpleasant publications, and watch some videos. Now, I consider myself as broad-minded as the next chap, and admit to being titillated by photos of scantily dressed, and undressed, young ladies, as much as any red-blooded male, but these films were positively sickening. To make matters worse, much worse, on either side of me in the jury box were the proverbial little old ladies, who were obviously shocked to the core. It would have been bad enough sitting next to a couple of men, but this made it ten times worse. To cap it all, after having sat through two or three of these vile films, we were asked to leave the courtroom, and when we returned we were dismissed by the judge, who said the defendant had changed his plea to guilty. So after all that, we hadn't needed to be subject to the horror. I must admit to hoping that the defendant would be given the ultimate sentence – but I don't suppose that is what he got. It was obvious that even the judge had thought we had had more than enough, because he proceeded to excuse us from any further service.

KAMASUTRA

I have included this heading purely to titillate the reader, as there is, sadly, so little reference to sex in this book. Indeed, if I am honest, there hasn't really been all that much in my life.(A-aah, how sad). What is possibly worse, is the fact that I haven't even actually read the book in question.

KISS

Not long ago I came across something called the Kiss principle – an acronym for Keep It Simple, Stupid – and I realised that it clearly set out my own attitude to things in general. It seems to me – and I don't think it is just because I am getting on a bit – that things are deliberately made as complicated as possible. There are those flat pack furniture items, which contain instructions "that a child could follow", but I can't. Instruction manuals to electrical goods, particularly if produced in China or Japan, seemed designed specifically to help you electrocute yourself. Car manuals are excessively thick but never seem to have a section telling me, in a reasonably understandable way, the answer to any query I might have. I will not even discuss computer instructions. The most difficult thing I can remember from my younger days was trying to put up an old-fashioned deckchair at the seaside. Today, that would be the simplest of all tasks.

KNOCK DOWN GINGER

Some of you older readers may remember the children's game of 'Knock Down Ginger'
- though why it was called that totally eludes me. It consisted of knocking on somebody's door, and running away before anyone came to answer. When I was about ten or eleven it dawned on me that there was very little point, or sport, in this, so I devised something a little more subtle. There were actually two parts to my scheme. Firstly, I tied a long piece of strong cotton thread to a door knocker, moved well away, and then, from hiding, pulled it. When the person came to the door, and stood there slightly puzzled, I pulled the cotton again and the knocker behind them would strike again, giving them quite a start. An advance on that was to tie the cotton to a knocker, and then tie the other end to the knocker of the house on the opposite side of the street - making sure that the cotton was above normal head height to avoid pedestrians. Then one waited, impatiently, for a vehicle of the right height to pass by, which would pull both knockers at once. The people would come to their doors, peer around, and then look suspiciously at their opposite neighbour who was also standing at their door. Childish, I know, but at the time it was great fun.

KNOWLEDGE

I am a great believer in knowledge for knowledge's sake. I know quite a lot about a few things, and according to some, think I know a lot about a few others, but I do know a little about a lot of things. Perhaps more importantly, I know where to find out. The great Dr Johnson said, "Knowledge is of two kinds. We know a subject ourselves, or we know where we can find information upon it." In my library, apart from the hundreds of books about athletics, I have reference books on almost every subject under the sun. They include music, religion, art, science, politics, theatre, movies, astronomy, antiques, animals, plants, archaeology, geography, history - you name it. There are also at least four encyclopaedias, three world atlases, guide books to various parts of the world, and about five good collections of quotations. I pride myself that I can find the answer to most queries that crop up. However, sometimes I am a little worried when I recall that *Ecclesiastes, Chapter 1, Verse 18* states "For in much wisdom is much grief: and he that increaseth knowledge increaseth sorrow". Then again, I realise that my increased knowledge also tells me that this reaction has always been organised religion's attitude to learning, so I don't worry too much.

LANGUAGES

Of the three or four languages that I have been taught, at one time or another, I suppose the only one that I am still conversant with is French. However, when I say conversant I do not imply that I can readily 'converse' with a French speaking person. I find that my latent lisp and inability to 'think' in the language are great hindrances. I think the problem goes back to my Matric French oral exam, which was conducted by an east European gentleman, who also took the German oral test. His accent, as far as I was concerned, was almost unintelligible, and caused me terrible problems. There were two things that haunt me to this day. The first was the standard test of being given a postcard, and asked to describe what the picture was in French. The scene was of a living room, with the usual accoutrements, and a cat sitting on something before a blazing fire. I thought I did quite well describing the table and chairs and the fireplace etc, but came to an abrupt and embarrassing halt when I couldn't think of the French word for what the cat was sitting on. Yes, you guessed it - it was a pouffe! He then asked a number of questions, which brought his terrible accent into play, and the interview came to a grinding halt when, in answer to his " Quelle leçon aimez-vous le mieux?" (What lesson do you like best?), I answered " Le printemps" (The spring). I thought he had said "saison" (season). From there on in I lost all confidence and it deteriorated even further. When the Matric results came out

TIMED TO PERFECTION
Stan Greenberg

the only subject, of the ten I was required to take, in which I failed, other than chemistry about which I have written before, was French Oral. My French master was perplexed as I had got a Credit in ordinary written French. In fact, in the Oral published results there was no mark shown whatever, and I know I wasn't *that* bad.

I am jealous of those who learn foreign languages easily. At various times I have 'studied' French, German, Spanish, and Russian, but I am not very good at any of them. However, I can make some sense of newspapers, menus and, particularly, athletics magazines. Annoyingly, I have many friends who are excellent linguists, having no trouble in switching from one language to another at will. Someone who I look on with awe is my cousin's wife, who teaches Russian at Stanford University in California. Born in the Soviet Union, she moved to Israel, married a Briton, and now lives in the United States. Not only fluent in Russian, Hebrew, German and English, she also has knowledge of a couple of other European tongues. But perhaps her greatest accomplishment was to learn Japanese. So now she reads languages which go from left to right, right to left, and top to bottom. If anyone knows one which reads from bottom to top, let me know - she would like the complete set.

Nevertheless, my limited knowledge has been useful at times. On a visit to Athens, some friends and I took a trip to Delphi. Late reaching the Athens coach station, we were met by row upon row of buses. Somebody called out "How do we know which one?", and I shouted "Over there - that one". Everyone rushed to the bus I indicated, and once aboard, asked how I knew it was the right one. I said that it had 'Delphi' on the front. My friends argued that it hadn't, and when we arrived we checked. Sure enough, on the indicator board was Delphi, in Greek. I realised for the first time that the Greek alphabet was like the Russian (i.e. Cyrillic), and subconsciously I had read it correctly. Similarly, in the Moscow Olympic stadium in 1980, the BBC commentators were eagerly awaiting confirmation of the 100m final result to see if Britain's Allan Wells had won the gold medal. Suddenly I called out "He's got it", and when asked how I knew I pointed to the vast stadium scoreboard. The others looked and saw what they considered to be gobbledegook, but with my limited knowledge of Russian I could read the names shown, and there was Wells in the first spot.

While in Tokyo for the 1991 World Athletic Championships I developed very bad stomach pains. It became so painful that I had to get some help. Wary of doctors, of any nationality, I was sent to a nearby pharmacy. It was a large, bright, well-stocked place, with many assistants - but, surprisingly, none of them spoke English. I used face and hand gestures, to explain that I wanted something to make be burp. In other circumstances, my effect on the assistants would have been funny. Finally, one of them went to get the chief pharmacist himself - who also spoke little or no English. I was beginning to despair, when Japanese ingenuity came to the rescue. The pharmacist produced two sheets of card on which were written, in English as well as Japanese, a series of ailments and symptoms, such as 'I have a headache', 'My arm is broken', 'I think I am pregnant' etc. Happily there was also one which said 'I have a stomach ache'. As I pointed to that, there were sighs of relief and smiles all round, and a package was produced, which actually had English instructions on it. Triumphantly I returned to my room, where the concoction did give me some relief. I wonder if Japanese tourists would find as good a service at a London chemist.

LEGEND

Some years ago, I was extremely flattered to be referred to, in a major newspaper, as a 'legend'. It was in an article about athletics statistics (surprise, surprise) by a well-known journalist, and it certainly gave my ego a considerable boost. However, when I showed the item to my in-laws, I was quickly brought down to earth by my mother-in-law, who, for some time after, would refer to me as the 'leg-end'.

TIMED TO PERFECTION
Stan Greenberg

LEVEL PLAYING FIELD

Currently, this is one of the most used phrases, along with 'moving the goal-posts', among political as well as sporting writers. While I cannot remember a situation when the goal-posts were moved, I recall many uneven playing fields that I have played on. One special occasion was when my Unilever soccer team played a London Transport team. The ground was near Bushey in Hertfordshire, and was unbelievably uneven. In fact, if you stood in the goal at the bottom of the slope, you could not actually see the goal at the upper end of the pitch. However, I found the pitch, which was water-logged in the bottom half, very much to my liking. Having toiled up to the levelled out section which lay between the halfway line and the top goal, I used my speed to easily outrun the opposing backs, and, although missing even more, I scored a lifetime best of four goals before half-time. Playing in the opposite direction was not so pleasant, as I continually slipped over on the wet, muddy, downhill grass slope, but we had a winning lead, and it didn't matter.

LIBIDO

I am not exactly sure what this is, and I am much too shy to give the dictionary definition here. It seems to me that when I was younger, people didn't have one - it was definitely never discussed in any of the company that I was in. I am virtually certain that my parents didn't know anything about it, and even if they did they would have pushed it to one side, both in their minds and in their lives. Sigmund Freud, the Austrian founder of psychoanalysis, (doesn't he have a lot to answer for?) thought that repression of it caused acute anxiety. Well, perhaps he was right - I certainly was very anxious when I was younger, even though I didn't really know exactly what it was that I was anxious about. However, I realise now that not only do I have a libido, but that it has worked pretty well in the past. Come to think of it, and I often do, it isn't doing too badly in the present either.

TIMED TO PERFECTION
Stan Greenberg

LIFE

I read recently that people sleep for about one-third of their lives. This seemed ridiculously high, so I decided to check it - and was quite horrified at the calculations that I made. Working on the basis that I have averaged about 8 hours sleep a day in my life, that works out at over 25 years. Then I calculated how much time I had spent working - based on an 8 hour day for about 50 years, that makes about 11 years. Now add the time spent eating - say about 1½ hours per day - which adds up to nearly 5 years. (I suppose while on the subject one should also allow some time for getting rid of it - say, a year or so). Therefore in a 70 year life, over 40 years of it is spent eating, working and sleeping, etc. That doesn't leave too much time for other things does it? While on this subject, I also calculated that the 1,000,000 miles of flying that I have done means that I have spent about 90 days in total in the air! I think I will stop this train of thought here and now before I get really morbid.

LIFTS/ELEVATORS

My dictionary defines a lift as "an enclosed platform moving in a well to carry persons and goods up and down". Our American friends call it an elevator, and often seem quite confused when a newly arrived Brit asks at an hotel desk for the site of the 'lift'. Another form of this conveyance that I discovered in the States was an open fronted one. It travelled continuously, albeit very slowly, and one walked on and off it at the various floors at will – hardly an 'enclosed platform'.

When we stayed at the Luxor hotel in Las Vegas, which is built in the shape of a pyramid, we found that they didn't even have elevators, they had something called an inclinator. It travels vertically and horizontally at the same time, thus travelling up the sloping sides of the pyramid. A very odd experience on the first occasion it is tried.

LIM LIM

As a small child, while in a pram or wheelchair out in the street, I would drive my parents crazy by suddenly screaming out "Lim Lim", "Lim Lim". For months relatives and friends puzzled at this, wondering what it was that so upset, frightened or intrigued me. There didn't seem to be any rhyme or reason for my outburst. The mystery was only solved when they realised that quite often my cries occurred at a time when the only person within sight was - a policeman. Apparently, the sight of these tallish men in their uniforms and helmets fascinated me. Nowadays, and particularly when in my car, the last person I look forward to seeing is a Lim Lim. It is a shame how one's early passions are dimmed by experience - well, in this case anyway.

LISTINGS

Quite a large, and important, part of my life has consisted of compiling lists. As long as I can remember I have put together lists about one thing or another. At school they were of countries, capital cities, rivers, mountains, or historical dates. When I got into athletics I first started compiling lists of British and World records, as well as individual performances. Then I realised that there was a niche in Commonwealth athletics marks (or rather the British Empire, as it was then), and I became the main source of such data. My first major compilation was for the 1958 European Athletics Championships, held in Stockholm. I went there as a fan, and the night before departure I stayed up all night trying to run off 28 pages of current European performance lists on an old Gestetner machine. Anyone who has ever used such a machine will remember the cold feeling of horror which came when the 'skin' would tear, and one would have to retype it. That night it occurred over and over again, until I was not only exhausted but also covered in ink. However, the dozen or so copies I had intended to make were run off eventually, and in Stockholm I was able to pass one to the Chief National Coach of the time, John le Masurier. He was delighted with it, as he had never had such information about the opposition at a meeting before, and on a number of occasions in future years he very kindly referred to the great assistance those lists had been to him at the time.

While on the subject of listings, one of the things that has puzzled me over the years is who decided that we should list items by the decimal system (i.e. on the basis of 10). Why not the duodecimal system (base of 12), or, indeed, the octal system (base of 8)? Thus one could have the top 8 or 16 of something. Come to that, why not the top 9, or 13, or 16? Don't you get fed up with everything being the top 10, or 20, or 100? Just think about it: the top 10 pop songs; the 10 best dressed people; the 100 richest people; at a quiz there are invariably 10 categories of questions; in books and films, torturers and gunmen always give their victims a count of 10 before the dirty deed; the National Census (in Britain) is every 10 years. Why can't the next century start in 2087? I think I will start a movement for the establishment of the top 17 of everything. Coincidentally, while writing this I have been watching the Ryder Cup golf, and it has dawned on me that that sport has got it right – they use the nonary system i.e. nine holes a round, and 18 holes for a match.

LIZARDS

I have never been particularly fond of animals of any kind, and I definitely don't like small things that crawl. Therefore I had a bit of a shock when I went to Mauritius in 1992 for the African Athletics Championships. We were put up at a wonderfully positioned hotel on the north coast of the island, where accommodation was in bungalows overlooking a bay. Soon after I entered my quarters I heard a scurrying sound behind a cupboard, which, I discovered on investigation, was being caused by a small lizard. Disturbed, it ran up and down the walls before disappearing under a chest of drawers. Not too pleased with my roommate, I complained to the concierge, who warned me not to force it out of the room, as I had intended, since, he said, it was quite safe, and kept other, less desirable things, out - he said this rather ominously I thought, but I didn't ask him to elaborate. After a rather nervous first night, I found that by the end of our stay I had almost forgotten about him, and certainly had no trouble from any insects or flies - or anything else. Back home, I found it very difficult to convince friends that I had shared my room with a lizard.

LOCUSTS

As a practising Jew, although not extremely orthodox, my diet is rather limited, as members of my faith have a long list of animals, fish and other foodstuffs that we are prohibited from eating. In this modern age it does seem that many of the restricted items should no longer be proscribed – most of the restrictions stem from the unhealthy conditions which existed in Bible times. However, in Judaism, habit often becomes law, and the Authorities, in their wisdom, have decided that such restrictions impose a different way of life which marks us out, for good or evil, from the rest of the world. Personally, I don't have any argument with this, although life would have been much easier for me without many of those food restrictions, especially when I travelled a lot. Nevertheless, I am often very pleased that I am not allowed to eat some of the slimy, crawly, ugly creatures which my non-Jewish friends seem to have. So I was quite shaken to read in a particular text in the Old Testament – *Leviticus,11:21* - that we are allowed to eat locusts. Can you believe it? I can only assume that, in the past, this was done to try and get rid of them when they invaded the Holy Land. In my youth I often took part in pea-picking and apple collecting to help farmers, but the thought of a group of us going locust gathering just blows my mind.

LONELINESS

Loneliness has rarely troubled me. The fact that I was an only child made me far less dependent on other people. Thus, I am quite happy to be alone for quite long periods, particularly if I have something to read or to work on. However, I recall one occasion when I felt truly alone. It was after a serious row, a very rare occurrence, with my wife, and I stormed out of the house in righteous indignation, intending never to return. I got into my car, and then sat there wondering what to do, as it dawned on me that I couldn't 'go home to mother' - my mother had lived with us for 30 years. It was an awful feeling - I had nowhere to go, nobody to turn to. After things returned to normal, I mentioned this predicament to a bachelor friend, and asked him if such a situation came up again whether I could go and stay with him. He said that I could, but he would prefer it if I stayed at home and I sent Carole to stay. Nice to know you can rely on friends in a crisis. Incidentally, regarding the merits, or otherwise, of being an only child, I understand that Genghis Khan, Stalin and Leonardo da Vinci were all only children. Make of that what you will.

LONGEVITY

We all wonder how long we will live, and at times no doubt consider our chances. Because my father died at 64, and two of his brothers when they were only in their fifties, I never really considered that I would last very long. In fact, I will admit to being quite nervous as I approached 64, and only relaxed when I passed that age. My mother lived to 98, and I sometimes wonder whose genes are more dominant in me, but I can honestly say that I no longer worry about the matter. What does concern me though is retaining my health and quality of life. It is easy to say, when I am quite well and fit for my age, but I am not sure I would want to go on if my health deteriorated badly and/or I was in terrible pain. It would then became a case of merely existing, not living, and though I have a number of interests that I could enjoy if I were confined to bed, it is not a situation that I think I could embrace easily. Beyond eating, drinking and living 'healthily', there is not very much one can do about it, so we have to take whatever may come – but it does 'give one pause'.

Around the time I was writing this item there was a report in the press about a Chinese woman who, it was claimed, had reached the remarkable age of 128. In one newspaper there was a photograph of the lady, looking unbelievably sprightly. My cousin

Alan and I came to the conclusion that it was not a contemporary photograph, but that it was probably taken some years ago – when she was a mere 120 or so.

LORDS AND LADIES (Actually, DAMES)

At Unilever I worked with a former international athlete, unfortunately after his running days were over. He was Terry Higgins, a 1952 Olympic 400m runner. A former President of the Cambridge Union, he was a top-flight economist in the E & S department. It was no surprise when he entered politics and won the Worthing seat for the Conservative Party (holding it from 1964-1997), and from 1970-72 was Minister of State, Treasury. He was later knighted, and in 1997 raised to the Peerage. On one occasion, an office 'do', my wife and I met his wife, Rosalyn. Later, at home, Carole and I concluded that Rosalyn was a "nice, cute, girl, and just right for Terry". Some time afterwards I found out that she had been Visiting Professor at Yale Law School, was an expert on International Law, and wrote the definitive work on the subject. Later, she became a QC, and then a Dame of the British Empire. Mind you, we still thought that she was a nice, cute, girl.

When I went to work for the *Guinness Book of Records*, I found that one of the 'bigwigs' at the office was Viscount 'Tommy' Sudley, the heir to the Earl of Arran. Though thought a snob by others, I found him very friendly, and often went to lunch with him. Sometimes that would be slightly embarrassing, as he would always have a glass of wine with his meal - even with beans on toast at the local Lyons. Later, he was a junior minister in the Conservative government, and succeeded to the title in 1983.

In 1987 I was intrigued to learn that Maurice Peston had been raised to the peerage, as Lord Peston. I believe he had been an economics adviser to the Labour government - he was a lecturer at the University of London. It was the first time I had thought, or heard of him, for forty years, when we had been at Hackney Downs School together. Particularly I remember him because he had a twin brother, causing much confusion, and secondly I remember he had an attractive sister. I am certain that I was as clever as he was at that time, often ahead of him in examinations. So - where did I go wrong? His son, Robert, often appears as a business pundit on TV news programmes.

In recent years my 'interest' in the House of Lords had been diminished with the abolition of hereditary peers, and the retirement of others. However, as I write this, two people I regard as friends have 'been raised'. That wonderful runner, Seb Coe, has become Lord Coe, and that delightful lady and Olympic champion, Mary Peters, has become a Dame of the British Empire. Since I am more than likely to meet them here and there, I wonder if I should shake their hands or curtsey. I mean, one does like to get these things right.

On a less savoury note, I am writing this on the day that Lord Archer has been found guilty of perjury and perverting the course of justice. Though I have never actually met the gentleman, my life has 'bounced' against that of Jeffrey Archer on a few occasions. The first time that I probably took notice of him was in the 1964 Oxford v Cambridge athletics match at the White City, when he caused a false start in the 100yds, before finishing a close second to a NUTS colleague, Adrian Metcalfe. I was later to come across him when I worked at the Greater London Council (GLC), at which he had become a councillor. Prior to that, while he was still at Oxford, I had given a lift in my car, from a meeting in Leicester to north London, to another University sprinter, whom I had heard roomed with 'the lad'. Trying to make conversation with a rather morose athlete, I mentioned that I had heard that Archer could be a bit difficult. The athlete broke his silence to mutter something to the effect that he had no trouble with him, and then relapsed into an unnerving silence for about 30 miles or so. Suddenly, he said, without any preamble, "Just be pleased that he doesn't want to be King. That chap will be whatever he wants to be." I was so surprised at the statement that the car swerved sharply, but I never forgot that comment. How perceptive that undergraduate was.

Lastly, when I read Francis Crick's biography of Archer, I was intrigued to learn that he had 'stolen' Mary, eventually his long suffering wife, from a fellow Oxford student, Jonathan Martin, who, later, as head of the sports department, was my boss when I worked for the BBC.

Many years ago I wrote to the Marquis of Exeter enquiring about some details of his great career as Lord Burghley, one of our best athletes in the 20s and 30s. I received a pleasant and informative letter in reply, indicating his pleasure at my interest. He made a major impression on me by signing the letter - 'Exeter'. Ever since I have had a burning ambition to be able to sign my correspondence as 'Friern Barnet'.

LOVE

Actually I knew my wife years before I met her. Perhaps this needs a little explaining. We were vaguely related even before we got married. Her father's sister was married to my mother's brother. We assumed that this was far enough removed not to breed idiots - but, at moments of great stress with my children I have had serious doubts. We obviously attended family functions without knowing about each other, and as I am some nine to ten years older than she, it was not until well into our lives that I would have deigned to take notice anyway. I have no recollection of her at all until a mutual cousin's wedding when she was just 15 and the chief bridesmaid. Because of the occasion I can pinpoint the date, 30th October 1955 - surely not many people remember the actual date when they first met their future partners. As best man I had to partner this rather chubby schoolgirl for the occasion. As a suave, sophisticated 24 year old man about town (well, it is my story) apparently I made a real impression. Two years later, I was best man yet again to another cousin, and Carole turned up as my partner once more. She was now an only slightly less chubby 17 year old, and I remember she wore a white mohair stole. At our table, on my other side, was another female relative, who had a red mohair stole. Of course, I wore a black tuxedo, of which I was very proud, and by the end of the evening it was covered with red and white hairs. I covered my embarrassment by explaining to my young, impressionable, partner the origins of the Tibetan Mo from which I said the wool came. She appeared to be fascinated - or perhaps wondered where I had escaped from. However, I gather that she did enjoy my company, although on my part I admit that by the following week I had forgotten about her.

Move forward about 12 months, to a cold September evening. I was out with a girlfriend and travelling up the escalator at Tottenham Court Road. It is very steep, and as one ascends, you tend to watch the girls coming down on the other side. I noticed one girl with nice legs, and thought that she was vaguely familiar. Once my memory kicked in I realised that it was the chubby schoolgirl - except she wasn't anymore. I didn't think too much about it for some weeks, but then one night, while playing badminton at the GEC building in Kingsway, I found myself thinking of her. I decided then and there to ring her up. Now that was most unlike me, and I still wonder just what grabbed me that night. Between games I went to the caretaker's office to use the telephone, but he wasn't about, so I walked around the corner to the main road and across Kingsway itself to a public phone box. I was only wearing my playing things - white tee-shirt and shorts, socks and plimsolls - which seemed to give the middle-aged lady already occupying the callbox quite a shock.

I found Carole's number in the phone book and made the call. Her mother answered and asked who it was. I answered that it was Stanley, but she had gone by the time I gave my second name. Then Carole was on the line, sounding very matter of fact in asking how I was and what did I want. I was a little puzzled, as getting a call from someone you hadn't seen for weeks, and who you didn't really know very well anyway, surely would elicit some surprise. Then, warily, Carole asked again who I was, and I gave my full name - that got some reaction. I found out much later that she already had a boyfriend named Stanley, and thought that I was he. After brief politenesses I asked if she would care to go out that coming weekend. She declined, saying that she was booked up. I got the same answer to a request for the following weekend, and had decided to let the whole thing drop, when she suggested the weekend after that. I often think that many couples fail to get together because the girl feels it is unladylike to make any move to show she is interested, or at least not disinterested. If Carole had not made that suggestion then I know that my innate shyness, or male pride, would have prevented me ever ringing again. It would have been an awful shame, for both of us, to have missed the past 55 years.

On reflection, our budding relationship could have been a total disaster, as neither of us was very experienced, as they say. Both of us had dated (what a quaint word) before, but neither of us were very accomplished in the verbal or physical interplay that constitutes a 'romance'. However, we were patient and tolerant, and learnt together. The happy thing was that we *liked* each other. That is not as common as one might suppose. I have known many couples who appear to really dislike each other, even though there is sexual chemistry between them. It may be great for a while, but then what. Once the love, sex, lust, has happened, you have to like each other to have a good, strong, lasting relationship. If I am honest, I don't think I was really in love with my wife when we married. Certainly I was very fond of her, and I enjoyed her company very much. I missed her when we were apart, always looked forward to seeing her, and was never bored when I was with her. But, in an amorous, passionate, sexual way - I don't think so. That grew gradually over the ensuing months and years, and that side of our marriage is as good as ever. There can't be too many men who admit to falling in love with their wives after they were married, but I do, and claim that I still am. I suspect that the same was true with Carole. Perhaps, as we were both an only child, initially what we wanted was companionship. Whatever the reason, I have never had any reason for regret.

LUCK

Quite recently I came across this quotation, apparently by an American football coach: "Luck is what happens when preparation meets opportunity". With that statement in mind, I think I have been lucky in most aspects of my life. Certainly, in my private life, and, for 99% in my working and sporting activities. Whenever I have had job interviews it seems that the right questions were asked, and that I gave the right answers. Whoever, or whatever, is in charge of such things, was assuredly watching over me when I made my choice of life partner, and, indeed, nudged her to accept me. By and large we have been lucky with our children, in that they have not strayed overly far from the pathways we suggested for them. The way my hobby and overwhelming interest in life, i.e. athletics, developed into a full-time occupation, had to be due to a benevolent deity or suchlike. In matters of health we have had a relatively easy time of it.

Of course, there have been upsets and disappointments, but, on the whole, I don't think there is much I would change if I was given the chance again. (No, Cyd or Raquel, not even for you). For most of my working life I looked forward to every new day, often with keen anticipation. Most surprisingly, not least to my accountant, I seem to have made the right decisions in financial areas. There is no question that I was lucky with the time period in which I was born - I doubt that if I was 20 again at the present time, with my lack of paper qualifications etc, I would have the opportunities that I had 60 years ago. Also, I am very aware that I was lucky to be in the right place, at the right time, on a number of occasions. Nevertheless, I am also aware that on those occasions, the preparation that I had done previously, often unknowingly, gave me the background to take advantage of the new opportunities presented. And yet, it pleases me to think that perhaps some presence is looking out for the interests of me and mine.

MACHU PICCHU

One of the greatest experiences of my life was when I finally

TIMED TO PERFECTION
Stan Greenberg

visited fabled Machu Picchu in Peru. I say finally, because I had wanted to go there for some 70 years. When I was about 12 years old, and stimulated by a movie I had seen, I made a list of places throughout the world that I would like to visit one day. At the time it was quite ludicrous really, as firstly, WWII was raging and I wasn't too sure that I would necessarily survive it, and secondly, at the time I had never even been outside England. Nevertheless, I made that list, and over the years I got to every one of those places – except Machu Picchu.

Being in South America made it an expensive place to go for many years after the war, and then getting married and having children meant that the wherewithal and spare time was hard to come by. When I reached the stage of my life when I had the money and could make the time, the Maoist 'Shining Path' followed by the Tupac Amaru guerrillas were murderously running wild in the country from the mid-1970s until the mid-1990s, seriously affecting tourist areas. Thus, now well into my 60s I thought the dream was over. Then, at the end of 2002, when I was over 70, I saw an advertisement in *The Times* newspaper for a trip which excluded the customary extensions to the Amazon basin and Lake Titicaca, and my interest was stimulated again. I sometimes feel that divine intervention had something to do with it, as over the next few days I couldn't pick up a magazine or newspaper, nor watch a television programme, which didn't have a picture or story about Machu Picchu. As Carole commented at the time, someone was trying to tell me something. So I booked a trip for early January 2003.

By good fortune I checked the Internet for projected weather in Peru at that time, and found to my horror that the date when I was going was right in the middle of the rainy season. Immediately I contacted the company to alter the date, and was able to transfer my booking to the first week of April, near the end of the rainy period. I should state that I was less worried about getting wet than the probability of low cloud and poor visibility at the site, which would have ruined the trip. Also, acknowledging my advancing years, I took the opportunity to upgrade the level of hotel. This move, put me into some truly excellent establishments, and also meant that the dozen or so other 'rich' people travelled around in their own minibus, with their own guide, as opposed to the big coach used for the main group. Among our smaller party were a very nice couple from Glasgow.

We flew from London to Miami, and thence to Lima, for a two day stay. Then we flew up, and I do mean up, to Cuzco (at 3326m 11,000ft altitude), something we had to do in the morning because the winds cause serious problems for landing planes in the afternoon. One of the worries at that elevation is succumbing to altitude sickness, an aggravated condition of which could mean having to immediately leave and fly down to sea level again. Happily, I and most of our party avoided that problem. To guard against it, we were advised to drink regular infusions of coca tea, which was provided free by our hotel, but I found the drink so awful that I only had about three cups all told, whereas others knocked back considerable quantities. I should point out that in that tea form it was not, apparently, as addictive as its derivative cocaine. I did a lot of walking around, and had an excursion to the remarkable ruins of Sacsayhuaman, which loomed another few hundred feet or so above Cuzco, but I didn't particularly notice any breathing difficulties. Finally, we took the 3½ hour train journey to Aguas Calientes (it gets it's name from natural hot springs), the little village at the foot of the mountain on which the famed ruins stand. From a bridge over the raging Urubamba river we took a rather rickety bus up, up, and up a rather scary 'road' to the famous Lost City. Although 'only' about 7500ft *2286m* above sea level, Machu Picchu stands on a precipitous outcrop, and is totally surrounded by much higher mountains. The day I arrived was bright, the feared clouds were high, and the sun was quite warm. The effect of my first sighting of the city was completely overwhelming, and for one of the first times in my life I was left speechless. The husband of the Glasgow couple I had befriended, took out a mobile 'phone, and to my utter amazement, in those mountainous conditions, contacted his family back in Scotland. He then offered it to me so that I could ring Carole. When I got through I was so overcome by the emotion of the moment that I had tears in my eyes, and found it difficult to speak. After all those years, it had come to pass at last, and I was, literally, fulfilling a childhood dream. What is more, unlike some other such dreams, this one surpassed anything I had hoped for.

MANGLE

When I was ten or eleven I was playing in my grandmother's garden with some friends. I remember we were putting wet cloths through an old mangle which stood under cover outside her back door. Inadvertently, I held onto one item for too long, and the longest finger on my left hand – the middle finger – partly got drawn between the wooden rollers, before my screams alerted my friends to what was happening. The accident ruined my nail for many years, and to this day – some 70 years or more later – the nail on that finger develops a split whenever it grows more than a millimetre in length. Though not the same word apparently, the verb "to mangle" means to mutilate or maim, which it sure did to me.

MANNERS MAKETH MAN

I have always found, from what contacts I have had with them, that the Japanese are very well-mannered, but a recent experience quite surprised me. Carole and I were on a sight-seeing trip to Monument Valley in the United States, and found that all the others in the party, about 30 or so mainly young people, were Japanese tourists. At one point we stopped for lunch and all of us sat down at a very long table to eat. Suddenly, I realised that there was not a murmur or sound from any of them as they were eating and drinking. It was uncanny, not a sound of cutlery scraping on a plate, not a glass clinking on the table, and certainly not a sound of conversation. Carole and I agreed that their parents had done a great job of bringing them up. Normally, on a similar occasion with Americans or Europeans, the noise would have been close to deafening.

MARRIAGE

That most famous source of quotes, Anon, has it that "A man is incomplete until he is married. Then he is finished." I can agree with the first part, but not with the second. Carole and I seemed to hit it off from the start. There were so many likes and dislikes that we had in common - but not enough to become boring. We share a very similar sense of humour, which is something I consider to be very important in a marriage. Our feelings about music and cinema are also similar, although I am not as keen as Carole on today's 'pop', and she doesn't appreciate my interest in Sci-Fi films. My relationship with Carole has given me great physical and mental contentment, and I hope that she feels the same way. She was clever enough not to try and change me too much - since she apparently liked what I was in the first place - but I think that I had enough sense to realise that I had to adapt. I always tried to make up for my many absences, especially when it meant me going abroad, and therefore I took her away as often as was financially possible. We have had remarkably few rows in our 55 years together - and those we did have were invariably about the children, but never over money. Another important point was that we both made a great effort never to go to bed without settling an argument, as such things can fester into something much worse. While I would not be such a hypocrite to suggest that I have never looked at another woman, I have never made any attempt to take it past the looking stage, and I believe the same attitude to be true for Carole - certainly I have never had cause to be jealous, and nor has she. We still hold hands and hug a lot, which I believe sincerely is how it should be, and we will continue to do so for as long as we are allowed.

MEANINGS

When very young I learnt that words can have double meanings, especially if you intend them to. I have always considered that 'double entendres' are a higher form of wit. My introduction to this form of words was in an English lesson, when the master read out the sentence "John sat by the fire, and felt rosy all over". I remember it took me some while to understand what everyone was laughing about. (As I have stated before, I was somewhat backward in certain areas). Then there is the following: "Rose's are red, Violet's are blue - how do you know?"

We all have favourite expressions or words, which we use incorrectly. Thus I would say "I feel rotten", only to be told that I shouldn't touch then. While on the subject of words and meanings, I always liked the story about the computer developed to translate English into Russian, and vice versa. It translated the maxim "Out of sight, out of mind", and then translated it back from the Russian. The answer came back as "Invisible idiot".

MEMORY

In a wartime speech, Franklin D Roosevelt said that no man and no force can abolish memory. Well, he may have been right, but age can do what no man or force can. I find that it is one of the most frustrating results of getting old that my memory keeps letting me down. Usually, not on important things, but to do with small, relatively unimportant matters, which nevertheless the lack of recall drives me crazy. The name of a long-ago acquaintance; the location of a one-time popular venue; the title of a favourite film; an early telephone number; the colour of your first car. We have all had the same problem at one time or another – and I fear that if you haven't had it yet, you will in time.

Memory is a strange and fickle thing. In all of my occupations, memory has played a most important role, and I have had to rely on it to a greater extent than most people. However, I have found in recent years that it plays unfortunate tricks on me. Sometimes, I forget my home telephone number, and I can never remember my car licence number. Obviously, it has something to do with getting old, but I do not think that is the main reason. It seems I have a very selective memory, but I don't understand how and why I select certain things to store and others to discard. For example, I have little difficulty in recalling athletic performances of the most unlikely

TIMED TO PERFECTION
Stan Greenberg

performers, eg Ghanaian 800m runners from the 1950s, a long jumper from Haiti in 1928, or a whole series of American sprinters from the 1930s onwards. Some years ago I was introduced to a distinguished West African businessman, whose name (Omubo Peters) stimulated the recesses of my mind to produce the fact that he had run 9.7sec for 100y about 20 years before. It delighted him, astonished bystanders and staggered me, for, at that moment, I couldn't remember the name of the man who was doing the introducing, a man I knew well.

Similarly, I have no trouble in remembering scenes and dialogue from old movies, the names of actors, capitals of countries or the titles of pieces of music. Conversely, I can't remember names of some people I meet regularly. To overcome this, I resort to carrying pieces of paper with 'aide memoire' notes eg Jeremy - large nose, Agnes - stringy hair, Belinda - big bust, etc, which, if discovered, would surely result in a series of lawsuits. Then again, I may meet someone abroad, not seen for ten years, and instantly recall him. Why does my mind work this way?

When I was at the GLC, I sat opposite a chap, i.e. facing with desks abutted, day in, day out, for about two years. We got on well - certainly there was no hostility which could account subconsciously for what followed. Then I went to a different organisation. About three weeks later I received a telephone call from my replacement, asking the whereabouts of a file. Having settled the query I began to ask about my former colleague, only to realise that I couldn't think of his name at all. I covered my confusion by asking about everyone in general, and left it at that. I didn't recall his name until about a week later.

However, once I really outdid myself. I forgot *my own name*. In my twenties I had an interview for an upgrading at work. Expecting questions about the job I was then doing, I had boned up on the answers I would give, and obviously had these on my mind. The interviewer turned out to be someone I knew well, and we spent some time talking about mutual sporting interests. Suddenly he switched topics and pulling a form towards him said "Let's get the formal stuff out of the way ... now your name is?" He well knew it, but presumably he wanted confirmation in case there were middle names or strange spellings involved. Completely caught off guard, I stared at him stupidly as he repeated the question. I couldn't think who I was. Nothing came to me. I started to splutter and cough, as I frantically tried to think. He was looking at me very oddly by this time. Then my mind engaged, and I blurted out "Stanley ...Stanley Greenberg". With a broad smile he expressed surprise that my middle name was the same as the first, and asked if perhaps it was a family idiosyncrasy. For the record, I got the upgrading, but I gather that he told other members of staff that I had acted rather strangely.

MEN AND WOMEN

Ever since I was old enough to realise that men and women were different I also learnt just how alike they are too. A great jolt to my male upbringing occurred when I joined the badminton club at work. The club met in a vast church hall in Balham, which contained two full-sized courts, with as much height as would ever be needed - quite superb facilities. There was a stage on which the members would sit awaiting their turn, watching the other games. As a young man, I took a vicarious pleasure in watching the girls play. Not surprisingly much discussion went on among the men about who looked the prettiest, who had the best figure or the nicest legs.

Then one evening I received a tremendous shock - I discovered that girls discussed boys in the same way. It was a revelation to me, in my 19 year old innocence. I was sitting alone, at the back of the stage, when I heard some of the girls talking about the boys who were on court. They were comparing their height, shape, shoulders, face, nose, hair, and even, to my astonishment, their legs. Then, horror, my name was mentioned, with the comment that they thought I had a good pair of legs. Just then I was called to play. Terribly embarrassed, I tried to pull my brief shorts down as far as possible. I must have been a wonderful sight with my bright white kit, and my bright red face. I don't remember how I played but it must have been very badly as I felt everyone's eyes staring at me and my legs, of which I had never been especially aware until that moment. I must have looked ludicrous, like Groucho Marx, dropping down in an attempt to get as close to the ground as possible. For the first time since I joined the club I tried not to play, making all sorts of excuses. The following week I wore track suit bottoms, which got me a rebuke from the committee. Later, I realised that if I did have something nice about me which girls liked - and I didn't think I had much else - I should be proud of it. So back came the shorts. It may have been coincidence, but that very week a girl that I was keen on made a point of getting friendly. In responding to that I found that I lost some of my many inhibitions, and I reckon that period was a watershed in my social development. I wonder if women realise that men need assurance about their looks and appeal, just as much as they do. Young men especially need to know that they are as fine as they may think they are, or, more importantly, much better than they may fear they are.

I suppose, when I was young, I was what is now called a 'nerd', only saved from total social oblivion by a love of, and some achievement at, sport. I wasn't good-looking - although compared to some of the Pop groups I was a Greek god - but I was slim and wiry, and looked healthy and athletic. I fondly remember that about the age of 12 it somehow stimulated a crush note from a very pretty girl at school. Unfortunately her interest soon wore off, due almost certainly to my non-reciprocation. Not that I didn't want to, but I didn't know how. That state affected my life for many, many years to come.

As a youngster I was always a loner, and although I had a number of friends, good friends, I was never particularly unhappy to be on my own. With the addition of a bad case of almost pathological shyness, I was well into my twenties before, outwardly, I showed an interest in girls. Luckily, my initial, tentative, excursions into the, nerve-wracking world of boy/girl relationships were not as fraught as I had imagined. Just one bad experience, a curt refusal, a cruel remark, a sarcastic comment, would have sent me back into my shell - perhaps forever. Actually, that nearly happened, as I found out much later.

I well remember the time that I summoned up courage to ask one of the girls in the office for a date. It had taken me weeks to get to the point, and literally with a pounding heart I spoke to her. After a brief pause, during which my mind was in a turmoil, she agreed to come out the following evening, and I returned to my desk aglow. I learnt later that the girl didn't really like me very much, but she had just had a row with her then boyfriend and agreed to go out with me to spite him. Oddly, my bumbling, awkward manner, plus a tendency, when nervous, to babble on about anything and everything, apparently quite fascinated her, and, to my great surprise she came out with me again, and again. She bolstered my confidence at a crucial time in my life, and when we eventually parted I was a very different person. Nothing ever 'happened', as they say, but we were very close, and we, and later our respective spouses, have remained friends ever since.

METRIC SYSTEM

Interested and working in a sport which is totally involved with measurements, both of time, weight and distance, the metric system has played an important part in my life. I first 'discovered' it when I began reading foreign sports publications in the 1950s, and soon became quite conversant with it. (It still causes great problems to the mass of the British population - and is totally unknown to most Americans). However, it was not always so. On my first trip abroad, in 1952 to Finland, I decided to buy sweets. I entered a shop, and pointed at a jar of small, multi-coloured boiled sweets. The shopkeeper spoke no English, and certainly I knew no Finnish (I was amazed that anyone did), but she was obviously asking me how much I wanted. Waving my hands about in a vague way I tried to indicate a basic quantity. She nodded, and proceeded to pour vast numbers of sweets into her scales. I went to the stadium with a kilo 2¼*lbs* of the sweets, and was very popular with those around me that hot day.

After that debacle I made sure I was au fait with all aspects of metrication. One of the problems, from a sports statistician's point of view, is that by losing Imperial measurements one also loses some interesting 'barriers'. For instance, seven feet in the high jump becomes 2.13m, and 20 feet in the pole vault is 6.09m - not quite as thrilling is it? However, there was one occasion when I was able to reverse the trend. At the Moscow Olympics in 1980, the winner of the men's long jump, Lutz Dombrowski (GDR), cleared an outstanding 8.54m, which equated to *28ft 0¼in.* Now, this performance, to athletics fans, was quite important, as nobody had ever jumped a measured *28 feet* anything before. The world record was a phenomenal 8.90m *29ft 2½in*, achieved in 1968. That had improved the world mark by *21¾in*, and in the meantime nobody had jumped better than *27ft 8¾in.* Anyway, realising the significance of Dombrowski's jump, I went to my old friend Vladimir Otkalenko, who was commentating for Soviet TV, and explained it to him. At first he was puzzled, but, being conversant with British and American measurements in magazines, he then got the point, and as far as I could tell began explaining to his Soviet audience what this performance meant within the intricacies of Imperial measurement. Either that, or he was telling them that he had just been interrupted by a mad Briton.

MINOR DISASTERS AND IRRITATIONS

Many occasions in life can cause serious difficulty and/or embarrassment at the time, but can be looked back on with amusement. Currently I do not like spaghetti, although it appears that at one time I might have. On a date with my future wife in the late 1950s, I accidentally tipped a plate of the stuff into my lap, while wearing my good suit (Actually, my only suit). I can't remember exactly what happened after that - no doubt my psyche has benevolently wiped the incident from my memory - but what does one do in such a situation. I vaguely recall being wiped down in the kitchens, and miserably taking Carole home with my coat hiding the stain and the damp.

In somewhat similar vein was the occasion when a friend and I attended an athletics meeting on a warm summer afternoon at Motspur Park in south London. We walked about the ground watching the events from up close. To his absolute horror my friend suddenly realised that the zip on his trousers had broken. Because of the good weather we had no coats with us and he spent the rest of the afternoon with his newspaper held firmly in front of him. The worst thing about it was that the meeting was the national Women's championships, and about 90% of the people there were female.

MODESTY

I know this is usually considered a virtue, but so often it is a case of false modesty – when a person decries his or her abilities, but knows full well that everybody knows that they are exceptionally good or clever at the subject in hand. I have always liked the comment of the poetess Dame Edith Sitwell, when she wrote in the *Observer* in April 1950 that, "I have often wished I had time to cultivate modesty. But I am too busy thinking about myself".

Thinking about Dame Edith, and her equally famous writer brothers, Sir Sacheverell and Sir Osbert, made me think of the musical Goossens family (I'm sorry, but that's the way my mind works, when it works at all). Eugene, Leon, Marie and Sidonie were all feted musicians, with the first two renowned for their connection with the oboe. When I was at school I remember a particular 'funny', which referred to "The shy musician, who wouldn't say oboe to a Goossens".

MOTHER

I suppose that my mother, was a typical Jewish mother. She fussed and bothered about me all my life. Despite what some would say, that has not been unpleasant. Certainly, it turned out to be very useful when I got married, for I found out that for years she

TIMED TO PERFECTION
Stan Greenberg

had been putting aside some of the money that I had been giving her for my keep. So there was a nice little nest egg to help with the mortgage down payment. An excellent cook and housekeeper, she was the peace-keeper between my father and I, always a volatile pair. Incidentally, she had quite a temper herself, but invariably kept it under control. However, she could bear a grudge forever, and she remembered many real or imagined slights, from over 60 years previously.

In her old age she became quite bitter about her in-laws and other family members, feeling that she was put upon because she was quiet and reserved most of the time. From what I remember, she was probably right in most cases. However, when she was a young girl it seems that she was quite a gad-about, particularly keen on dancing. My father was just the opposite, being much more staid, serious and hard working. Their marriage was an arranged one, quite common in those days. Their characters seemed to complement one another, and, on the whole their life was quite contented, albeit uneventful. Neither made friends easily, and though there was a lot of interaction with family, I can rarely remember other people coming to the house on a social occasion. For a long time I was unaware that she could write, as all letters etc were written by Dad, and for years I never saw anything by Mum. However, she had a lovely writing style, and a much tidier and legible signature than I had, until well into her nineties. Mainly due to her, I can look back on my childhood as a generally happy time.

Since I wrote the above, my mother has died - aged 98. The end came very suddenly, following a session in hospital with an infection. Although she recovered from that, she deteriorated very fast after returning to the home. The cause on the death certificate merely stated "Old Age", and it does seem as though she finally gave up. I suppose that I should be grateful that she didn't suffer from any deadly disease or Alzheimer's. I hope, and believe, that we made the last third of her life as happy and as pleasant as we could, and that she took great pleasure in watching her grandchildren grow up, in her presence as it were. I probably knew my mother better than most children do. I lived with my parents until I got married, at the age of 29, and then mother came to live with my wife and I six years later, after my father died. She was with us for the next 32 years, until a hip operation necessitated that she enter a nursing home in 1998. A year later she broke the other hip in a fall, and survived yet another operation.

While I do not think that I could be called "a mummy's boy", I certainly got to know her every mood and fancy, especially as she got older. This point would be the right place to pay tribute to my wife, Carole, for graciously accepting the fact that mum had to live with us. In all those years any serious friction between them was rare - in fact there was far more between my mother and me. However, one must, in all honesty, state that mum was an invaluable built-in babysitter when the kids were young, and a loving "overseer" as they grew older. I think the close family feeling that both Karen and Keith evince, owe much to what they learnt from their grandmother, and Carole's and my relations with her.

MOTOR VEHICLES
It is amazing to realise that I have been driving for over 50 years, as it seems like only a short time ago I was taking lessons. Aged 33, and never having sat in the driving seat of a vehicle before, I couldn't believe I would ever learn. I did horrendous things to my instructor, at times similar to that very funny record by Bob Newhart about Mrs Webb. Never at ease with anything mechanical, I was always on edge for my lessons. At first this wasn't helped by my car, which I had bought too cheaply. It had a fault, not detected till later, which caused it to stall at will. One terrible afternoon, in a busy high road packed with cars and shoppers, I stalled about ten times consecutively at a traffic light, with a bemused policeman looking on. By the time I got the car moving again the jam stretched for miles.

Another time, while learning hand signals, I descended a steep hill with my left hand on the gear lever and my right hand stuck out of the window. My greatest feat was when I reacted to an urgent request to "brake a bit", followed by a call "not too much", by placing my left leg over my right (on the brake) to reach the accelerator. A strange thing my instructor did was during the first few days out. We were in a quiet road, and I was driving along very hesitantly, when he told me to very carefully take my hands a few inches off the wheel. This I did, and after a little distance he told me to replace them, and we stopped. Then he pointed out that the car had not swerved wildly to either side, and that therefore there was no need to grip the wheel tightly, ,just firmly enough to control it. In other words to relax. I remember the incident impressed me tremendously.

MOVIE MEMORIES

Having spent much of my young life in the cinema, I tend to relate everyday things to scenes or comedy situations from old movies. This can be disconcerting to those around me, but my immediate family understand what I am up to, and even get in on the joke. If any of them hear a knocking sound, someone is almost certain to say "Is you there Zom?", referring to a Bob Hope film, *The Ghost Breakers* (1940), in which Hope and Willie Best, the archetypal gangling black comedian, trap a zombie in a cupboard. When the occupant goes suddenly quiet after much thrashing about, Best fearfully knocks on the cupboard door and asks the question.

I have an intense dislike of formal committee meetings, and while I realise that some semblance of order must be kept, I deplore continual references to constitutions and the rules. So often groups want to take actions with which everyone agrees, but they are stopped from so doing by some barrack-room lawyer who says it is against this rule or that constitutional point. So progress is stopped. At one meeting where this happened, with someone on his feet intoning from a constitution, I stood up, agenda in hand, and slowly tore off the top inch or so with the remark, "The party of the first part". Some people there got the point and dissolved in laughter. They realised that I was imitating the famous Marx Brothers sketch between Groucho and Chico about the fatuous wording of legal documents.

There have been a number of films featuring athletics action, some quite entertaining while others have been rubbish. Perhaps the best, in my opinion anyway, was *Chariots of Fire (1981)*. However, there are a couple of others which have stuck in my memory. Buster Keaton made a silent comedy *College (1927)* - before my time but I saw it later - in which he practised various events to find one he was good at. Needless to say, there wasn't one. There is a hair-raising episode with him twirling a hammer over his head, unable to release it, which he has described as one of the most dangerous stunts he ever tried. The visually funniest effort was when he tried a sprint. The camera comes in close, and he seems to be moving very fast - then a couple of small children easily pass him while skipping on the grass.

In 1970 the British director Michael Winner made *The Games* , with an excellent cast, including Michael Crawford and Ryan O'Neal. Unfortunately, it was not very good, but despite having read the critics' generally bad reviews, my wife and I went to see it, along with some other friends who were also athletics fans. I am afraid that, at least athletically speaking, it was awful, and led to numerous hilarious remarks among ourselves, which was obviously disturbing other patrons. The capper came in the scene in which Ryan O'Neal is competing at the US Olympic Trials. He wins an event in which he and a few other competitors come around the final bend of the track IN LANES, and throws himself over the finishing line to win the event. His coach then says "That decides it - you run the marathon". Now I presume that the event was supposed to be the 6 miles (or *10,000m*), which would make some sense, but the longest event that involves athletes finishing in lanes is the 440y (or *400m*), which would make the comment of the coach ludicrous. The raucous laughter which greeted this scene resulted in the manager of the theatre appearing at the end of our row, with threats to evict us if we didn't quieten down. Some time later, I questioned Ron Pickering about this scene, as he had worked as one of the advisors on the film. He said that he had, of course, pointed out to the director just how silly the scene would appear - apparently Michael Winner answered that it presented a much better cinematic shot with the athletes in lanes than in single file, so he would keep it in. So much for realism.

MUSIC

Music is very important to me, and without it my life would have been very empty. I have always whistled and hummed - although I know it is considered bad manners by those who make those type of rules. To my lifelong regret I never learnt to play an instrument. But from the day a relative gave me an old wind-up record player, which I kept beside my bed, music, good music, has been a constant companion. By 'good' I don't necessarily mean classical, but music which is tuneful, melodious and/or moving. There is some music which I find very restful, such as Bach's *Air on the G String* (Yes, I know that is not its proper title, but everyone knows it as that), whilst other pieces excite me tremendously. In this category I would put the final bit of Tchaikowsky's *Fifth Symphony*, *The Great Gate of Kiev* from Moussorgsky's *Pictures at an Exhibition*, and *The Entry of the Nobles* from Act II of Rimsky-Korsakov's *Mlada*. A particular favourite is *Symphony No 2 in B Minor* by Borodin, which, I think, incorporates the most wonderful series of melodies ever put into one composition. However, I also find the music of Jerome Kern, Irving Berlin, Cole Porter, and, particularly, George Gershwin very enjoyable. The latter's early death was a great loss, and I rate a performance of *Porgy and Bess* at the old Stoll Theatre, Kingsway, in 1952, as one of my greatest experiences in a theatre or concert hall.

Another unforgettable musical occasion came in 1958 in Stockholm. Perhaps it was so memorable because it combined two of my passions. The Swedish capital was hosting the European Athletics Championships. During the opening ceremony the famous Swedish tenor Jussi Bjorling sang *Morgon* by Einar Eklof. With a magnificent voice he captivated the crowd. However, my own taste

TIMED TO PERFECTION
Stan Greenberg

in male singers generally tends more towards baritones and basses. Two of my favourites were Tito Gobbi and Boris Christoff, although on records I love to listen to Chaliapin. That may be because my father told me that as a child he had stood in the snow outside a Russian concert hall just so he could hear the great bass through an open window.

Without question, the piece of music that I have listened to most often is *Trumpet Blues and Cantabile* played by Harry James. I first heard it in a film, and when I discovered that a friend had a record of it, I borrowed it so often that my friend complained that he had to 'borrow' it from me. I am afraid that I ruined the record due to overplaying, the hard metal needles of the time gradually wearing their way through the old-fashioned 78 record. On the rare occasion that I hear it today my feet still tap away. Another record that similarly I ruined by overplaying was *Clair de Lune* by Debussy - for years I rarely went to sleep without playing it.

In 1947 I saw an inconsequential film, *Fiesta*, which introduced me to two of my favourite pieces of music. One was *El Salon Mexico* by Aaron Copland - and it led me to the rest of his excellent work. The second piece was a little Mexican folk tune *La Bamba de Vera Cruz* , which years later became a major pop hit - but as I told my pop-mad daughter, Karen, I found it first. While on the subject of pop music, there was another rave where I was in at the start - skiffle. I was at Lever Brothers at the time, and one of my colleagues in the shipping department was a keen musician. Although he had passed examinations to become a customs officer, he was also forming his own group. He used to practice in the office after work, and so I learnt the lyrics and tunes of most of the forthcoming hits of this style of music. He was Chas McDevitt, and soon after leaving the company he had become one of the leaders in the field, with his recording of *Freight Train* in the charts for some four months in 1957.

As a frustrated conductor I would perform in front of a mirror, and also when in bed. Soon after Carole and I returned from our

TIMED TO PERFECTION
Stan Greenberg

honeymoon we were listening to music in bed. I got carried away, and forgetting that I was no longer alone, spread my arms wide to 'bring in the orchestra'. One arm hit Carole across the throat, happily not doing any serious damage, but making her choke. The piece was the *Overture to Russlan and Ludmila* by Glinka, and it is now known as 'Carole-bashing' music. When I was young, and single, I spent a lot of time going to concerts, particularly at the Royal Albert Hall in London. I usually sat in 'the gods', way at the top of the seating, in a sort of gallery. At that time the acoustics had not been updated and when the piece played was loud and vigorous, people in the gallery would hear it about three times, such was the echo up there.

One real disaster that befell me in my quest for musical highspots, occurred in Rome at the time of the World Athletics Championships in 1987. The attending media were offered tickets to a performance of *Aida* at the Baths of Caracalla, and Ron Pickering and myself eagerly accepted. Not having any special clothes, other than sports jackets, to wear, we were somewhat overawed by the extremely smart, and beautifully dressed, men and women around us as we took our seats, and very good seats they were too. Then, ,just as the opera began, the heavens opened and one of the heaviest downpours I have ever witnessed fell on the unprotected people. Everyone scattered to find shelter, but there was little, and by the time most people got under cover their clothes and coiffures were ruined. The opera was abandoned for the night, and we did not have the time available to go again. It would have been a memorable experience - indeed, for the wrong reasons, it was.

I am afraid that much modern classical-style music leaves me cold, and my feelings were very well summed up in a poetic note that my wife, Carole, wrote to the BBC progamme *Points of View*, about ten years ago. It went as follows:

I settled down to watch the Proms, as I have done for years
When they played some modern music, it had me close to tears

TIMED TO PERFECTION
Stan Greenberg

If that is today's composition, I do not want to know
The sound it was quite awful, I would rather watch grass grow

How can you compare it, with what followed after that
It sounded just like somebody was strangling the cat

It had nothing to commend it, that I could tell at all
And not what I expect to hear, in our Royal Albert Hall

So please let's stick to standards, which have some melody
And keep the last night of the Proms, the way it used to be.

Carole and I were lucky enough to attend a Proms last night once. Although I was somewhat appalled at the outrageous nationalism of the occasion, I must say that it was a most entertaining, and indeed thrilling, evening of excellent music, wonderfuly played, good humour, and a remarkable display of nationalistic fervour.

On the subject of classical music, I find myself questioning exactly what it is. Dictionary definitions vary from music composed prior to the 20th century, to 'serious' music. I find it interesting that the classical music station (Classic FM) on British radio, which has a massive following, often plays music by George Gershwin, including his *Piano Concerto*, his opera *Porgy and Bess* and *Cuban Overture*, composed in the 1920s/1930s. I remember that when I was at school, the music master going nearly berserk when, in answer to his question about our favourite classical piece, one boy answered W*arsaw Concerto.* Now that was a piece composed by Richard Addinsell for the film *Dangerous Moonlight* in 1940, and was, to a musical snob like my teacher, totally beyond the pale. However, it was tremendously popular, and undoubtedly led many people to listen to more 'serious' music than they otherwise would have. Interestingly, I was stimulated to write this paragraph by hearing it played on that popular radio station because many people had voted for Addinsell's piece in it's annual classical Hall of Fame compilation. As his and Gershwin's music is now from 70-90 years old, and still popular, there is every reason to suppose that both their compositions will reach their centuries. Surely then they will be taken seriously, as 'serious' music if not as classics.

NAÏVETÉ

Most of my life I am afraid that I have been somewhat of a dreamer, and very naïve in so many ways. When I was younger, I always thought that people would judge you by what you are and not by who you are. I always expected that people would treat you by how you behaved, or how well-educated and well-mannered you were, but it has nearly always been down to one's colour, religion, size, age, or monetary standing. In other areas, I always expected: the post would be delivered on time (nowadays if it is delivered at all); plumbers and electricians would arrive at the time agreed; shops would stock things one wanted; trains would run to their timetables; footballers and other sportsmen would not cheat; banks would give a fair interest on your money; that schoolteachers who could read, write and spell properly would teach our children; investments would always increase in value; my damned computer would give me years of trouble-free use; I would only get older in years but not physically. There are many more things that I expected, and have been disappointed in, but, as I noted in the beginning, I was so naïve when I was younger – in other words when I was about 50 years old! But, I'm okay now, aren't I?

NAMES

Some people are so famous that their first names are rarely used, eg Churchill, Einstein, Picasso, Tchaikowsky. The first time I was addressed only by my surname was at school, and then usually when I was in trouble. Names have held a fascination for me, mainly because of the humour that seems to be inherent in some names. Little things please little minds I suppose. That may be why I get a kick learning that a friend of ours, on marriage, changed her name from Ros Silver to Ros Gold. I think of her husband Len as the world's greatest alchemist.

TIMED TO PERFECTION
Stan Greenberg

I have had various problems with my own name, and not just because it sounds Jewish or foreign. My first initial is 'S', and is my only initial as I have no middle name. It seems that when my name is taken over the telephone, often the writer passes over the message with the initial written too close to the title. The result is that I receive an inordinate amount of mail addressed to Mrs Greenberg, instead of to Mr S Greenberg. Even more unfortunate things happen when I give my first name in the form that I prefer
- that is Stan. Prior to the 1988 Olympic Games, I regularly received publications from the Korean Organising Committee, addressed to Satan Greenberg. This was of particular delight to my son. Quite regularly I pick up the telephone to be asked "Is that Mr Goldberg?", to which I usually reply, "No, its Greenberg, but I presume you're colour-blind". Not a nice thing I know, but it pleases me, and also puts me in a 'One-up' situation (à la Stephen Potter, of which I write about elsewhere).

I consider that there is, or should be, an aptness about first and last names. Thus, I am amused when a Smith or Jones, or Levy for that matter, has a rather pretentious first name. In this category I would place Wilberforce, St John and Peregrine. Now they go quite well with a D'Arcy-Fortescue or Cholmondeley-Smyth, but surely not with a Jones or a Smith, and certainly not with a Levy. Similarly, Fred doesn't really go with the aforementioned posh last names, does it. As I say, there is a certain aptness - which all too often parents forget. My father enjoyed telling a story of when he was at Cliftonville before the War - a resort then very popular with our faith. One afternoon he heard an elderly Jewish lady call to her little grandson "Montgomery, Montgomery, come to Booba". My father said he had rarely seen anybody less like a Montgomery in his life.

I have written before about difficult names in athletics, but there are others which have since come to mind. In the 1991 World Championships there was a distance runner from Mongolia with the mind-boggling name of Tschuuluunbaatar Ariunsaikhan. Happily for the commentators, he didn't run very well. Perhaps an even more terrifying source of difficult to pronounce names is Madagascar - virtually all athletes from there cause apprehension as their team includes such as 400m runner Randriamahazomanana, and a decathlete, Razafindrakovahoaka. I never did find out their first names. The Madagascan women's 4 x 100m relay team at the 1999 World championships was composed of the following: Lantoniana Ramalalanirina, Ony Paule Ratsimbazafy, Rosa Rakotozafy, and Hanitriniaina Rakotondrabe. No wonder the phrase "the little Madagascan" is heard so often. The Spanish-speaking world's habit of adding the matriarchal name causes serious problems, especially so in the computer age, with the tendency to merely show the first initial and last name of a competitor in starting lists and results. Thus the world record holder in the high jump, known throughout the world as Javier Sotomayor, was listed in one major championship as J Sanabria, and much confusion ensued - at least until he started jumping.

On a personal note, it has been suggested to me that I should change my surname, so that I should not be automatically taken as Jewish. The fact is, of course, that no amount of name changing would alter the fact that I look Jewish, so what would be the point. A few months ago I found out that I had a hypocoristic, but not any diacriticals, in my name. As I already lack a middle name, I felt so much better, and can face the world anew. To those few (?) who don't know the meanings of the words, I should note that an hypocoristic is a shortened form of the given name i.e. in my case Stan. Diacriticals are marks or accents in a name - eg any Czechoslovakian name is full of them.

NATURE
I have had a few brushes with the forces of nature. One of the funniest, though I don't remember laughing at the time, was in Tenerife, when walking up the last few hundred feet of Pico de Teide (3718m *12,195ft*), the highest point on Spanish territory. Teide (or Teyde) is a dormant volcano, and near the top there are places where smoke and steam issue from small vents. The last

TIMED TO PERFECTION
Stan Greenberg

eruption was in living memory, and the ground can be very warm. Being on holiday, I was wearing rope soled sandals, which, apparently, were held together by glue. As I neared the top I suddenly found that the glue had melted and I had left the soles behind and was walking on bare feet. I then had to descend quite a way to the cable car station like that, on rough stones and fairly hot earth, serenaded by the hysterical laughter of my loving family.

Another experience with natural forces, very frightening at the time, came on my first trip to Hawaii in 1974. Many of my older readers will probably remember watching 'escapist' movies in the 1930/40s , set in the South Sea Islands, when the highspot of the film was when the 'Volcano God' got angry and all hell would be let loose. Well that first time in Honolulu I thought that something similar was happening to me. It was mid-morning on a beautiful, clear, sunny day and I went to the harbour to take a trip on a glass-bottomed boat - to see the fish and coral. While I was waiting on the quayside I noticed that the sky was becoming progressively gloomy as dark clouds began to appear over the nearby hills. Within about fifteen minutes the sky had turned black, not just cloudy but black, and I was quite nervous - I had never seen anything like it before. My thoughts went to those movies, and I wondered what on earth was going to happen. Then thunder crashed and lightning flashed wildly, and torrents of rain lashed down - boy, the 'Volcano God' was really annoyed about something. Then, almost as quickly, the sky began to clear and within about another fifteen minutes everything was back to normal again, with clear, blue, sunny skies. I contemplated that perhaps they had sacrificed the required virgin, but on second thoughts dismissed the idea - in the 1970s it was so difficult to find one, wasn't it. Whatever, the whole episode was a very frightening experience, which I don't wish to have again. Incidentally, I have a photograph which I took at the height of the storm, which shows the British flag flying against the blackness. I had not realised before that in the corner of the Hawaiian flag is a small Union Jack, commemorating early British discoverers - Captain Cook was the first European in 1798.

NAVY

Just before World War II my father took me to one of the Navy Days that were held then. We joined a party which was taken on a tour of the battlecruiser HMS Hood, then the most powerful ship in the Royal Navy. I was overawed by the size of the guns, and I seem to recall being sat on one of them by a naval rating. In May 1941, when the terrible news came of the tragic sinking of the Hood, by the battleship Bismarck, I took the loss very personally.

NERVE WRACKING

Not long ago, while waiting in a hospital waiting room for a not too pleasant examination, I found myself contemplating other nerve-wracking occasions. There was, of course, the morning of my wedding day - I was so tense throughout, that, except for a few minor incidents, I cannot remember a thing about the whole day. Another time was awaiting the birth of our first child - by the time of the second I was almost blasé. Other occasions which come to mind include: waiting for the whistle to start the school inter-house soccer match; any time I was in my starting holes - it was too long ago to have used blocks - about to race; walking up the school steps to read the Matric results pinned to the door; checking lottery numbers when you've got the first three right - the others were all wrong; sitting in the waiting room before an interview for a new job; anytime I am at an airport waiting for my luggage to appear on the baggage carousel; driving a new car for the first time and realising that I haven't read the manual properly. Then there is the occasion when up in an aeroplane and the pilot announces, " We are returning to the airport. There is nothing wrong, but .....". Similar attacks on one's nerves occur when you are inside a lift which stops between floors, and, the bane of my recent working life, hitting the wrong key on the computer and something totally unexpected happens.

NEWSPAPERS

For as long as I can remember I have always read newspapers – not just glanced at them, but read them carefully. Nowadays, at

TIMED TO PERFECTION
Stan Greenberg

home, we read two daily ones and another on Sunday. However, there was a time when I read all national daily newspapers plus most of the Sunday ones. This was because it was part of my job, in the Economics and Statistics dept of Unilever, at the time. Every morning I would carefully read practically every word of each 'paper, including the adverts, looking for anything that might be of interest to the Company. Some of my colleagues would be perusing magazines for exactly the same reason. Then, late in the morning, we would produce a newssheet with brief reports of items we had noted, which was circulated to our economists, senior managers and directors. Anything which was thought of importance would be followed up with photocopies of the articles, reports or the adverts themselves. Often, an advert for a job, allied, say, to a report of increased activity in a certain chemical market, would give an indication of a business competitor's expansion in a particular field. Whatever, the exercise was considered very important to the Company, and, for a person with my 'research' interests, quite fascinating.

Round about that time I remember that one Saturday morning I was accosted in the street by a market research lady with a clipboard. In a good mood, I agreed to answer her questions and thereby hangs a tale. One of her first questions was "What newspapers do you see?", I answered that I saw all of them. Doubting that, she then began to list them all out, to which I answered in the affirmative to each one – she gave me a very odd look, although I explained what my job was. Then she asked "What newspapers do you actually read?" Again I said all of them, which caused her distress once more. Her next query of "Which sections of the 'papers do you concentrate on?" She was no happier when I replied that I looked very carefully at the whole of the newspapers listed. When she asked "Which adverts have you particularly noticed?" the interview came to a quick end when I said that I carefully took note of all adverts, written and photographic. I promised her that I was not trying to be difficult, but that it was the nature of my job, but I don't think she believed me, and as I walked away I noticed that she tore up the top sheet from her clipboard.

NIGHTCLUBS

On visits to Paris, with my wife may I add, I have attended performances at the Folies Bergères, Moulin Rouge and the Lido. The shows were always spectacular, colourful and entertaining, and I would recommend them to any tourist, although they do tend to be somewhat expensive. On one visit to the Lido, with another couple, we had waited quite a long time to get in, and the other chap's wife was not in a very good mood - also being something of a feminist she was not fully in favour of the whole idea anyway. To make things worse we were given a table behind some shrubbery and fronds which almost totally obscured our view of the stage. I was just about to complain, when the offending greenery suddenly disappeared, descending into the balustrade on which it stood, giving us a most excellent view. The show, albeit slightly erotic, was excellent and we all agreed it had been well worth it.

In 1973 I was in Minsk with the BBC to cover the USA v USSR athletics match. Standing beside the track before the meeting my attention was caught by the Soviet lady 400m runners, Kulichkova and Kolesnikova, warming up. They were both beautiful platinum blondes, with long shapely legs, and I must admit that I pretended to be taking a 'professional' interest in their running, when that activity was probably furthest from my mind. I suddenly noticed a Soviet coach nearby watching me, and to cover my embarrassment I made some remark about what good form they were in. In very good English he replied, "Yes, but they should be in Folies Bergères, not here". How true, how very true.

NOBEL PRIZES

I have known two people in my life who have won Nobel Laureates – and in both cases was nearly instrumental in causing them hurt. Professor Sir Bernard Katz was a distant relative, and I was delighted when he was awarded the Nobel Prize for Medicine in 1970. Some years later I narrowly missed knocking him down, when he ran in front of my car not far from his office at the University of London building. I always found him to be a most pleasant and self-effacing man on the family occasions that we met.

When I was at school I called a classmate "a bighead", and was called out for a fight. I suppose that there was very little chance of him getting hurt, as he was a very fit, very well-built young man, and I was then small, skinny and weak. I always consider the remark was a major tactical mistake on my part, but not a factual one. It is a shame that he had not yet developed his infamous conscientious objector attitude of later years. In the event he gave me a right pasting. However, he did become quite famous, albeit still, in my eyes, bigheaded and opinionated, and he, Harold Pinter the playwright, was awarded the 2005 Nobel Prize for Literature. Whatever my past feelings, I do not begrudge him the honour, as, although I do not like nor really understand his plays, obviously he was a major talent.

NO PROBLEM

Mondai Arimasen, Selvä juttu, Nada Problema, Kein Prolem, Pas de Problème, Non Problema. A terrifying phrase, used throughout the world, it is intended to put people at their ease. However, in my experience, quite considerable in 40 years of travel, it is actually the harbinger of doom, gloom and disappointment. The worst perpetrators are hotel clerks, waiters, taxi drivers, athletics officials ,and foreign TV people. The number of times I have had a request answered in such a way is incalculable, and in almost every case nothing, or the wrong thing, was forthcoming. On travels now, if I need something or other, instead of asking anyone for assistance, I do without it - it is much simpler, causes no disappointment, and I sleep better.

NOSTALGIA

I read the following in a novel recently - "I feel nostalgia for every era that preceded my birth" – and realised that it expressed my own feelings to a remarkable degree. I do find that the past interests me much more than the present. Whereas I hardly take notice of the current political situation, especially in Britain, I am fascinated by what happened in politics, say, a hundred, two hundred, three hundred years, ago. In sport, I am definitely more able to quote the Olympic champions of the 1920s and 1930s, than I am about those of the 1980s and 1990s – even though I was actually there in those latter days. Certainly I find the music of bygone ages far superior in every way to current compositions, and the fact that telephones didn't exist until the end of the 19th century gives anything before a big plus in my estimation.

NUT BY NAME AND ....

There are some who think I am somewhat odd. One thing is absolutely certain - I am a NUT. By that I mean I am an enthusiast, a devotee, a fervent fan, of the sport of athletics. In that capacity I am a founder member of the NUTS - the National Union of Track Statisticians. I should state that this union has nothing to do with worker's rights. The word, union, is here used under its other dictionary definitions of 'agreement' and 'harmony', although in practice such states of grace have rarely existed within this group, which is composed of some of the most opinionated, pig-headed, argumentative and downright ornery people that you could meet. Nevertheless, they are a great bunch, who, over the years, have done a tremendous amount of work for British, and indeed, world athletics, often at no small cost to themselves and their families. Although some of them, including myself, have ended up making a living from our involvement, I think that, mainly, it has also been to the benefit of the sport.

The organization was founded by a band of athletics fans to promote the spread of information and statistics about the sport in Britain. Although the official founding date is given as January 1958, the seeds of the group were first sown in August 1952 on the way back from the Olympic Games in Helsinki, Finland. On the boat from Turku to Stockholm, myself, Alf Wilkins and Len Gebbett, agreed to attend future meetings together and swap data. Thus, I claim that the NUTS is the only British society to be born in the middle of the Baltic. The term 'nut' is a transatlantic one, and refers to someone who has a passion for a particular pastime. The group produces ranking lists and booklets about athletics in Britain. The common bond is a love of the sport, and an obsession with its statistics. To this end we all read various magazines, newspapers and books, from all over the world - and annoy our spouses by leaving them all over the place. One of the sport's keenest fans and supporters was Sir Eddie Kulukundis, the impresario, who sponsored many British athletes over the years. His wife is the actress Susan Hampshire, a delightful lady. The first time we met, at a sports dinner, she, Carole and Mel Watman's wife, Pat, got on very well, and discussed their problems being married to an 'enthusiast'. At one point Susan exasperatedly commented that "He leaves piles of magazines and books all over the place - even in the dining room". To her surprise, Carole and Pat, in unison, said, "So what's new?"

OBSESSIVE COMPULSIVE DISORDER

There is a very clever, and funny, programme on TV called *Monk,* about a detective who suffers from OCD, and, although driving his colleagues and acquaintances crazy, it enables him to solve otherwise unsolvable cases. I must say that his character does disturb me somewhat in that I do sometimes exhibit some of the more minor aspects of his persona. However, I prefer to call what I have as an excess of tidiness. I am a great believer in the phrase coined by the English essayist, Samuel Smiles in 1875, " a place for everything, and everything in it's place". With my hobbies of athletics statistics and history, and the incredible number of books and pamphlets that it generates, I would be overwhelmed in my study without some idea of where everything is. This overlaps into the house in general, and I tend to tidy up after my family. My son, Keith, seems to derive a lot of pleasure by deliberately leaving very small bits of paper on the lounge carpet, and guessing how quickly I will notice and pick them up. However, as I tell him, it's better to be somewhat 'obsessed' with tidiness and cleanliness, than be a slob.

OCCUPATION

The other day I realised that I had been working for some 68 years, officially starting in 1947. Based on having some earnings, albeit quite small, on which I have to pay tax, I consider that I am still working at the present time. I have been extremely lucky in that for the latter part of my life, about 34 years or so, I have been working solely at my hobby. I was at Lever Brothers (later Unilever Ltd) for twenty-one years, the GLC for nine, the *Guinness Book of Records* for five, and the rest as a freelance statistician and writer. Within those years I was with the BBC TV athletics commentary team for twenty-six of them, the same length of time I was with the British athletics selection committee. However, the longest 'job' I have had seems to be that of supplying *Whitaker's Almanack* with annual athletics results and records – which I did for thirty years.

Then again there is one occupation that I have had, and happily still have, at which I have worked hard, and successfully I believe, for over 55 years, and that is my marriage.

OLYMPIC GAMES

As the reader may have gathered, the Olympic Games hold a great fascination for me. Ever since I attended those in London in 1948 (unfortunately, only for one day) they have taken up quite a large proportion of my life. I was lucky to be able to go to the 1952 Games in Helsinki, and had a wonderful experience, but due to finance, work and marriage, did not attend another one until 1972 (Munich), when working for the BBC. However, I had worked on the 1964 (Tokyo) and 1968 (Mexico City) Games in the London studios of ITV and BBC respectively, so It was only the 1956 (Melbourne) edition, which had no television coverage, and the 1960 (Rome) celebration, during which I got married, that I missed out on. From 1972, at which there was the horror of the Israeli murders, until I retired in 1994, I was at six more Games. Happily, in 2012, I was able to get a press accreditation, and attended the athletics every day.

TIMED TO PERFECTION
Stan Greenberg

Until I was 21 years old, I had not been outside England, i.e. not Wales or even the Isle of Wight. However, that summer I attended the 1952 Olympic Games in Helsinki. In those days, flying was rare and expensive, and my journey consisted of a boat trip from Tilbury to Gothenburg, across Sweden by train, and boat from Stockholm across the Baltic to Turku in Finland. An unexpected delay at Gothenburg meant the final part of the journey was a 160km *100 miles* dash by a Finnish coach to reach the Olympic stadium in time for the Opening Ceremony. The trip across the North Sea was my first time on a 'big' ship. Practically everybody else aboard was ill, due to the slow rolling of the ship on a calm sea, but I was so excited that it never affected me. On the contrary, I had a tremendous appetite, and, after the rigours of rationing, the food aboard this Swedish ship was like a dream. At each mealtime, during the day and a half on board, the dining room got steadily emptier and emptier. At the end there were only a group of young Swedes and myself left. It took two days to get to Helsinki then, and the cost, including board and tickets for the stadium, came to £65.12.6d (£65.62½p). The last time I went there, in 2005, that was almost the cost of a single meal, albeit a very good one, and the flight took 3 hours. However, in 1952 that sum was a lot, and I was only able to afford it due to an aunt's generous 21st birthday present. Later I discovered my mother had asked her sister to make her present monetary, and early.

In Helsinki we shared double bunks in a school hall, and I discovered that the chap above me had won the AAA Junior mile walk title in 1950. I was surprised because he wore a back brace, a cumbersome metal thing which I helped him with. He mentioned he intended emigrating to New Zealand, but I only remembered four years later when he, Norman Read, won the Olympic 50km walk for his adopted country. I remember him for something else too. The Opening Ceremony was in pouring rain, and as we had arrived with only minutes to go, we rushed for our open seats, dressed mainly for summer, our rainware with our luggage. A dark young girl offered to share her pac-a-mac with me, but most were not that fortunate. Norman, surrounded by umbrellas and raincoats, suddenly took off his shirt, and sat on it, leaving him topless in the rain. He was the centre of attention for camera buffs, in particular the Japanese, who scrambled to get photographs of the crazy Britisher. Actually he was far from crazy, as afterwards he would have a dry shirt to put on - but he was a sensation for a time. I wonder if any of those fans ever realised they have an unusual photo of a future Olympic champion.

Aside from famous sportsmen and women, I have met one or two celebrities while at the Games. One afternoon, at those Helsinki Games, I noticed a very attractive, dark haired woman coming up the stadium stairs. To my delight, she sat in the seat next to mine. Then I realised she had a male companion, someone I thought I recognised. It was obvious that neither of them really understood what they were watching, so I gave a few helpful details about the proceedings. We became quite friendly, and they introduced themselves as Mr and Mrs Viktor Barna. Before the war he had won 15 World and 20 English table tennis titles, and was on a Scandinavian tour with his stage act - which later I saw at the Palladium. It was an exhibition with another great player, Richard Bergman, culminating in a rally during which they backed into the wings of the enormous Palladium stage, until both were out of sight, with the ball continuing to bounce on and off the table in either direction. It was an astonishing thing to behold if you had ever played the game.

At Montreal, in 1976, the BBC commentary team was visited by Joe Jagger, his son and daughter-in-law. Joe was an old physical education lecturer buddy of Ron Pickering, and he had brought pop star Mick, and Bianca, with him. They created quite a stir, especially the exotic looking Bianca, who came and talked with me about the events on the track. She was wearing diaphanous harem pants, which left little to the imagination, and I felt that every eye in the stadium was on us. I made what small talk I could, including information about the few Costa Rican athletes who were competing. Despite the furore she must have known she was causing, I found her to be very pleasant.

TIMED TO PERFECTION
Stan Greenberg

ON TIME
The song pleads *Get me to the Church on time*. I have never had that venue in mind, but I am sure even if I had, it would prove no problem. I was brought up such that I am always, sometimes annoyingly, punctual for appointments, visits, trains or planes. Usually I arrive early. I much prefer that, knowing many people who favour arriving a minute or so before a plane's departure, which often ends up as a minute or so after. I don't understand this attitude. It stems, I believe, from a paranoiac fear of wasting time, at stations and airports, but I do a lot of work waiting for trains and planes. Surely that is better than arriving in a lather, frustrated and angry at the traffic, and probably finding that you have forgotten something. There is an old proverb which goes "The fool wanders, the wise man travels". I don't know what light that throws on the topic, but it seems apropos.

To this day my wife and I are among the first to arrive at a party or other function. One of the things about my wife that appealed to me when we first met, was that she never kept me waiting. If we agreed six o'clock, then that is exactly what it was. I would heartily recommend her conduct to others of her gender. I get a certain glow of satisfaction at functions when certain goodies run out before the latecomers arrive. So much for virtue being its own reward.

ONE OF US
As a member of a persecuted minority – now there's a way to grab a reader's attention – it has always fascinated me the way my co-religionists show intense interest when a fellow Jew makes good. This is no more so than in sport. Therefore, there used to be great curiosity about the 'affiliation' of certain athletes from the Soviet Union. In particular, there was one woman, who held the world discus record from 1971-1976, Faina Melnik, who we were sure was 'one of us', but it seemed impossible to confirm. Whenever Soviet athletes of the time went abroad they were very closely guarded and watched, especially if they had interviews with the

TIMED TO PERFECTION
Stan Greenberg

foreign press. An Israeli acquaintance of mine was determined that he would find out once and for all, and as he knew he would not get an answer to a straight question while her minders were about, he hatched a clever plan, to be put in operation at the Munich Olympic Games in 1972, where she won the gold medal. At the post medal-ceremony press conference he and his colleagues asked her some fairly innocuous personal questions, about her age and place of birth, but then, suddenly, asked for the names of her mother and father. She hesitated a moment, and then replied, "Sarah and Shmuel". Very pointedly my friend said "Thank you", and she answered "You're welcome", with a big smile. We had the answer we wanted, as the names of her parents were extremely 'Jewish' ones.

On another occasion, another member of the Soviet team, about whom we also had our suspicions, approached another Israeli journalist, and asked him if he could have the badge which the journalist had in his lapel. It was a miniature Israeli flag. "I want it especially for my father" the athlete said. Another one noted.

OOPS
Generally I think I have made the right choices in my life - at least they've been right for me at the time. However, in one important area, athletics, I have made two very bad decisions. The first was on Bank Holiday Monday, August 1945 when I was playing in the street. A friend asked if I would like to go with him and his father to the White City that afternoon. I replied that I wasn't interested in dog racing, but he said that it was an athletics meeting. I hadn't become obsessed with the sport yet, and although I enjoyed running myself, I had never been to watch it. As I was playing marbles, and beating everyone, I declined. Years later I realised that the meeting had been my only chance to see the legendary Swedes Gundar Haegg and Arne Andersson, as well as Britain's great Sydney Wooderson.

The second occasion was on 5 May 1954, when, looking at a wet and wild night sky I decided not to go to Oxford the next day for the AAA v Oxford University match. I even had the coach ticket in my pocket, but, having had trouble at work getting time off, I decided it wouldn't be worth the aggravation. The following evening came the news that Roger Bannister had become the first man to run a sub-4 minute mile. At work, my boss tiptoed around me for days afterwards. As a postscript to this story, I was fortunate to be at the 40th anniversary dinner of that great Oxford occasion. Thanks to the kindness of Sir Eddie Kulukundis, Carole and I were invited to participate in a wonderful evening of nostalgia. Every living world mile record holder from Sydney Wooderson (1937) to the present was there, with the exception of Gunder Haegg (too ill) and Steve Ovett. In addition to Wooderson, there was Arne Andersson, Roger Bannister, John Landy, Derek Ibbotson, Herb Elliott, Peter Snell, Michel Jazy, Jim Ryun, Filbert Bayi, John Walker, Sebastian Coe, Steve Cram and Noureddine Morceli. It almost made up for missing the original ..... almost.

OPERA

I am not particularly a devotee of the human singing voice, and that may be the reason that, generally speaking, I don't like classical opera. I know that one of the main reasons for my antipathy can be laid at the door of a performance of Puccini's *Turandot* that I attended many years ago. The basic plot of this opera is about a princess who is so beautiful and desirable that suitors take the chance of not being able to answer three riddles and thus be put to death. All very well, and one must take all forms of art with some modicum of leeway. However, when the role is played by a very, very large Bulgarian soprano, it is difficult to believe that the gentlemen concerned would take the risk, any risk, even if she is the Emperor's daughter and exceedingly rich. Perhaps compounding the problem was my next visit to an opera. This time it was to see Cav & Pag, or rather the twinning of Mascagni's *Cavalleria Rusticana* and Leoncavallo's *Pagliacci*, two of the most miserable stories in a generally miserable genre. It was very noticeable to me that the famous, and lovely, *Intermezzo* from the former, was not even actually a part of the opera itself, but was played in between scenes. So it is that I most certainly enjoy the orchestral versions of various operas, but, with a few notable exceptions, can do without the vocal ones.

OPINIONS

Some time ago, a friend's wife commented that I seem to have an opinion about everything. I don't think she was being unduly unkind, but it did bring home to me the fact - THAT I DO. Well, not about everything, but certainly about a lot of things. The problem is that I have a very wide range of interest, and also a habit, others might call it a fault, to get very involved in things that stimulate my curiosity. When an idea, or subject, or person, catches my attention, I invariably want to know much more, and read as much as I can get hold of. Then I tend to form an opinion, hopefully my own opinion and not necessarily that of the writers of the books or articles I have read. Thus, if the subject or person comes up in conversation, I have a ready made opinion all ready and waiting to be aired - at least it is one that has been thought out, and not just manufactured on the spot, nor reflects the ideas of some political or religious demagogue. The fact that it is not always the most generally popular sentiment seems to unsettle people, and also the fact that I tend to get quite ardent in my attack on, or in defence of, a given attitude, probably offends those of a more reserved demeanour. They can take some solace from the fact that I know I am doing it - but I am afraid that in certain cases I can't control it.

ORWELL

This is not really about the book by George Orwell, but it owes a passing bow to his famous nightmarish novel *1984,* which appeared in 1949. In the middle of the 1960s, while I was with the Economics Department of Unilever, I helped read the proofs of a highly secret report, which looked forward to the consumer markets of 1984 – a date almost certainly taken because of Orwell's work. I remember that my assistant and I were told, only partly jokingly, to check the spelling and grammar but not to read the contents, as it was as confidential a document as had ever been produced in the company, and even many of the top brass were not allowed to see it.

It had been compiled over a long period by experts in all sorts of fields relating to future sales of convenience meals, soaps and washing products. It predicted, correctly, that in the future many more women would continue working after marriage and children, and that easily prepared meals would be extremely useful for such women and their families when they got home. At that time convenience foods were in their infancy, and it was considered, rightly it proved, to be the biggest potential market of them all. I recall particularly, although of course, according to orders, I didn't really read it, that the psychologists in the reporting group were insistent that it was always going to be highly necessary to leave at least a small amount of preparation for the wife in such products, as otherwise she would lose her self-esteem if she didn't have anything to do at all. Thus, it was suggested, that it was most important that she could add some milk, or salt, or herbs, or suchlike, to those meals, so that she could feel, and her family perceive, that she had, even if in a small way, prepared them. Perhaps the experts should have listened less to the psychologists, and talked more to some ordinary women, and see what they thought. That report had far-reaching consequences to the food and household goods industries in both Britain and America.

OTHER SPORTS (PLAYING)
Just before I left school, exams over and waiting for the end of term, a master introduced me to badminton. I loved it, and, at Lever Brothers, became fairly proficient. In fact I reached the final of the London Business Houses championships, quite a good standard. At the peak of my prowess I attended the All-England Championships, as a spectator, and left with 'my tail between my legs'. I couldn't believe what I had seen. Shots that I could make with only the greatest effort, and luck, were commonplace and

made to look easy, and the power and accuracy of the top player's shots nearly made me destroy my racquet. It took a long time to come to terms with my own game, and enjoy it again.

There was another sport, fencing; I tried at Lever Brothers, mainly because my friends and I had heard that some nice young ladies attended the classes. At the time I was probably as fit as I would ever be, with football every weekend, running competitively regularly, and playing badminton twice a week. The fencing club was run by a pleasant, but strict ex-military chap, and, instead of us doing any Errol-Flynn-like activities, he had us practising the lunge virtually all that first evening. This involved standing in ballet's Fourth Position, and then extending the leading leg forward and down at full stretch. We did that about thirty times before he was satisfied. Next day I thought I was crippled, hurting in places I didn't even know existed. Fit as I was, I had rarely used those muscles before, and I paid for that non-use. Nice young ladies or no, I didn't go again.

Unfortunately, volleyball was virtually unknown in Britain when I was young. I would have loved to have played it, and I think that I would have been good at it. I always had good springing ability, excellent timing, and a good eye for ball games, and all these would be useful in such a sport. In fact, I did play once, but it was not until I was 53 years of age, and I will always regret it. I had spent many happy days around the pool at a resort in Tenerife, and was at peace with the world. One day an enthusiastic hotel activities organiser talked me into playing a game of volleyball. Despite warnings from my better half, I decided to have a go, and found to my great delight that I was playing quite well. Then, when I was up at the net, suddenly I felt as though I had been kicked violently and fell to the floor. I turned to swear at the perpetrator, only to find that no one was near. The immediate thought that came to mind was that my Achilles tendon had snapped. Luckily, there was another hotel guest spectating, who turned out to be a physiotherapist to the Swedish national soccer team. He appraised the situation quickly, lifted me up and carried me back to the swimming pool, and sat me with the leg dangling in the comparatively cold water. It wasn't the Achilles, but obviously something quite serious. I didn't fancy going to a doctor in Tenerife, and as we were going home a couple of days later I waited until then. In the meantime my leg had swelled to almost double the normal size from internal bleeding, and had turned blue and mauve. Once home, my local doctor immediately referred me to a Harley Street specialist, who, after making some very sarcastic remarks about someone my age doing what I had done, commented that it was one of the worst cases of tearing he had ever seen, without the Achilles actually going. The only thing to do was rest, alternate with frozen peas and a hot water bottle on my leg, and I was on crutches for about two months. Unfortunately, or otherwise depending on your point of view, I have not been able to take part in any sport since then. In another of those coincidences which seem to litter my life, the specialist turned out to be the uncle of the top Canadian 800m runner of the day.

I should specify that the game mentioned above was old-fashioned court volleyball, and not the extremely popular beach volleyball which has become an Olympic sport, and draws vast TV audiences, not least due to the skimpy costumes worn by the players. Perhaps if I could get into this type of volleyball, I might gird my loins again - for the game that is.

OTHER SPORTS (WATCHING)
For the last fifty years I have spent so much time with athletics that I haven't had much time for other sports. However, I have attended a few rather special events. Not truly a 'sporting' occasion was a visit to see the Harlem Globetrotters basketball team in the 1950s. Still clear in my mind is their star player, Meadowlark Lemon, arguing with the referee on the centre spot, and defiantly throwing the ball high and hard behind him. It went right into the basket to an enormous roar from the audience. I gather his hit/miss rate with this trick was about 50-50. My only top class basketball occasion was just before the 1984 Olympics. I was with Ron Pickering and Stuart

Storey, returning from the British athletics team quarters outside San Diego. As we passed the main auditorium there Stuart noticed that the US Olympic basketball team (then amateurs) was playing a professional All-Stars squad that evening. The Americans were so good that the IOC gave them special permission to play this type of opposition in warm-up meets. Stuart was to commentate on the Olympic basketball, as well as his athletics duties, and used his BBC clout to get us in. The US team had a couple of young players named Michael Jordan and Patrick Ewing, and I sat mesmerised.

Whenever at an Olympic Games, I would try to see other sports before the athletics began. At Munich in 1972, Ron Pickering insisted I come and see the <u>gymnastics</u>; in particular a little Russian girl who he said was stupendous. Indeed Olga Korbut was, and so too was her lovely teammate Ludmila Turischeva, perhaps the last of the 'real women' to take part in Olympic gymnastics. At later Games I always tried to attend at least one evening of gymnastics competitions. At Montreal, in 1976, I spent 1½ hours at the <u>swimming</u> and witnessed three world records. I had similar success at other Games. One evening in Seoul in 1988, I had just entered the <u>weightlifting</u> hall, when the great Naim Suleymanoglu of Turkey stepped up and lifted a stupendous new world record in the featherweight category.

OVERHEARD

Being an inveterate eavesdropper, I have often heard some highly unusual, shocking, and amusing things. Elsewhere, I have told of the first time I went to New York, in 1972, and overheard, in a restaurant, the most vile language I had ever heard outside the London docks, being used by a couple of smartly dressed old ladies. Against this I can report that in 2004 at Las Vegas airport, there was a general announcement on the tannoy system that "a set of false teeth has been left in the men's restroom".

OXYMORONS

You may have noticed that there are certain forms of language that appeal to my tiny mind. Among them is the oxymoron, which describes the combination of two apparently contradictory terms. The most common examples of this are "cruel kindness", "falsely true", and "make haste, slowly". However, there are two others, often used in ordinary speech and writing, which afford me a great deal of amusement. They are the terms "military intelligence", and "journalistic ethics". Also I was delighted to be told at a party, not long ago, that they were serving "diet chocolate cake".

You may be interested to know – and then again you may not – that the above mentioned phrase "make haste, slowly", in fact the Latin phrase "Festina Lente", was probably the first ever oxymoron, as it was coined by the first Emperor of Rome, Augustus, after whom the month of August was named.

PARADISE OR LUTON AIRPORT

A memorable TV advertisement had Lorraine Chase answering a lovelorn swain's ardent "Were you wafted here from Paradise?", with a broad cockney, "No, Luton Airport". In 1980 my family and I welcomed the New Year (the English one) in Jerusalem, and then went to Eilat on the Red Sea. Incidentally, to show how cosmopolitan we are, Carole & I celebrated the following New Year in Cairo - that's got to be rather unique. Anyway, in Eilat, my son, Keith, then 13, met two boys, and they in turn met three girls, with whom they chummed up. One day Keith told us that unbelievably the girls were really from Luton Airport. Not just a case of having flown from there, but they actually lived there. Apparently their father was an airport mechanic and had a house on the site.

PARIS

"I love Paris in the summer, when it sizzles, I love Paris in the winter, when it drizzles", as the song by Cole Porter puts it. I do like the city. The tourist attractions are usually very well run, the Metro

TIMED TO PERFECTION
Stan Greenberg

is excellent - I particularly like the maps with coloured lights which indicate the route you need to take - and the bateaux mouche are clean and efficient. But as in every city in the world one must be careful of the traffic and the prices - both can be deadly. My first introduction to Paris drivers came many years ago, when our tour driver stopped at the Arc de Triomphe, in the centre of l'Etoile - the Silverstone of France. The cars tear around it at break-neck speed and only the stupidest pedestrian would attempt to cross other than by the underpass. Of course, there is always one - guess who? I had realised that I could not get a really good camera shot of the Arc from just below it, so I decided to take one from across the road, and without thinking made my way into the maelstrom of traffic. Actually I didn't have too much trouble reaching the outside pavement, and happily took my pictures. However, when I tried to get back the same way I realised just how idiotic I was being, but by then it was too late, and I was trapped halfway across. I swear the drivers deliberately increased their speed when they saw me, and came as close as they possibly could - one car definitely touched my loose jacket thought I had.

Another time I got my comeuppance in Paris was one hot afternoon when Carole and I were strolling down the Champs-Elysées. I suggested that we stop and have a drink at one of the restaurants which had tables on the pavement. My wife warned me that it would be expensive, but I thought that I wouldn't mind lashing out a bit. It was more than a bit! The table was outside Le Fouquet's, a Paris landmark, and the two Coca-Colas cost some £5 each. Carole does seem to have an affinity for Paris, and indeed for things French. Perhaps this has to do with her mother's family originating in France. Anyway, on yet another trip to Paris, having gone all the way up to the top of the Eiffel Tower, she suddenly needed a 'powder room'. I remember thinking "Oh Lord, not here", when a commissionaire directed her to a door, and up a few more steps to a just such a 'powder room'. I was flabbergasted. I wonder how many people realise that such a place is there, and that one can climb a little higher than most tourists think possible.

TIMED TO PERFECTION
Stan Greenberg

One way and another we Greenbergs have made our mark on the Eiffel Tower staff. On my first trip to Paris, in 1954, rather surprisingly I found that one of the windows at the top of the Tower was unlatched. I lifted it up and leant out to take a photo looking straight down. I had a very old camera in those days, which was one of those with a concertina-type lens, and a viewfinder on the top. Thus to see exactly what I was taking I had to lean out rather alarmingly to look through the viewfinder. I have never been afraid of heights, and felt quite safe, but suddenly all hell broke loose behind me. A screaming 'banshee" was yelling at me in French, and hands roughly grabbed and pulled me away from the window. I couldn't really understand him, or his slightly more composed colleague, but I think the gist of it all was that they thought I was trying to commit suicide. I kept pointing at my camera and waving my hands about in an approved British-French way, until they calmed down and escorted me to the lift. I got some very funny looks from the other passengers, and some of them pulled their children closer to them, away from le folle - that much French I understood.

PARTIES
As a child, and also as a young man, I had a pathological fear of parties - at the latter age, good lord, there was the probability of meeting girls! However, once I had my girl, i.e. my wife, Carole, I got to like the idea of parties, and have hosted a number of quite large ones at our home. Usually they are related to New Year, special birthdays, anniversaries, or just because we want a party, and at times we have had up to 50 guests - which in an ordinary suburban house is pretty good going. I think that I can say, not without some immodesty, that they have generally been quite successful. One, perhaps rather unusual, thing about our get-togethers, is that our guests have to pay - not in financial terms, but by intellectual effort. By this I mean that invariably I hold a quiz during the evening, covering all sorts of subjects, and to "oil the wheels" I arrange guests into teams of three or four, based on my knowledge of their interests. As expected, people complain before,

during and after these competitions, but despite the moans and groans, I believe that they quite like the stimulation of such a contest.

PEA PICKING

While evacuated at Kings Lynn I was roped into helping the local farmers with their harvests. During the long summer evenings, after school, I would cycle out to the fields and spend a few lucrative hours picking apples, strawberries, and, in particular, peas. I greatly preferred this latter as it was on piece-work terms, while the fruit was on daily rates. I had an aptitude for the peas - perhaps because I didn't like them and didn't spend time eating them. Whatever, I was nearly as fast as the gypsies who were at all such sites. They were amazing, hands moving at remarkable speed as they stripped the vines. To my great delight I could fill the large sacks almost as quickly, earning quite large sums. So much so that when my beloved bicycle was stolen, by one of my fellow pickers, I didn't worry as I knew I could easily buy another if necessary. Actually, it was returned the next day.

PETS

Unlike the great bulk of the population of Britain, I have never particularly liked animals. I tolerated the odd cat that my parents had in their house, mainly because it was very necessary to keep down the mice which infested houses in the East End of London in the 30s and 40s. However, I never got too attached to them - one of my friends cried like a baby when his little cat got run over, even though he was in his middle twenties when it happened. Dogs I actively dislike, though on reflection it may be more due to their owners than to themselves. Why local and national governments continue to allow dogs to foul pavements and pathways in the park is a mystery to me. To my mind it is the same sort of scandalous misuse of power as that exhibited by American governments relating to the control of guns in the United States. I suppose that in that case they can fall back on the provisions of the US

Constitution, but I am certain that there is no section of the Magna Carta which allows dogs to do what they do where they do it. To be fair, one should really put the blame on their owners - but what can you expect from someone who would want a dog in the first place. Oh, oh, now I'm in trouble.

Soon after we were married one of our friends bought a kinkajou, a sort of raccoon, as a pet, which they allowed to roam around their house quite freely. It wasn't too difficult to cope with on our occasional visit, but when it was suggested to Carole that she get one, she replied that she already had her own kinky Jew as a pet.

PHILOSOPHY
There have been many great philosophical topics which caught my interest over the years, but one has outlasted all the others. Why, when it falls to the floor, does toast and jam always end up jam side down ? No matter how it falls, how many times it rolls around, some inexplicable power will turn it onto the sticky side. Now this phenomenon doesn't only happen to me alone, but is known throughout the world. It may be that there is a good scientific explanation for it, but I find that difficult to believe.

PITH

A strange heading you may think, especially if I am not lisping. True, but it has figured quite often in my life. When I was a young boy, and evacuated during the war, I delighted in making little boats out of elderberry stems. As you may know, the plant has soft, spongy tissue (pith) in its branches, and by scraping out some of it you can end up with a miniature 'dug-out canoe'. Among family and friends, I have garnered a reputation for dealing with the pith of oranges – some think that when I peel the fruit it becomes a work of art, as I do not finish until every vestige of that white lining has been removed. As well as improving the taste of the fruit, I find the preparation of it very relaxing.

There is a scene in the Marx Brothers' film *Animal Crackers* in which the cast greets Groucho, playing a returned explorer and wearing a pith helmet, with a song, "Hurray for Captain Spalding". My wife and I have a habit of breaking into the song whenever we see anyone wearing such a hat. Now, that is not too often in this day and age, but we had a field day when we first visited Disneyworld in Florida, and found that quite a number of the other visitors were wearing them. We received a number of queer looks as we kept breaking into song.

PLACES

I have been very fortunate to have travelled extensively around the world. Rarely have I been anywhere that I found dull or uninteresting, though probably that says more about me as an inveterate tourist than about the places I visited. The following is a short list, not in any set order, of some of the things that made a particular impression on me.

The thing that makes the most vivid impact on the visitor to Cairo, at least initially, is the traffic. It is the only place I know where the cars will not stop to allow pedestrians to cross, and so a common sight is that of little old ladies threading their way through madly driven traffic without any leeway given. Later, that memory is dimmed by the Pyramids. On the approach to the plateau at Giza I was perturbed to note that the modern city seems to encroach to the very foot of the ancient monuments - I had always imagined them to be aloof and away from civilization in the desert. However, once one gets close, the sheer immensity of the structures sweep away any trite intrusions. The largest, that of Cheops, is 137m *450ft* high, and 225m *737ft* along each side, although it must have been bigger originally with its long vanished limestone and granite facing. On entering it, many tourists find the consciousness of that immense weight of stone above too much for their nerves. For those who are claustrophobic it is the last place on earth to go. The central chamber is only reached via a low narrow passageway, which is not for the faint-hearted. As I crawled along it, bent over to avoid hitting one's head on the roof, a lady up ahead panicked, and insisted on going back, causing a near riot. The chamber itself is a vast room with dim lighting and containing little of interest. Leaning against a wall I became intensely aware that I was in a tomb with only one, rather difficult, way out. The room has a very high ceiling, but one wondered how much air it held, and I must admit to a very uneasy feeling - but glancing around it was fairly obvious that I was not the only one in such a state. Those talking to friends had a touch of hysteria in their voices, and those, like me, alone, looked nervously in the direction of the small entrance, getting ready for the return trip. I am very glad I made that journey into the heart of the pyramid, but I am not sure I would do it again.

The oddly named Old-New Synagogue in <u>Prague</u> is the oldest one in Europe, dating from about 1270. The old Jewish quarter miraculously survived the Nazi occupation without damage or desecration, apparently because of a decision to preserve it as an historic relic of 'a vanished race'. It is now a major tourist attraction, especially the old cemetery, dating from the 15th century, in which the headstones were all piled up against one another as space became scarce. It is estimated that there may be twelve strata of graves, with some 12,000 gravestones. The most famous is that of Rabbi Yehuda Löw, a great scholar and cabbalist, who lived from 1523-1609. He is famed as the creator of the legendary Golem, a giant clay figure brought to life by a sacred writing placed in its mouth, to defend the community against persecution. The story is said to have been the inspiration for Mary Shelley's *Frankenstein* .

Near the Dead Sea, in Israel, lies the ruins of the rock fortress <u>Masada</u> , which stands some 396m *1300ft* above the shore line. It is the site of the last stand, in 72AD, of a Jewish sect called the Zealots, against the Romans. When the besieging Roman army of some 10,000 men finally breached the defences they found that all 953 survivors, men, women and children, had committed suicide rather than submit. Undoubtedly, there is a strange atmosphere about the place, which has a stark beauty in its loneliness. From the summit there is a wonderful view over the Dead Sea itself and the surrounding country, and its impregnability can be better understood if one descends, not by the cable car, but by the aptly named twisting Snake Path.

Just outside Mexico City is the ancient City of the Gods, Teotihuacan, which more than lived up to my expectations. It is vast and covers several square miles. The pre-Aztec ruins include the Pyramids of the Sun and the Moon, and to climb up the many ceremonial steps to the summit of the former was a rewarding, but exhausting, experience. The early Central and South American cultures have fascinated me since childhood, and it was a dream come true to be there. However, I was deeply disturbed by the terrible poverty of the shanty towns one passes on the way. In fact I have rarely seen such extremes of wealth and poverty as I witnessed on the streets of Mexico City. I should also mention one of the most striking buildings I have ever seen, and that is the mosaic- covered library of the University of Mexico.

POLITENESS
I was brought up to be polite and well-mannered, and trust that I have been for most of my life. I never particularly thought about it until I visited the United States for the first time. If I held open a door, or stood back to allow someone through first, people seemed surprised, and I was quite embarrassed by their heartfelt thanks. Also I got the impression that politeness to a waitress was a Federal offence. I remember the remarkable reaction Carole and I had at a restaurant we frequented on Miami Beach. We didn't behave any differently than we would in a London restaurant, but the waitresses began fussing round us like mother hens after our first meal - and I am not a big tipper. On our final evening, when we mentioned that we were leaving the next day, the owner insisted that the meal that night was on him, in appreciation for the nice way we had treated his staff.

POLITICS
Basically, I am not a political animal, and must admit to not voting

TIMED TO PERFECTION
Stan Greenberg

in a number of local and national elections over time. Usually this has been because I have found nothing to support in any party's manifesto, and/or I have not had any faith in any candidate or leader. By upbringing I lean to the left, if anything, but by inclination, born of experience, I am of the centre, but this has not stopped me voting to the right when I have felt they offered better solutions to current problems. I have never understood those who vote the same way, year after year, no matter how their circumstances, or those of the country, change. To blindly follow a party line, whichever party or ideology, despite the often obvious deficiencies of that party's policies, candidates or leaders, is, I think, virtually a criminal act.

Despite my comments at the beginning, I have quite strong views about the general political situation. When I worked in the Transportation Department of the GLC, the planners and engineers all agreed that if you want a traffic jam, put the police in charge. Well, I feel the same about governmental 'policing' of projects in Britain - if you want them to take forever, or indeed even fail, bring in the politicians. We've seen it with the building of major roads, we've seen it with the building of major housing projects, we've seen it in the refurbishment of major historical and cultural sites, we've seen it with the lack of building a national stadium. This state of affairs is not the fault of either Labour or the Tories - IT IS THE FAULT OF BOTH THEIR HOUSES. The problem is that most of the party hierarchies, or at least those strong enough to be able to do anything about it, of the last forty years, apparently have had no general sporting nor cultural interests. I know Mr Heath was a yachtsman, and that Mr Major loved cricket, but I doubt that Mrs Thatcher ever went to a football or cricket match of her own free will, or that Mr Blair has attended the opera or a pop concert of his own volition.

There is a general problem, in this country particularly, and it is that politicians at local or national level have no conception of economic cost. They can only see the balance sheet relating to actual financial outgoings from their own coffers. Thus, the fact that such and such a road holdup is costing the country so many millions a week, or the building of this bridge might save thousands for industry, or a quick decision on that project will eventually save hours of work, all these notional costs or savings mean nothing Whatever your political opinion is about the Millenium Dome and the Olympic Stadium, the thing that impressed me was that they are about the only major constructions done in this country in my lifetime that were planned, discussed and then built, all within the set time limits.

There is an old Jewish joke - if it is a joke - that goes: So how do you know when a politician is lying? There are a number of psychological indications. If he rubs his nose, he isn't lying. If he pulls his ear, he isn't lying. If he scratches his cheek, he isn't lying. If he opens his mouth - THEN he is lying.

PSYCHIATRY
When I was in my late teens, my parents and I attended a family party at which we were introduced to a very attractive lady, who, apparently, was a quite well-known psychiatrist. My father, always an enquiring mind, monopolised her for a time, asking all sorts of deep questions about her work, which seemed to please her. After a while he suddenly turned and indicating me asked, to my intense embarrassment, what did she make of his strange teenage son. (I think that this was symptomatic of a time when he and I were just not on the same wavelength with anything, and he thought my general behaviour and attitude 'off the wall'). I remember that she smiled, looked me up and down, in what I did not consider to be a medical fashion, and, to my even greater embarrassment, said that she would be delighted to get me on her couch. Being very backward in such matters, and a social ninny of epic proportions, I quickly beat a hasty retreat to a distant corner of the room. As I got older, I often thought about the encounter, not without a little sadness. In whatever capacity, no doubt her couch would have done me some good, at a time when I most certainly needed help - of any sort!

PUBLIC SPEAKING

One of the biggest regrets of my life has been my complete inability to speak in public. Now, anyone who knows me will find that an hilarious statement, as I have a reputation for speaking far too much - in public and private. But I am referring to 'proper' public speaking i.e. in front of an audience. Certainly when I was younger the prospect filled me with horror and invariably I would just 'dry up'. In fact, even at my wedding all I managed to say when it came time for my speech, was "Thank you all for coming". As I sat down I remember that I got a tremendous ovation - probably from thankful family and friends who wanted to get on with the dancing. On the rare occasions I couldn't get out of giving a talk, I went through agonies. At the Guinness organisation I had to give a talk about the Book of Records to a local women's club - I choked and stuttered, and turned every shade of magenta - the organiser was kind enough to say they enjoyed it, but I think she was being very kind. On another occasion, I was teamed with my colleague Peter Matthews at a similar talk to another, much larger, local group. Unfortunately, from my point of view, Peter was/is an excellent speaker, and I am sure that made me look and sound even worse than I probably was.

When I was at the GLC Dept of Transportation Library, my boss insisted that I should give a short series of talks to Library Association students - he meant it as an appreciation of the work that I did, but I nearly died at the thought. However, I came up with a life-saver of an idea. I gave a slide show. That way I was able to stand at the back of the room, in the dark, using the projector, and talking over the pictures that were shown. I didn't have a sea of faces staring at me - I realise now that that is what always put me off. The slide shows were a great success, and my boss was very pleased - little did he know how close to farce it had been! Over the years I have often been asked to give a talk at athletics conferences, coaching weekends and club get-togethers, but I have always refused. Now people may understand why. I read somewhere that my mind (and, of course, yours) is the greatest information storage system, the fastest computer, and the best word selector, known to man. So, why is it that whenever I get up to speak it is the most useless piece of technology ever created. Even if it does think of suitable words, it totally loses its ability to string them together in intelligible sentences. The Canadian actor and radio panellist, Bernard Braden, once said that "The human brain is the most sophisticated and complex computer in the world. It only ceases to function when you get up to speak". I know exactly what he meant.

PUBLIC TRANSPORT
One of my earliest recollections of public transport is of a bus ride I took in Manchester, where I was evacuated for a time during WWII. I was about 12 years old and had just asked the conductor, in a London accent, for a 'happeny' ticket. I was then, loudly and publically, told off for not talking properly and calling it a 'halfpenny' ticket. Very embarrassed I paid up and got off the bus as soon as possible. The Manchester Corporation lost quite a few happennies from me after that.

A more recent bus encounter happened in Malta a couple of years ago. The buses there are rather old and seem to be looked on as the personal property of the drivers, who, I was informed, took the vehicles home at night. Perhaps rather foolishly, I had arranged our last day schedule to climax with a bus ride from the far western end of the island back to the capital Valletta, with just enough time to get to the airport for the journey back to Heathrow. Our driver was a big brute of a man, who obviously had never heard of a timetable, that is if could read at all. He virtually sauntered, if you can do that with a bus, for the first part of the journey, leaving me anxiously checking my watch. Then, about halfway back, he stopped in the main street of a little town, and waited. What for, we wondered. After quite a long time a chap came out of a grocery store with three large bags of goods and handed them up through the driver's window. Apparently the damn man had been picking up his weekly shopping. Money changed hands, and after some pleasantries, the bus moved on, slowly. We arrived back at the bus station in

TIMED TO PERFECTION
Stan Greenberg

Valletta, with barely enough time to spare, and only a fairly expensive, albeit fast, taxi got us to the airport on time.

One of the most outstanding subway networks is the Moscow underground. Not so much for the reliability of its trains, although I remember in 1980 being enamoured of the clocks on the station platforms which indicated how long it would be before the next train came - this was well before London Transport had similar noticeboards on its system. No, it was rather because of the stations themselves. Some of the central area ones were positive works of art, more akin to art galleries and museums than to train stops. At the time it was a total contrast to the New York subway system, which was then as dirty, dangerous, and graffiti-ridden as it is possible to imagine, although, I am reliably informed, it is much better now. One of the best public transport systems that I have used is the subway in Seoul, Korea - which deals with vast hordes of people swiftly and efficiently every day. During the 1988 Olympic Games I gave up using the BBC cars to return to the hotel from the stadium. Instead I followed the crowds to the underground trains, stood in line at specially marked spots on the platform, and within minutes was in a clean, bright train, with a minimum of fuss. Soon I was back in the hotel - a remarkable experience.

Two fascinating forms of transport were in Bangkok - a city perhaps better known for things other than locomotion. The most pervasive is the 'Tuk-Tuk' - a three wheeled vehicle with a motorcycle engine. The movement, noise and smell of this contraption is diabolical, but it does its job very well. On the Chao Phraya river are the fast, long, narrow, high-prowed river taxis, driven by propellers at the end of long poles, which are also used to steer with. It is a most exhilarating ride. Not surprisingly, the most efficient transport systems I have used were in Switzerland. Taking a trip halfway across the country entailed changing trains and postal buses on four occasions. The timings of each form of transport dovetailed perfectly with the next one, with the trip totally relaxed and delightful - but expensive.

PUNISHMENT

I believe in deserved punishment, whether for misbehaving children, or, for that matter, misbehaving grown-ups. Indeed, I seriously believe that one of the reasons for many of the ills of our time is due to the lack of censure and reprimand in society as a whole.

However, such castigation should be justified, should fit the 'crime', and be seen to have an effect. Personally, I have been on the end of a 'punishment' which I welcomed with open arms. It came about when I worked in the shipping department of Unilever, early in my working life. My section head, Mr Johnson, didn't like me very much, and was sometimes most unpleasant just for the sake of it. In our line of work, it was often necessary for someone to come in to work on a Saturday morning to clear various shipping documents in the city. He decided, out of the blue, and, it seemed to me, with sadistic pleasure, that I should be the one to do this, and, despite my loud protestations, insisted that I do this overtime. What he never realised was that I was only too happy to come into the centre of London on a Saturday morning. Especially was this true when it enabled me to (a) add to my meagre earnings, and (b) be close to the main railway stations I needed to catch the trains to various venues at which I was playing football or badminton matches on the Saturday afternoons.

PUT-DOWNS

We have all suffered the occasional experience of being 'put in our place' by someone's barbed remark. Having been on the receiving end on a number of occasions, sometimes even deservedly, I take some satisfaction from two examples of the genre – which were not applied to me, I should add. The famous Dr Johnson once said about someone that, "He seemed to possess but one idea, and that is a wrong one". But, pride of place must go to a physicist, Wolfgang Pauli, who said of a colleague, that "He doesn't even rise to the level of being wrong".

TIMED TO PERFECTION
Stan Greenberg

QUEUEING

The British have always been considered to be the organisers of queues par excellence, and all over the world people have been fascinated at how, at the slightest provocation, British travellers will form an orderly queue. However, I am afraid that their crown has been usurped. I had never realised that the management and organisation of a queue is a science, indeed almost an art form, until I visited Walt Disney World in Florida. At the more popular exhibits they have three or four parallel pathways for each queue, and,
remarkably, no matter which one you join, you will arrive at the front alongside the people who joined the other pathways at the same time you joined yours.

On my first trip abroad, to the 1952 Olympics in Helsinki, I recall that I broke the queueing rules I had been taught during the war. A few of our group went to buy some ice cream, and tried to form an orderly line. However, the Finns and other nationalities obviously had never seen such a set up and just barged their way forward ahead of us. After a while we thought ' blow this', or words to that effect, and formed a flying wedge, which got us through the scrum in no time. No one seemed annoyed at this, indeed they smiled to acknowledge our efficiency it seemed. Nevertheless, I still think the British queue is far superior to the continental free-for-all, especially at bus stops.

QUIZZES

Carole and I have always enjoyed taking part in quizzes, and, with a small group of friends, we have done very well in them over the years. However, I have had the opportunity, and great fun, of setting and/or checking the questions for some well-known quizzes on TV. The first of these was *Quizball* in the late 1960s, one of the first programmes that David Vine presented. I was given questionnaires filled in by the contestants, soccer players from the major teams, and remember being appalled, in many cases, at the answers given to queries about their standard of education, newspapers and magazines read, and the last books they had finished. Every now and again, but very rarely, there would be an answer which indicated a grammar school or even university product, but generally the overall standard was poor. One other thing that I had to be careful about - I was not to set questions about the rules of the game. I wonder why?

Another programme to which I contributed, but only occasionally, was *Mastermind*. The subjects were usually athletics or the Olympic Games, and the standard of question had to be quite stiff. One contestant, a Dr David Delvin, had taken a medical subject for the first round, but for the next took athletics as his subject. He was one of those people with a photographic memory, and had boned up on the subject. On the night of the programme, I sat at home, watching with my son, knowing all the answers, and yet he answered them before I could. On another front, I was involved with *A Question of Sport* for about 20 years, primarily checking anything to do with athletics or the Olympic Games. David Coleman got me involved when he was questionmaster on the show, and I will always be grateful to him for that.

I don't think that people realise just how difficult it is to set questions for a quiz. In amateur quizzes, not only are the answers often wrong, but on far too many occasions the questions are as well. I remember one quiz I was at just after joining the *Guinness Book of Records*, and one of the questions was "Who is the fastest swimmer in the world?". Now, at that time, it was obvious what answer they wanted - Mark Spitz, who

held the world record for 100m freestyle. However, I had recently formulated a new category in my work which calculated that the greatest swimming speed achieved had been by the holder of the indoor 50m mark. Thus, the question was wrong - for the answer they expected. Our team, at my suggestion, had 'incorrectly' put Mark Spitz, and therefore got the point, but I smugly enjoyed taking it up with the group asking the questions - especially as they had announced at the start of the proceedings that they would accept no arguments from the floor. I am afraid that over the years, at such charity-raising quizzes, I and my cousin Alan, have acquired something of a reputation for querying 'official' answers, as well as some of the questions.

QUOTATIONS

I like a good quote, whether historical, sporting or topical, and I have used some in this book where I feel they are appropriate. Here I append some of my other favourites.

"A man is as old as the woman he feels"
Groucho Marx

"There are three kinds of lies: lies, damned lies, and statistics"
Mark Twain

"No Rabbi ever lost his job because his sermons were too short"
Traditional

"That money talks, I wont deny, I heard it once, it said goodbye"
Anon

The multi-talented American entertainer, Sammy Davis Jr, when he had turned to Judaism after his horrific accident, was asked what was his golf handicap. He answered " I'm a one-eyed Jewish Negro - who needs a handicap?"

The great Irish dramatist George Bernard Shaw, commented that the United Kingdom and the United States were "Two great nations divided by a common language".

In the film *The Third Man*, Orson Welles states "In Italy, for 30 years under the Borgias, they had warfare, terror, murder and bloodshed, but they produced Michelangelo, Leonardo da Vinci, and the Renaissance. In Switzerland, they had brotherly love, democracy and peace, and what did they produce? The cuckoo clock".

TIMED TO PERFECTION
Stan Greenberg

An unknown philosopher said *"Never be afraid to try something new. Remember, amateurs built the Ark, professionals built the Titanic."*

"It's not that I'm afraid to die. I just don't want to be there when it happens"
> Woody Allen

"My formula for success is, rise early, work late, and strike oil"
> John Paul Getty

"A creature made at the end of the week's work, when God was tired"
> Mark Twain (Definition of a man)

"Imagination is intelligence having fun"
> Anon

"Against stupidity, the Lord Himself is helpless"
> The Talmud

"Without music, life would be a mistake"
Friedrich Nietzsche

"I always turn to the sports pages first, which record people's accomplishments.
The front page has nothing but man's failures"
> Chief Justice Earl Warren

"Living with a conscience is like driving a car with the brakes on"
> Budd Schulberg

"The covers of this book are too far apart" (Literary criticism)
> Ambrose Pierce

"I am strongly in favour of commonsense, common honesty, and

common decency.
   This makes me ineligible for any public office"
      H L Mencken

"Everything you see, I owe to spaghetti"
      Sophia Loren

"Children today are tyrants. They contradict their parents, gobble their food, and tyrannise their teachers"
      Socrates (Greek philosopher c400BC)

"The old believe everything, the middle-aged suspect everything, the young know everything"
      Oscar Wilde

"A lie can make it halfway around the world before the truth has time to put its boots on"
      Mark Twain

"Either don't attempt it, or carry it through to the end"
      Ovid (Roman Poet c10BC)

RACISM

As we all know, this can take various forms. One incident that I remember, occurred when I was on a sports weekend at Bisham Abbey, near Henley-on-Thames, in the early 1950s. At the time I was the newsletter editor for an organization called The Whip and Carrot Club - which was set up to help British high jumpers improve. Among the members who attended the weekend, for coaching and lectures, was Charles Van Dyck from Ghana, an extremely black gentleman and a really good high jumper from Ghana, who was studying in the UK. He was very popular with the athletics fraternity and I considered him to be a friend. Bisham Abbey was well laid back from the main road and was purported to be haunted by a lady ghost who prowled the grounds at night. The warden of the place was very strict, locking the doors and turning off the outside lights, quite early in the evening. If residents wanted to visit the hostelry in town they had to sneak out of a back window and make their way in the dark to the main gates. As a few of us made our stumbling way along the path one of the group said something about meeting the ghost, and Charles said "Hey, you chaps aren't scared of a ghost are you?". I replied that he was okay as all he had to do was stand still, and in the dark she wouldn't see him. Charles thought that was very funny and we went on our way. However, the next day I was approached by another member of the group, an upper-crust type, who reprimanded me for the joke, saying that he thought it was in very bad taste. When I spoke to Charles to find out if an apology was necessary for what I thought was just a funny quip, he said there was nothing to apologise for, and that it was only the guilty, neo-racist, conscience of the other chap, who he had 'dealings' with before, that prompted the comment. In fact, Charles told me that he had written down the remark, which he thought was quite appropriate, to tell other friends.

RATIONING

Those of us old enough will remember it lasted throughout the war, and in one form or another into the 1950s. During the war food rationing hit hard, with quite small quantities of key products, particularly meat, allowed per person. A married aunt, with two grown children, used a butcher near where my family lived, and my mother would sometimes collect my aunt's allocation, so that I could deliver it. The journey required two bus trips, and once, with a whole month's ration, I suddenly realised that I no longer had the bag of meat with me. I had been daydreaming I suppose, and had left it on the previous bus. I rushed back to the depot and made frantic enquiries but, perhaps not surprisingly, the bag had not been handed in. It never did appear, and I always considered that my aunt took the loss remarkably well - but my parents didn't, and I had several privileges withdrawn for my carelessness.

TIMED TO PERFECTION
Stan Greenberg

RECHTHABEREI

A German word which roughly translates as the state of thinking and behaving as if you are right and everyone else is wrong. Now why does this word trouble me? Can it be that I suffer from this state of mind? Surely not. If I was a politician, I could understand. If I was a certain kind of doctor, I could understand. But, little, old me? No, never. Then again..........

REFRIGERATION

In this day and age, when most people in this country have refrigerators, I often think back to when my family, that is my parent's family, didn't. Originally, I remember, we had what was called a 'safe' in the concrete floored room that led to our back garden. Incidentally, I call it a garden, but it was actually a ten foot square of more concrete, edged on three sides with a thin strip of very bad earth, and a further circle of earth in the middle. At the beginning of the war it was nearly all taken up by an Andersen shelter. Anyway, back to the 'safe'. It consisted of a wooden cabinet, about six foot tall, with the top 18 inches being a cupboard with a very thin metal-mesh door. Apparently this would keep food reasonably cool during hot weather, but I am not sure, with hindsight, that it worked all that well, albeit it did keep flies away. Somewhat later we used to put stuff down the coal cellar, under the stairs and hallway of the house. This was nearly always very cold, but as it was the abode of numerous creepy-crawlies I never liked going down there. We finally acquired a fridge – or it was called a fridge. It was approximately eighteen inches by eighteen inches by eighteen inches, weighed about 'a ton ', and held a maximum of two pints of milk and a packet of butter – but, at last, the Greenberg family had entered the modern age!

REGRETS

Henry David Thoreau wrote that "To regret deeply is to live afresh". We all have regrets, I am sure, usually about things we have done in the past. However, thinking back over my life, most of my regrets

265

are about things that I haven't done, but wish that I had. I deeply regret that I never learnt to play the piano, or, indeed, any instrument. I love music, and dearly wish I could actually make it myself. Similarly, I wish I had learnt to dance properly, and specifically to tap dance - I always thought that behind my two left feet was a veritable Fred Astaire. I fear I am now too old to learn to ski - something I always dreamed about. Another skill I wished I had acquired is that of public speaking - or perhaps I should say that I wish I had developed the nerve to do it. Also, I am full of remorse that I did not spend more time learning to speak foreign languages, especially French and German, after having made quite a promising start in learning both of them at school and at evening classes. I would also have liked to really understand Yiddish, but never knuckled down to it.

I wish I had spent more time with my children when they were young - they grow up so quickly - as their early years coincided with my BBC work and travel. It meant that actually I had two jobs at once, and that I had very little leisure time, especially at weekends. However, it did mean that we had more income at a time when we badly needed it. I should have learnt to drive much sooner - I was 33 before I began lessons. However, on reflection, I couldn't afford a car in my twenties, and even if I could have done, it would probably have meant that I would not have met and married Carole, and I have no regrets on that score. I regret not having gone to university – I know I had the ability, but not the wherewithal – although if I had I think the whole course of my life would have been different, and most probably not any better nor happier.

I very much regret that I never learnt to swim properly, as it is an activity I love but don't do very well with my self-taught style. Lastly, I believe I could have been quite a good sprinter if I had concentrated my efforts and training, and spent less time playing around at various other events - and similarly the same may be true of my ability at badminton.

TIMED TO PERFECTION
Stan Greenberg

RELIGION

My father was quite religious, indeed he was for a time a senior lay official in our synagogue, and so when I was young and lived at home it was required of me as well. Therefore, I attended services regularly, and when old enough, about five or six, went to Jewish religious classes. Our local rabbi, Maurice Lew, was one of my teachers, and I often queried what he was telling us. When he eventually transferred to another, more important, synagogue, he was given a farewell party, after which he delivered his last speech in which he referred to all the things he would be missing. Surprisingly, among those things he said were "the searching questions from young Greenberg", and I doubt that my father had ever been so proud of me as at that moment. Rabbi Lew, an extremely clever man, later became a Dayan, or a senior judge in the Jewish faith, and if he hadn't been physically a small, rather podgy looking man, he would probably have been Chief Rabbi.

A later rabbi at our place was a young, good-looking, firebrand, whose sermons really shook people up with their intensity and fervour. Interestingly, the younger element liked him, and his stock went up even more when I recounted a visit he made to my house. After a service my father invited Rabbi Melnick in for a drink before his long walk back to his own house. In our dining room we had a bookcase with a large set of the classics - Shakespeare, Dickens, Bronte etc. The rabbi happened to ask me how many of them I had read - actually over half of them - but before I could answer, my father complained that I was too busy going to the cinema to read. The rabbi then asked if I had seen the film then being shown at the local cinema, a musical, and agreed with me that it was very good. Dad expressed surprise, and indeed a little shock, that a rabbi would visit a cinema - I know that dad was thinking that it wasn't proper that a man of the cloth would be watching scantily clad chorus girls etc. Rabbi Melnick obviously realised the drift of dad's thinking, and replied "Mr Greenberg, I may be a rabbi, but I am also a man".

It is a well known fact that religious Jews have periodic rows with

TIMED TO PERFECTION
Stan Greenberg

their synagogues and/or community leaders. Thus it is not unusual for a Jew to change his place of worship on occasion. My grandfather continually attended different places, making it very difficult for me to visit him during the Day of Atonement - a most sacred day on which older, devout people stay in the synagogue all day, but the younger element tend to go out and visit their relatives and friends at other sites. He was a very religious and learned man, and continually disagreed with others about the order of service or the meaning of text. One year, when he was praying at one place, a private house, I was refused permission to enter to see him. Despite strong protests the doorkeeper was adamant, and I finally got him to send a message for me. When my grandfather came out to see me, he took me to one side, and, with a twinkle in his eye, told me that "This lot are crazy - they only let people in with beards. Luckily I have one."

There is an old joke about a religious Jew who was shipwrecked on a desert island, and lived there alone for many years, becoming quite proficient at making and building the amenities he needed. When he was eventually picked up he showed his rescuers around his island, pointing out various living areas and storehouses that he had built. With especial pride he indicated a particularly resplendent hut which he noted was his synagogue. One of the ship's officers pointed to another equally impressive hut some distance away and asked what that was. The castaway scowled and said that it was his old synagogue, but that he had had a row and no longer went there.

One religious occasion that I recall with particular pleasure was when Carole and I were sight-seeing in St Peter's in Rome. As far as I know it was just an ordinary day. Suddenly there was a bit of a commotion among the other few tourists about, and as we watched, the then Pope, the lovely John XXIII, was carried past us on a palanquin. He was almost close enough to touch. I was so surprised that I forgot to get my camera out of my bag until it was too late. The occasion made an already memorable trip even more so.

TIMED TO PERFECTION
Stan Greenberg

Carole and I were invited to a Methodist wedding some years ago. According to its tradition, the church was a very bare establishment, with very little adornment inside. Indeed, I remember that the inside walls were very rough brickwork on which one could scratch oneself very easily. I was really staggered when the minister gave his little speech to the bride and groom after the ceremony, as it was all hellfire, brimstone and damnation, and hardly what one expected on the happy occasion of a wedding. It was explained to me that this was 'low' church, but even for that line of belief it was a bit much.

RESIDENCE

I was born in London, and have lived there all my life – but there seems to be an international plot to make it otherwise. Let me explain. A few years ago I joined one of the proliferating loyalty agreements, in this case the Holiday Inn Priority Club. Each stay at one of their hotels gets points which can lead, eventually, to various awards eg free nights' stays. After some months I contacted the company to find out why I had not received my Priority Club card, and realised that their call centre was in Amsterdam. I was told that the card had been sent some time before and that I should have received it. Checking my address with them I found out that they had me down on their computer (surprise, surprise) as living at my London N12 address, but in THE YEMEN. "Where?" I yelled down the 'phone. The Yemen they said. "Why?" I asked. Did it not seem odd that a chap named Greenberg, living in a fairly obviously British-sounding address, would be in the Yemen? Two thoughts occurred to me. Firstly, it would appear that the poor Yemeni Post Office is still trying to deliver that strangely addressed letter. Secondly, and even more strangely, that it may have been delivered! It was explained that the error had come about, probably, because the person entering my details in their computer had hit the wrong code for the country of residence. Quite understandable, but doesn't anyone check?

TIMED TO PERFECTION
Stan Greenberg

Come forward a couple of years, and I had decided to get up-to-date and go online on the Internet. One of the first things I did was to contact the British Airways Executive Club website. I found that I had great difficulty getting into the site, despite carefully following all the instructions. However, then I noticed that in the security section box for my Country of Residence there was the word Morocco. I tried to change it, but it wouldn't change. When I telephoned the Executive Club help line I was asked if I had now changed countries. With some difficulty I controlled my temper, and pointed out that I had never lived in Morocco, and wondered how such an error had occurred. I was informed that I must have entered the wrong country myself. Still under control, about which I am very proud, I explained patiently that, in the first place, I had only just gone online, and that I had never been on that page before. Also, in the second place, it was highly unlikely that I would put such a country down as my country of residence. Nepal or Tibet, yes, but why Morocco? Happily, it was all put right, with an apology for the 'computer error'. Why am I not surprised? To appease my many computerised friends, I am well aware that it is not the computer's fault, but that of the operator. Still, if he or she were using pen and paper, it probably wouldn't have happened.

However, to show willing, let me give you a happier example of international computer use. A year or two ago I arranged, via the Internet firm E-Bookers, a fairly complicated trip to and in the United States. I had occasion to query one of the legs of the journey, and telephoned a given number. Although the number was apparently a British-based one, it turned out that I was talking to a chap in Bombay (actually Mumbai nowadays). He was very pleasant, helpful and efficient, and everything went off without a hitch, and I delighted in telling friends about my Indian travel agent, Mr Tuti.

RESPONSIBILITY
There is a movie in which the actor, Bruce Dern, playing a middle-aged man whose father has just died, thus making him the head of

the family, is given the line "I don't want to be the daddy!" I am sure that the principle behind that cry struck a chord with many men, and probably with some women too. There is a time in nearly all our lives when we suddenly have to take responsibility for other people, perhaps at work, sometimes at play, but usually at home. It is particularly difficult when it happens early in life, and/or unexpectedly, and you find you have to make decisions about other people's lives and finances, when you aren't that sure you are making the right decisions about your own. However, on the whole, most people seem to cope with the added strains, and it helps a lot if they have the support of friends and family. In this respect I have been very lucky when such responsibilities have been passed to me.

REVENGE?

This is not a story that I take any pride in, nor one that gives me any pleasure, but it does show how an accident can be blown out of all proportions. The BBC used to cover an athletics meeting in Coblenz, Germany, regularly in the 1980s. At first we did not have a very good commentary position, but then a bigger, better one was built for us. It was constructed such that spectators could, and did, stand around and beneath our bridge-like structure, often causing it to vibrate, to our annoyance. We were provided with very heavy chairs, which were difficult to push back easily if one got up from the table. During one broadcast, David Coleman called out for some information and I jumped to my feet, pushing back the chair with some force. Unfortunately, it tumbled back and fell through the gap between the hand rail and the flooring behind me, falling some three metres or so onto the people below. I leapt to the rail to see it land on a local chap's head, and fell him like an ox. He lay there with an enormous cut on his head from which blood gushed. I thought I had killed him. The crowd looked very threatening as I rushed down the ladder, and followed as he was carried away to the medical tent. The situation was not helped by David calling out something to the effect that "You finally got your revenge then" - obviously referring to the Holocaust. He could have got me lynched.

TIMED TO PERFECTION
Stan Greenberg

Happily, the medics brought the man round, patched him up, declared that he was only slightly concussed, but that there would be no permanent damage. I offered profound apologies, which the man graciously accepted, and I very was pleased to notice him watching the rest of the meeting - well away from our position, as were the other spectators. I don't know if it had anything to do with it, but the BBC never sent us back to Coblenz.

ROYALTY

I have been privileged to be invited to Buckingham Palace twice. The first time was for a Royal Garden Party in July 1986, when an invitation arrived from the Lord Chamberlain's office for Carole and I. My name had been put forward by the British Amateur Athletic Board, for whom I had been honorary statistician for nearly 20 years. It was a marvellous afternoon. There were hordes of people, and the police allowed parking on the grass verges around the Palace grounds. My little Renault felt very grand among the Rolls-Royces, Daimlers, Mercedes etc that seemed to be used by everybody else. The Palace grounds are superb, and it was very pleasant to stroll around, away from the milling throng on the lawns. When tea and cakes were served, the resulting 'bun-fight' would not have been amiss at a village fete. The Queen, Duke of Edinburgh, and Prince Charles, made an appearance later in the afternoon, and pathways through the crowd were organised for them to meet certain people. Two of those were a couple we had been talking to when an equerry, who was an old acquaintance of the husband, came by and invited them to be presented. So, it really is a case of who you know!

In January 1988 I made it inside the Palace. It was for a ceremony presenting commemorative pins to all British Olympic medal winners. I had helped the British Olympic Association in tracking down some of those eligible, and was invited to be present when HRH Princess Anne, herself an Olympian, presented the insignia, in one of the grand halls of the palace. Apart from the venue, it was wonderful to have the opportunity to speak to many legendary sporting heroes and heroines.

TIMED TO PERFECTION
Stan Greenberg

SAILING
I am writing this just after Ellen MacArthur had broken the single-handed non-stop round the world record (in just over 71½ days), and it reminded me of the time I met her predecessor, Sir Robin Knox-Johnston, the first to achieve the feat (doing it in 312 days in 1969). He was taken up by the BBC to cover the 1972 Olympic sailing events, and I met him at the airport on the way to Munich. A very hale and hearty individual, he was most pleasant and friendly, and answered my questions, about his epic trip, with great good humour. He did a pretty good job of the Olympic events (actually held at Kiel) as well.

SALT BEEF
One of the foods that I do enjoy is salt beef. Many was the Sunday morning that my father would take me to the Petticoat Lane market in London's East End, where, invariably, while exploring the stalls, we would stop at Bloom's or Barnett's and have a large salt beef sandwich and pickled cucumber. This was despite dire warnings from my mother that we were not to spoil lunch by eating anything.

When I first visited Hawaii in 1974 I came across a delicatessen which had a wall poster which, under a photograph of a typical Hawaiian, stated that "You don't have to be Jewish to enjoy Levy's salt beef". How could I resist? Unfortunately, with a memory of sparse British rail sandwiches at the back of my mind, I ordered two. The waitress expressed some surprise, which should have warned me I suppose, but I explained that I was hungry and could cope. Oh no, I couldn't! Two giant sandwiches arrived, with a vast amount of meat in each one, and in addition there were two large pickled cucumbers, two large portions of coleslaw, and two portions of potato crisps. Very embarrassed, I didn't want to leave anything, so, when no one was looking, I surreptitiously 'fed' the large plant pot nearby with practically three-quarters of my meal.

Visiting New York with Carole, we were invited to lunch by a friend. The New York Deli was very good, and the sandwiches matched those I had had in Hawaii. Carole was shocked by their size, and could only eat half of hers. I fared slightly better, but still had to leave quite a bit on my plate. Our friend, who had ordered the same as us, then proceeded to mop up what we had left. There is no question that Americans in general, and New Yorkers in particular, have far bigger appetites than we poor Brits. Nevertheless, they also waste a phenomenal amount of food.

SCHOOL

I was not a brilliant scholar, but usually made the top quarter of any given class. My favourite subjects were always history, geography and English Lit. I enjoyed the challenge of learning, but did not take kindly to the discipline of doing homework. I much preferred to ride my bicycle or play football - or, indeed, do anything else. Even so, as one of those lucky people stimulated by competition, I did well in examinations. At grammar school, with a special effort in maths, I gained the necessary grades to pass the Matriculation exam. I took 10 subjects (everybody did), including some I hated. My main dislike was chemistry, not really the subject but the teacher who taught it, as I have recounted elsewhere.

My early schooling suffered badly from two things. Firstly, being a timid child, I copped it from all the anti-semitism rife in the schools I attended. Although I did nothing to precipitate trouble (except perhaps do too well at school), I was in more fights than most professional boxers ever will have. I was always on the losing end, as, even on the rare occasion that my opponent was as small and thin as I was, he was invariably backed up by two or three others. Additionally, I had been brought up to 'turn the other cheek', and ironically that attitude gained little favour among my mainly Christian tormentors. Also, many of the teachers showed the same anti-Jewish tendencies as their pupils and, although the victim, I was often treated by them as the perpetrator. This went on throughout my primary schooling, and only stopped when I went to grammar school. No doubt that was because half of that school was also Jewish. On reflection, I still had the odd knock at this school, but at least then it was because I was annoying or a twit, and not just because I was a Jew.

TIMED TO PERFECTION
Stan Greenberg

The second thing that interfered with my education was the War. From the day before War was declared, when most London schoolchildren were evacuated to the country, schooling was upset for some 3-4 years. For various reasons (including that mentioned in the previous paragraph) I would be brought home by my parents and then re-evacuated. During one three-year period I attended 10 different schools, in London or the country. Therefore, I missed out on some important areas. However, everything came together when I won a scholarship to the grammar school. This in itself provides an example of the peripatetic life I was leading then. I sat the examination in Luton in 1942. The news of my pass came when I was back in London. The school that I wished to attend, Hackney Downs (formerly the Grocer's Company) School, was evacuated at Kings Lynn in Norfolk, so I ended up 'based' on Parmiter's in East London. Lastly, I went to Kings Lynn in August 1944, via a brief stay in Manchester, and remained until after VE Day, 1945.

It was in Kings Lynn that my sporting abilities flourished. Always a fast runner, here it was channelled into other sporting activities. For the first time I was available for school teams. Prior to this my father, a religious man, would not let me play games on the Sabbath (Saturday), but away from home, and over 13 years old, he said the responsibility for my religious behaviour was now mine, and that I could do what my conscience dictated. I didn't find it difficult to convince myself that, with the horrors going on in the world, the Almighty wouldn't be too upset if I played football and things.

So, despite a lack of real skill, but a good sense of timing and innate speed, I made the school teams at soccer and cricket. In the latter I stood at the crease with the bat around my neck, baseball style. Sometimes I would score a four, now and then a six, but more often, if it was a straight bowl, I would be out. My bowling was similar - if I could get it straight, its speed and slight spin would get wickets, but I also gave away a number of wides. Unusually, I was selected for the team for my fielding. I rarely let a near ball reach the boundary, could catch well, and I had a good accurate throw.

Briefly I was a schoolmate of Maurice Micklewhite. In the 1945 schoool sports, I gained some second and third places in the under-14 section for Lucas House. The under-12½ 100 yards was won by young Micklewhite, a fellow House member. In later years he achieved somewhat greater fame as movie actor Michael Caine, and mentions the school in his autobiography. Among other schoolmates, who went on to greater things, was the playwright Harold Pinter. At school he was an excellent actor, good sprinter and cricketer.

SHAVING
Greenberg men have tough beards, and I had to shave from a young age. Oddly, my skin was quite tender, and I spent my late teens and early twenties with a permanent sore and cut-marked face. Aside from the agony, it didn't help with my already meager social life. In my late twenties I discovered, or rather could afford, an electric razor, and my life was transformed. It had been a dictum of my father that a man should shave every day, especially if he was in contact with other people. I was now able to shave without the awful cuts and abrasions that I had grown up with. Needless to say I totally abhor the 'macho' pop idiots, and other show biz characters, with their 'designer stubble'. What a nonsense. Call it sheer laziness and I can partially accept the 'fashion'. Similarly soccer players and other sportsmen who take the field unshaven, in the ridiculous assumption that their strength is unimpaired, merely show their sloppiness. A sloppy appearance equals a sloppy performance, on or off the field of play, in sport or in life. A lifetime of observation has indicated nothing to change that view.

SINS
During the service in the synagogue on the Day of Atonement (Yom Kippur), there is one particular passage in the sequence of prayers which lists all the sins for which we ask the Almighty's

forgiveness. I do not intend to be flippant about such a solemn subject, but I don't really understand exactly what some of them are. However, I am sure that I have not committed most of them. Perhaps that is because I am, I think, basically a good person, or perhaps, more likely, I am a bit of a wimp, but I fail to understand why I should admit to crimes and indiscretions of which I am not guilty, neither in deed nor thought. I believe the rabbinical answer is that I am asking forgiveness for all Jewry, and not just on my own behalf. That too I find difficult to accept, as surely even the best of us have enough "dark thoughts" in our souls to atone for, let alone get involved in the sins of others. I understand that other religions have the same attitude to collective guilt, but that doesn't necessarily make it right either.

SKIING

It is a sport that I always meant to try. However, when I was young I only had two weeks leave a year, some of which I took to cover the main Jewish holidays, and there was no way I would sacrifice a summer holiday with what was left. Also, I doubt that could have afforded what was then a very expensive pastime. By the time my leave entitlement had increased, I was married and the children had arrived, and even though my income was better, both time and money were not readily available. Finally, when everything seemed right – time, income, and responsibilities – I felt I was too old for the sport. Now that I am in old age, Carole and I have finally become skiers – but in this case it means we are Spending the Kids Inheritance. And we are really enjoying it!

SLOWLY DOES IT

Among a number of things that Margaret Thatcher, the former Prime Minister, said, which I consider to be nonsense, is the comment that, "A man who finds himself on a bus after the age of 30 can count himself a failure in life". I get the point, but like so much else, she got it all wrong. In my own case I reckon I was a slow developer, not, I think, in an educational sense, as I did quite well at school, but more to do with my social life and work. I was 21 before I went outside England, and up to the age of 35 had only travelled to seven countries. I have currently visited 50 countries. I didn't get married until I was 29, and took my first flight a year later. I only learnt to drive at 33, started working for the BBC, part-time, when I was 37, and became Sports Editor of the *Guinness Book of Records* at 45. I wrote my first book at 50, visited Asia at 57, Africa at 61, and finally made it to South America aged 72 - and I often travel by bus.

SPOKEN WORD

Twice in recent weeks I have been reduced to laughter by quite straight forward announcements on the radio/TV. The first, related to a music programme, and the statement that the next piece was to be performed by the West Kazakhstan Symphony Orchestra - I can't explain but I found that very funny. The second item only means anything to anyone who has heard the famous comedy baseball routine by Abbott and Costello. The BBC commentator at an athletics match between the USA, Britain, Russia and China, listed the runners in the Chinese relay team with the words "Hu's on first and Wen's on third". My wife and I curled up. It's no good trying to explain. If you don't know the routine, it just isn't funny.

SPECIALISATION

I realise that it is probably necessary these days to specialise in a subject, but I fear it has been taken too far by education experts (if there are such people). It was brought home to me on one occasion while I was working in the Economics and Statistics Department at Unilever. Back in the sixties, not much interest was shown in, and little known about, Ethiopia. Then, the Queen visited the country, and things started to take off. At Unilever there was some thought given to the sale of its products there, and consideration was given to the possibility of even manufacturing in that country. Therefore, some of the department's economists were given the job of writing a detailed report on the country. When it was eventually published, on a very restricted circulation, it received tremendous praise from former embassy staff and other expatriates, who found it difficult to believe that such an excellent job had been done by people who had never been to the country. What they didn't know was that initially the team who compiled the report weren't even sure where the country was. I used to have a map of the world on the wall behind my desk, and, on the day that the order came down from the Board, the members of the team, all quite brilliant in their own area of expertise, congregated around the map – and couldn't find the country. At first, they were actually searching for it in South America - I had to direct them to East Africa. So much for a general education.

SPEED
I have always liked the sensation of speed, and therefore have taken an interest in it. When, some years ago, a friend of mine offered to give me a ride back down the M1 from Leicester in his new Mercedes I was very pleased. However, I was also somewhat worried as we hurtled along, albeit not on a crowded motorway, at speeds exceeding 100mph, passing at least three police cars that I saw. Remarkably they didn't seem to take any notice - either they thought they could never catch us, or perhaps they were just admiring the car. On another occasion, again on the M1, I was with Ron Pickering, who also liked driving fast. He was particularly annoyed when, although well exceeding the speed limit, he was hooted by another car behind us. Despite increasing his speed slightly, the hooting didn't stop, so very reluctantly he moved into an inside lane, as the other car shot past. A Porsche, it had the frightening number plate of 140 MPH.

Not being able to afford, or indeed to want, a powerful car, nevertheless I have tried, in safe circumstances, to see what my own vehicles could do. The highest speed that I have reached, going downhill on the M1, has been fractionally over 161km/h 100mph - at which speed my cars tend to strain and leap about a bit. The greatest land speed that I have travelled at is the 300km/h

186mph achieved on the Eurostar train when it gets onto French rails.

SPICY FOOD

My father could and did eat the spiciest food imaginable, and so I grew up with a taste for some spicy items, but I came across one such food in Seoul which, I am sure, even my father would have avoided. On the last night of the 1988 Olympic Games, Ron Pickering insisted that I join him and the others at a meal in our hotel's famous rooftop restaurant. He knew that I had been working so hard that I had not had a really decent meal throughout the Games, and said that the restaurant was excellent, with a tremendous choice. When I met them upstairs there was a truly magnificent buffet laid out, containing every type of food imaginable, so that even with my picky ways I had no problem finding things that I liked. Including, I thought, pickled cucumber. Now that is a 'delicacy' to which I am very partial, and I was slightly surprised to find it available there. So it was that with my first bite of food I took up a sizeable piece of the pickled cucumber - and probably set a world record for the standing high jump. I leapt to my feet, gasping, my mouth burning, and my eyes full of tears. I grabbed the cold drink in front of me and swallowed all of it at one go. Spluttering and yelling I danced about like the proverbial dervish. After they had calmed me down, Ron casually remarked that he had been surprised that I had taken that particular item, but had not wished to put me off, as so often, in various parts of the world, he had chided me for not trying the local delicacies. It seems that what I had thought was pickled cucumber, was an extremely 'hot' Korean dish called Kim Chi. Remember the name, and avoid it like the plague.

STAMP OF APPROVAL

The day I was married is almost a total blank in my memory. I think I passed the day in a trance. Not that I had any last-minute doubts about taking the step, but due to my nervousness of 'performing' in front of people. I knew I had to make a speech during the proceedings, and I was in a blue funk about it. Thanks to much pre-planning, all the arrangements went perfectly and I understand from guests that it was a wonderful wedding, but I can only recall a few minor details. There was one which drew a lot of attention to myself, the last thing I wanted. In the Jewish wedding service there is a point when the groom breaks a glass tube, symbolically remembering the destruction of the Temple in ancient times.

During the service, my mind, already in a turmoil, wandered from what the rabbi was saying, and I had terrible thoughts about missing the glass when I stamped on it. I was wearing new shoes and worried that it might slip beneath the heel and leave me jumping up and down like a lunatic trying to break it. When the moment came I was wound up like a spring, and stamped down with incredible force, causing the whole synagogue to shake, and everyone there gave an involuntary jump. I certainly broke the glass - and probably part of the floor too.

STARS
When I was evacuated to Manchester during WWII, a chap who lived next door to the people I stayed with was very interested in astronomy. He taught me quite a lot about the heavens, in particular the star patterns, and how to find them. Even today, I find myself looking up on a clear night - all too few in the London area I am afraid - and pinpointing Orion's belt, the Big and Little Dippers (or the Great and Little Bears, okay, Ursa Major and Ursa Minor if you insist), and the North Star. On my first trip to the Southern Hemisphere, to New Zealand, I excitedly looked for the Southern Cross. Having trouble finding it, I asked the hotel desk clerk for guidance. Despite the fact that the constellation forms part of the national flag, neither he nor his colleague were able to help. Eventually, another guest pointed it out to me. As a postscript, when I went to Cuzco, in Peru, the stars were clearer and bigger than I had ever seen them. Undoubtedly due to the altitude, the Southern Cross was enormous in the night sky.

TIMED TO PERFECTION
Stan Greenberg

In the film *Singing in the Rain*, there is a scene in which the 'villainess' Lina Lamont (played by Jean Hagen) refers to herself as "A star in the cinema firmament". This quickly became a family catchphrase in the Greenberg household, slightly corrupted to "A star of the firmament". Imagine my delight, and the family's chagrin, when on a recent visit to the optician, she revealed that I actually had 'stars in my eyes'. Apparently, some people (very few I hasten to add) have a sparkle effect in the main liquid of the eye, thankfully not dangerous, but quite entertaining to an optician. It is not something that one would make a fuss of, of course, but if one does have something special about one..........

STINGY
I don't think that I can be accused of stinginess, but I will admit to being careful with money. Coming from my comparatively poor background I think that this attitude is understandable. I don't mind spending money, if we have it to spend, but I do tend to think first about what else it could be used for. (See "Debt" re my I.S.)

However, on one occasion this carefulness almost cost me very dear, and I don't mean in money terms. On the way to the 1991 World Athletics Championships, to be held in Tokyo, I realised I had the chance to fulfil a long-held ambition, and I stopped off at Delhi for a few days. The specific intention was to visit the Taj Mahal in Agra, though I also took the opportunity to see something of the Indian capital. I hadn't reckoned on how far away Agra was, and the only sensible method of getting there was by hire car. When I went to book it, the prices of the vehicles, albeit with driver/guide, went from quite pricey to excessive, and I originally decided on the cheapest. However, on enquiring how long it would take, and being informed that we were talking about four hours each way, my financial caution was overcome by the need for some comfort on such a journey. So I went for a more expensive vehicle, thank goodness - and probably saved my life. What I hadn't considered, or indeed enquired about, was that the cheaper models did not have air-conditioning, and with the temperature up in the low 40s centigrade, I think I would have died. As it was, it was a very tiring journey, but comfortable, with a most pleasant and knowledgeable driver, and was well worth whatever I paid. In a number of ways it taught me a lesson.

STYLE

At the end of 1979 I attended the Jerusalem Book Fair representing the *Guinness Book of Records*, and helped man a stand containing the other books that the company published at that time. I was there with the managing director, David Hoy, who insisted that, despite the intense heat in the Fair building, we maintain a high standard of dress. Therefore we wore jackets and ties every day, and although I protested continually that we would look much tidier and smart if we weren't perspiring so much, he was adamant. It seemed that his attitude would be justified on the last day, when it was announced that the President of Israel, Yitzhak Navon, was coming around to view all the stands. When he came by, it was very noticeable that he, and his entire entourage, were dressed casually, all with open-necked shirts, albeit extremely smart, and I pointedly noted the fact to David.

SUITCASES

When I first began travelling a great deal with the BBC I used an old expanding suitcase to carry all my stuff. This included an inordinate number of books, as it was prior to the computer era – or, at least, I was – and I needed all my sources of information with me. The case, made of compressed cardboard I believe, had belonged to my father, and served me well. That is until the fateful day when leaving a hotel somewhere abroad I found myself carrying just the handle – the rest of the case just sat there on the pavement. Unrepairable, this caused me serious problems on that trip, but I was somewhat mollified by the producer telling me he would stump up for a new suitcase when we got home.

With his agreement I decided to lash out and get a good, strong, case, and went to a major store in the West End to buy it. I emerged with a solid, hard-bodied, wheeled case, with a very strong, well-embedded, handle. The point of the story is that at the end of the financial year I passed the invoice, with everything else, to my accountant. It should be noted that the hand-written invoice merely stated the word 'Delsey' followed by a rather large sum of money. So perhaps it was not so surprising to receive a phone call from said accountant asking, quite indignantly it seemed, what I was doing trying to claim on a large purchase of toilet rolls.

SWANS

I have vivid memories of that beautiful bird, the swan. The first was when friends and I spent a pleasant afternoon rowing on the River Lea in London. Two of us, side by side single-oared, were trying to raise a 'good head of steam', exhorted by another friend acting as cox. As we passed by, a swan, which, I later realised, was guarding a nest, became very agitated. To my horror, it spread its vast wingspan, rose up on the water, with neck and beak outstretched, and, surprisingly quietly, made straight for us. My fellow oarsman and I were facing it, and, as one, proceeded to stroke in a manner likely to get us into the Olympic team. Our friend, the cox, unaware of the danger, cheered lustily, congratulating himself on his fine coaching. We really did move at a remarkable pace for a short time, long enough to leave the swan's territory. As it was almost upon us it suddenly subsided into the water with a mighty splash. At this the 'cox' turned and for the first time was made aware of what had caused our spurt. The look on his face was well worth the total exhaustion that was coming over me. It took us a long time to muster enough courage to return past the spot - in order to return the boat. This time we hugged the opposite shore and very, very slowly eased our way past, as the swan eyed us all the time. It was a long while before we rowed on the Lea again, and then it was in the opposite direction.

Another recollection of swans was more pleasant. On our honeymoon, Carole and I stayed at the Hotel du Pont in Lucerne, and our room overlooked the famous Chapel Bridge and Water Tower on the River Reuss as it enters the Lake. Every morning and evening there were flocks of swans beneath our window. It added a wonderful, romantic, touch. Sadly, the hotel is now defunct.

SWEET TOOTH
All my life, I have had a 'sweet tooth', eating far more sweets and chocolate than is good for me. When young, it didn't affect my weight as I was so active. However, undeniably, as I have got older it greatly contributes to a weight problem. Munching a toffee or some chocolate undoubtedly helps me in time of stress. So it was, one evening during our courtship, after a rare tiff with Carole, I approached the chocolate cream bar machine on Golder's Green station. This machine had cheated me on many occasions, not delivering the bar after taking my money. Usually it was too late to complain to station staff, and invariably the last train was ready to go. This particular evening I was seething, because of our row, and I intended to deal with the machine forcibly, if it failed again. Luckily it didn't, and I got in the waiting train, slouched in a seat, muttered about the foibles of women, and broke open the bar - to find that it was solid all the way through, with no cream. My anger really welled up, and stayed with me until I got home, well past midnight. A name, Bond's, was on the wrapper, but no address. The phone book listed a Bond's confectionery firm in North London. So at 1.00am I wrote a pointed letter about their product, and the dastardly machine which dispensed it, or rather didn't. I also enclosed the broken bar.

A day or two later, I received a pleasant reply from the company, noting that the product was not theirs, but of another company, Bond's of Bristol, which they were "happy to say" had no connection with them. Also, they said, they were "pleased" to pass on my complaint. A week later a letter came from Bristol, unstamped, on which my mother had to pay excess postage. It was very formal and trite, informing me of the wonderful mechanical process by which the product was made, and that such an error could not happen. However, as I had enclosed the evidence, somehow it had, and I would be receiving a suitable replacement. Now, friends had told me stories of similar occasions when they had complained about various foodstuffs, and had received wonderful boxes of goods, as an apology for the inconvenience. I had visions of, at least, a large box of chocolates. Some days later, my irate mother informed me that she had had to pay yet more excess postage, this time on a small parcel, which again had no stamps on it. On being opened it revealed a small, very small, package of chocolate creams, worth about the same value as the bar I had returned. Although annoyed, I had to smile as I wrote direct to the managing director of the Bristol company, giving details of the whole sorry tale, and ending with the statement "Please do not answer this letter as I CANNOT AFFORD IT".

TACTICS
The reader would have noticed that I have a tendency to note sayings and quotations, and apply them to myself or my life when I think there is a connection. I pick them up from all sorts of sources, and the latest one is from the world of chess. The Polish chess master Tartakover once said that "Tactics is knowing what to do when there is something to do. Strategy is knowing what to do when there is nothing to do". I particularly like the comment, and have a feeling that it is relevant to something, sometime, in my life, but I cannot think exactly what at the moment.

TALKING TO ONESELF
Come on, we all do it, some more consciously than others. Usually it is a case of cursing oneself, or indeed others, under one's breath. However, I admit to having quite long talks with myself when I am alone. Actually, I find that I can often clear my mind about something troubling me if I discuss it with myself. Speaking aloud seems to focus the problem much better. For one thing, I am a very sympathetic listener to me, and, of course, I fully understand any foibles or shortcomings that I suffer from. Similarly, when in the process of writing, I find that ideas and phrases are more likely to present themselves when thought about out loud. My wife tells me that I sometimes do it when I am asleep, but apparently I am mainly unintelligible, and that annoys her tremendously. As far as I know I don't do it in public, but anyway even if I did, I don't think I would

worry about it too much. There are at least a couple of strong motives for my talking to myself: (1) I know I am going to get a decent, intelligent, conversation, with no obscenities; and, (2) I never try to put myself down or score points. I ask you, what more can the two of us possibly want? Yes, doctor, I'll lie back quietly now.

TARZAN

My earliest hero was Tarzan - the mythical character dreamed up by Edgar Rice Burroughs. When I was young I read every book featuring him that I could get my hands on, and saw and re-saw every film which appeared about him. I could, and did, climb trees better than any of my contemporaries, having practised tirelessly on a very tall tree which stood at the end of the garden of the house my family occupied for the first seven or eight years of my life. I would regularly go to Epping Forest, in north-east London, and spend countless hours climbing, and one of the few things that made wartime evacuation bearable was the joy of being out 'in the country' where there were ever more trees to test myself on. Up to the age of 65, I took great pride in climbing the apple tree in my garden each year, collecting the fruit. Coincidentally, considering my later interests, the two best film Tarzans were Johnny Weissmuller, a five-time Olympic swimming gold medalllist, and Bruce Bennett (né Herman Brix) who won the silver medal in the 1928 Olympic shot event.

TAXIS

London's taxis are famed for their remarkable manoeuvrability - indeed with the city's narrow twisting streets they need it. The best comment to illustrate this was made on television some years ago, during an interview with the ultra-wealthy Nubar Gulbenkian. He was asked why, despite his riches, he rode around London in his own taxi. He answered that it was much easier to get around that way, and, with a wicked twinkle in his eye, said, "You know it is said that they are able to turn on a sixpence - whatever that may be!"

One of the greatest treats I could be given when I was small was

TIMED TO PERFECTION
Stan Greenberg

to be taken in a taxi. It didn't happen very often, but now and again, after visiting relatives, particularly on a rainy night, my dad would hire a taxi to take us home. Remember, this was in the days before most people had cars, and therefore to ride in a vehicle other than a bus was very, very rare. In fact, at that time, I suppose about 1936-37, nobody we knew had a car, and mass private ownership was still well in the future.

What is it about driving a taxi that affects financial morals? That will not endear me to friends who operate taxis, so I will say that there are always exceptions. However, I have been 'done' on so many occasions by drivers of taxis, minicabs and the like. No matter what country, what city, in what language, I, and fellow travellers, seem to be easy meat. The fact that we have usually arrived after a long, tiring, journey, probably makes us even more susceptible. Whatever the reason, I have been 'taken to the cleaners' in Paris, Mexico City, New York, Los Angeles, Rome and Bangkok, as well as London.

TEA
Plain tea is my hot drink of choice. I abhor herb and fruit teas, positively dislike coffee, and don't mind hot chocolate in cold weather. In my parents' house tea was virtually an elixir of life, to be had at times of great joy and of great sadness, of stress and celebration, and when one just wanted a drink. I found it a true lifesaver on my athletics trips around the world. I never travelled without a portable 'kettle', tea bags and some of those little pots of UHT milk which one can obtain at motorway service stops. With my collection of various plugs, I could make myself a cuppa whenever I wanted or needed it. Often it was the only thing between me and night starvation on trips when I had to work late into the night, not having eaten nor drunk for hours. I only had a problem on one or two occasions when there were apparently no sockets in the hotel room. One such time, in the Soviet Union, I was up very late and badly required a cup of tea. Room service was out of the question, and there was no socket available. I wandered out into the corridor, and found a socket near the lift. As it was so late I doubted that

anyone would be about, so I plugged in - there was a small explosion and all the lights in the corridor went out. I quickly scurried back to my room, and went without that night. Ironically, the next night I found a 'hidden' socket behind my bed, and all was well. On another occasion, somewhere else, the only socket I could find was the main light in the centre of the room - it worked very well, although I had to support the kettle in my hands as it heated up, as the cord was not long enough to reach any surface.

One of the most memorable cuppas I can remember was on a trip to Scotland with my wife and children. Forward planning had ensured that we had a small camping gas appliance, with appropriate canister, and a kettle, tea and milk. We stopped in Glencoe, scene of the massacre of the MacDonalds in 1692, a truly eerie place flanked by high (3000ft *915m* plus) mountains. We brewed-up with ice cold water from the meandering brook and had our drink listening to the wind - at least I think it was the wind - moaning through the glen.

TECHNOLOGY
When young I was amazed at the telephone, but today there is new technology everywhere. In ordinary homes, there are word processors, personal computers, satellite television, video machines, Ipods, Ipads, Kindles, CD and/or DVD players and music centres. However, I used to think that one of the most remarkable innovations is facsimile transmission - or fax. I recall a key scene in a Film Noir thriller in the 1940s when a picture of the killer was being sent from New York to Los Angeles by such a transmission. The suspense was terrific as it came through, building up the photo with horizontal lines, until the audience saw who was the villain. I thought then how marvellous, little realising that one day I would have such a machine myself.

My friends will be disappointed if I don't make some comment about computers. My attitude is summed up by a notice in my study, which states: "To err is human. To really louse things up takes a computer". Of course, it is not the machines themselves which cause the trouble, but their adherents, who look on the damn things as divine instruments. So we have the situation, with no paper backup kept, when, not if, but when, the computer breaks down, all hell breaks loose. A while ago I was going abroad, so I called into the building society to get some money. I couldn't because the computer was being overhauled. Then I went to my bank, to be informed that their computer was 'down' and nothing could transpire for a few hours. The following day I arrived at Heathrow, early as usual, and pleased to note there was only one couple in front of me at the check-in desk. Forty-five minutes later I was still there. The airport computer was not operational, and nothing worked. No baggage could move, no boarding tickets could be issued, no indicator boards worked.

With the memory of those two days, and the wider proliferation of computers since then, I firmly believe that any day now, the world will break. In other words, nothing will work - anywhere. Remember you were warned here first. One last thing, and I won't mention the beastly things again. My views gained more credibility at the Atlanta Olympic Games when the much-heralded computer information system was a complete mess. Of course, that was reflecting the rank arrogance of computer companies, who will never ask advice of people who know the problems which need solving. Incidentally, I did use a computer for this book - so perhaps there's hope for me yet.

TELEPHONE BOXES

I have fond memories of some strange things, and among them are telephone boxes. One I clearly remember was in the wilds of the Scottish highlands. Miles from any habitation, there was a faded red box sitting forlornly at the crossroads of two minor roads. On closer inspection I could see that the framework of the box was peppered with buckshot, leaving it resembling a good quality Swiss cheese. One presumes that the local poachers gave vent to their frustrations every now and again. I didn't check to see if the phone actually worked.

TIMED TO PERFECTION
Stan Greenberg

Another box with conflicting memories was one which used to be just off Moorgate, in London. It was from there that I rang to try and arrange my first ever date with a girl. Really, she was far too sophisticated for me, but I had met her and been smitten at a party held by a cousin, and had been trying to get up the nerve to ring for some time. On this particular evening I had just left evening classes, very boring stuff on the law of sea transport, and had finally mustered the courage to make the call. However, I had spent what seemed like hours walking up and down the pavement - the groove can still be seen - before I entered the box, and dialled. The girl in question, whose name I cannot now remember, agreed to come out at the weekend, but I do recall that the 'date', expensive and embarrassing, was an unmitigated disaster - which put me off such things for many a year.

TELEPHONES
The telephone was once described as being the work of the Devil, and, no offense to Alexander Graham Bell, I sometimes agree. When I started work I was terrified of the thing, and if on my own when the telephone rang, I would run out of the office. On one auspicious occasion I took an urgent call that a car was required for a director, without finding out when it was required, or actually who it was for. I have always had difficulty recognising voices on the telephone, and have been in the predicament of being given a personal message, and then having to ask them who they are. When it turns out to be one's daughter, wife, or best friend, it can be quite disconcerting - to them if not to me.

Akin to Attila the Hun, one of the worst scourges of all time is the mobile telephone. Naturally, it is of great help to certain types of businesses, and undoubtedly to lone women out at night, but the misuse of them seems to outweigh their advantages. Idiot drivers are constantly seen trying to negotiate heavy traffic or a roundabout while speaking on one, and we have all been passed on the motorway, usually at excessive speed, by similar morons. One is continually disturbed in meetings, restaurants, even at weddings and the theatre by the little horrors. Once, in Florida, I was relaxing by the pool when I heard the tell-tale ring. I glanced up, to see a chap in the middle of the pool talking on his mobile. What puzzles me is this. If the 'phone was by the side of the pool when he was swimming, he didn't have time to pick it up when it rang and then walk back into the centre of the pool - nor would he have wanted to surely. Therefore, it can only mean that he was actually swimming with it. How important can your business be? Or is it merely ornamentation and ostentation.

TELEVISION TIMES

Despite my 26 year connection with the BBC, the first television work I did was for ITV. Early in 1964 I had a call from a senior producer, Tim Hewat, an Australian, inviting me to lunch to discuss my helping in their London studio during the forthcoming Olympics. He was with another producer, Graham Turner, and they explained that while the main ITV operation would be in Tokyo, the linking would be done from London, by Kent Walton, the wrestling commentator. He would be aided by journalist Frank Keating, but they needed someone with specialist knowledge to check that no errors were made. As Tokyo was 9 hours ahead of London it meant that most of the action would take place early in the morning. I did a good job, got a bonus on top of the agreed fee, and went home to my wife and young baby feeling very pleased. As well as the money, I had seen far more of the Games than the average viewer, and as a fan that was great.

I thought that this was a good way of widening my sports viewing, as well as an additional source of income, so I wrote to ITV enquiring if they would want me again for the Commonwealth Games in 1966. The Games came and went and I heard nothing, so I asked about the 1968 Olympics. Again no answers, either to letters or 'phone calls. Having given up hope, just before the Mexico Games, out of the blue, I had a call from Norris McWhirter. I had met him initially in the late fifties when he and his twin, Ross, published an excellent athletics magazine. As it was available only by subscription, and his office was near my workplace, I would go there on publication day - thus getting my copy a day or two earlier

TIMED TO PERFECTION
Stan Greenberg

than my friends (a great act of one-upmanship). Over time I got to know the twins and later helped them in compiling athletics ranking lists for their column in the late-lamented evening paper *The Star*. Norris, who was also a TV commentator, explained that he had been left in London deliberately by the BBC, to cover any breaks in the sound transmission. Apparently, the TV pictures were transmitted by satellite, but the sound travelled by land/under-sea line, and not infrequently the line broke. Norris was to add commentary to any pictures which arrived sound-less. He suggested that I might like to help him. A small fee was also mentioned. As the time factor worked in my favour (Mexico was about 7 hours behind London), I was able to go straight from work to the studio, and be taken home by taxi early in the morning. We were called into play on at least one occasion and I proved my worth. Also we sent bits of information down the line to the office in Mexico City which they used. Specifically, when Bob Beamon did his amazing long jump of 8.90m *29ft 2½in,* I suggested that if the viewer was in an ordinary suburban home, it was as if someone leapt in their front room window and left by their backroom window. That was used over the air. After that, in 1969, I was asked to provide statistics and other information for Norris, and then Ron Pickering, in coverage of some minor meetings. Finally I was invited to the White City to assist David Coleman at one of the big Bank Holiday occasions.

It was the start of 26 years of fascinating travel, intense work, high excitement, and incredible interest. My first important broadcast, on site, was at Edinburgh for the 1970 Commonwealth Games, when I worked myself, literally, into a state of exhaustion. The day after the Games ended I offered a friend a lift back to London. Not far from Edinburgh he offered to drive, and we changed seats. Apparently, as I fastened my seat belt my head went back and I was gone. He couldn't wake me when he stopped for refreshments, and I only woke when we arrived home in north London. However, it was worth it, as from then on I was a permanent member of the BBC commentary team, and attended all the major championships around the world, plus many other meets, for the next 25 years.

TIMED TO PERFECTION
Stan Greenberg

Initially, it was still a hobby, as from 1968 to 1976 I was working for the GLC - luckily with excellent holiday entitlement. Then I was with Norris at the *Guinness Book of Records* till 1981. In that year I found the two jobs were just too much for my advancing years, and I became a free-lance, working primarily on a BBC contract. "From little acorns ......etc etc".

I am proud of the fact that, in my own small way, I think I helped change the face of television athletics coverage. By providing ever increasing data about competing athletes, I enabled more confident and interesting commentaries to be given. Due to this the sport gained more appeal to viewers, and the powers-that-be gave more and longer broadcasts of home and foreign athletics. Foreign TV and radio companies saw the help I gave to our people, and they began to employ statisticians, in turn leading to their better coverage. In Europe athletics grew into one of the most popular sports on television, and thus provided it with increased sponsorship and revenues. Not all of this was due to my efforts, of course, but I reckon I did have something to do with it. I was fortunate to work with some of the best people in TV sport. It is invidious to name only some of them but particularly significant to me were David Coleman, Ron Pickering, Stuart Storey, Paul Fox, 'Ginger' Cowgill, Harry Carpenter, David Vine, Barry Davies, John Shrewsbury, Paul Dickenson and Martin Webster. Mostly it was wonderful, with many highs - albeit a few downs. I will never forget the companionship, the banter, and, not least, the great feeling of a job well done.

TEMPER
Earlier, I mentioned my father's temper. There were two unfortunate consequences of it - both myself and my son, Keith, have inherited it, in spades as our American friends say. I don't lose mine often, but when I do it tends to be fairly 'spectacular'. When I was with the BBC athletics team, my stand-up rows with David Coleman became legendary. They were never really personal, but invariably brought on by the stresses under which we worked, he in his field and me in mine. When I retired, he referred to them with

TIMED TO PERFECTION
Stan Greenberg

some nostalgia. Elsewhere, on a more personal level, I lost my cool completely at work once when I was in the library at the GLC. One of the women, at my grade but much younger, was, to put it mildly, somewhat bossy, and tended to give advice where it wasn't appreciated. She was not an unpleasant girl, and usually I wasn't bothered by her attitude. However, on one occasion she really got to me. I just erupted, screaming a few home truths at her - but no obscenities, I hasten to add - in an excessively loud voice. She was shell-shocked, and backed away hurriedly, while other colleagues and visitors to the library looked on in horror. Nobody had ever seen the 'mild-mannered' Greenberg in temper mode before. I immediately reported myself to the head librarian, apologising for my behaviour in relation to the library's reputation, but not for my reaction to the lady in question. Interestingly, he only gave me a mild reprimand, as I think he had also 'suffered' on occasion. She was very careful in her dealings with me after that, and it seems that the experience, not to be repeated, had a good effect on working conditions in that office.

TERRORISM
The recent screening of a film, about the murder of 11 Israeli sportsmen at the Munich Olympics, brought the whole ghastly episode back to me. It was the first Games I had been to in 20 years, and was the first that I had attended with the BBC, for whom I was working very hard to prove my worth. Already there had been five hectic days of athletics, and the 5 September was a rest day, for the athletes and also for people like me. Two days before, my friend Alf Wilkins had introduced me to the Israeli lady hurdler, Ester Shakhamurov, and her coach, Amitzur Shapira. She was in good form and they hoped that she would become the first from her country to make it into an Olympic athletics final. By pure coincidence, the BBC commentary position in the stadium was next to that of Israeli TV, headed by Nissim Kivity, later to become a good friend. However, that rest day morning I was awoken by loud knocking on my bedroom door. It was an ashen-faced Ron Pickering, who told me to get dressed quickly as there was serious trouble. By the time I reached the BBC office I knew the story. Arab

terrorists had stormed into the Israeli team quarters in the village, killed some people, and now held hostages. The BBC office was overlooking the street where it was all happening, and going outside I had a 'front-row seat' to what was going on. At one point I could see the balaclava-wearing terrorist on the balcony - a TV picture that went around the world - while all about me were hundreds of armed German police and soldiers. I found that it all got to me quite badly, and I eventually had to go back to my room. The TV gave details of what had happened, what was supposed to happen, and finally the debacle at the airport which ended tragically with the deaths of all the Israelis - including the aforementioned Shapira. The following day there was a very moving memorial service in the stadium, to which David Coleman gave perhaps his greatest-ever 'commentary'. After much debate, it was decided that the Games should continue - a decision that was supported by the Israelis, with the attitude that the terrorists must not be allowed to win. There were some great sporting achievements in the following days, but my heart really wasn't in it any more, and I was very pleased when I got home. Incidentally, and perhaps not surprisingly, I didn't go to see the film.

In the 1980s, I visited Belfast on a couple of occasions. It was rather worrying to find the front of the hotel protected by a sandbag barrier, and when I went for a walk, forewarned about where not to go. There was a very odd atmosphere, to put it mildly. On one early season trip, Ron Pickering, Stuart Storey, myself and a producer were driving along a main road, all bundled up against the cold in anoraks and scarves, when we were flagged down by armed soldiers at a checkpoint. They were quite brusque about us getting out of the car, until one of them recognised Ron, and everyone relaxed. It occurred to me later that probably we did look rather suspicious - four 'toughies' in a car, undoubtedly exceeding the speed limit, as was Ron's wont.

TEXAS
Sometimes one hears a funny punch line that one would dearly love to use, but, because it requires special circumstances to exist

TIMED TO PERFECTION
Stan Greenberg

before it will make sense, you cannot. I heard such a punch line in a movie, and after years of hoping, despaired of ever being able to use it myself. Then the opportunity came, in, of all places, the Soviet Union. In Kiev, for a GB v USSR match, our hotel was shared by a group of American students on a tour. One was a pretty, talkative, girl who was very proud of her home state, Texas. My heart skipped a beat when I heard this and shamelessly I egged her conversation on in the direction that I prayed she would go. Indeed she did, and, goaded by the teasing, made the claim all Texans eventually make - about how big the state is. As I held my breath, she gave me the lead line for which I had waited so many years. With a ringing voice she declared that she could leave her house in the morning, drive off in her car, and by nightfall she would still be in Texas. In the momentary hush that followed I uttered the line that I had rehearsed so many times. "Oh", I said, "I used to have a car like that". I felt as though a great weight had been lifted from me.

A few years later it happened again, in a clothes shop in Hawaii. Nearby was a lady, whose husband wore a big stetson proclaiming his origins. When the saleslady asked where they came from, he boomed out that they were from Texas, and before I could collect my thoughts, he followed that with the optimum remark about driving his car etc etc. As my wife coughed in embarrassment, I quickly made my treasured comment. It got a puzzled reaction from the Texan gentleman and his wife, but I was more than recompensed by the peals of laughter from the quick-witted saleslady. Carole quickly removed me from the shop, and I now await my third opportunity.

THEATRE
The theatre has always appealed to me, but my preference has been mainly for comedies and musicals rather than heavy drama. There are three particularly entertaining occasions which stick in my mind. Early in 1948 the London Palladium began a series of variety shows which had a famous show business person (usually a film star) as the headliner. Remember, in those pre-TV days, film

TIMED TO PERFECTION
Stan Greenberg

actors and actresses were the pre-eminent personalities, much more recognisable and admired than pop singers or stage actors. The first headliner had been Mickey Rooney, who was panned by the critics. The next 'star' was Danny Kaye, relatively unknown in Britain, although he had made two very funny films. Having enjoyed those, my friends and I had booked to see him at the end of his first week, by which time he was a smash hit. He was a good-looking man with a shock of red/gold hair and a pleasant voice. That alone doesn't explain the atmosphere he created. It was electric, and the audience wouldn't let him leave the stage. The show we saw lasted until past midnight, by which time he was seated on the edge of the stage, feet dangling into the orchestra pit, singing a variety of songs. Some of these were the 'nonsense' ditties, written by his wife, Sylvia Fine, which were his trademark. He involved the audience in them, persuading staid, stuffy, people to make the oddest noises as part of the background to a song. In fact, his audiences worked quite hard - and loved it. Perhaps that was the secret, the one all the great vaudeville performers had known. Get your audience involved. Kaye was a sensation, was held over for an additional two weeks, and even the Royal Family came. Tickets for his show sold on a black market like those for the Cup Final.

As I have written elsewhere, I am a fervent Gershwin fan, and a dream came true in October 1952 when a touring company of *Porgy and Bess* appeared at the old Stoll theatre. The cast included a young Leontyne Price, William Warfield, and the jazz scat singer Cab Calloway. The opera, was wonderful, and I was overwhelmed by it all. I whistled the tunes incessantly for the next six months. Then, in February 1967, my wife and I had the good fortune, courtesy of her uncle, to be in the stalls during the first week of *Fiddler on the Roof*, starring Topol. I was mesmerised by the show, as virtually everything that I saw on stage seemed to be exactly what my father had told me of his early days in the Ukraine. As most of the audience seemed to have the same basic roots, it was a great evening.

Over the years I have kept the programmes of every show, play

TIMED TO PERFECTION
Stan Greenberg

and concert I ever attended - they make fascinating reading now, especially looking at the casts with the benefit of hindsight. For many years my friends and I regularly attended the variety shows presented at the Palladium and London Casino theatres and the supporting casts would include various up-and-coming British acts. Among these I note that I first saw the then new comedians Max Bygraves, Ted Ray and Norman Wisdom. Among the many stage musicals I saw in the 1950s were *South Pacific,* in which I note that one of the minor roles was taken by somebody named Larry Hagman (later the infamous J R Ewing in *Dallas* on TV). Also in that show were the then virtual unknowns, Ivor Emmanuel, June Whitfield and Joyce Blair. Similarly, in the 1949 production of *High Button Shoes* , I see from the threepenny (old money) programme that two of the chorus girls were Alma Cogan and Audrey Hepburn. Well down the cast list in Cole Porter's *Can Can* in 1955 was Warren Mitchell, while in 1975's *Kismet* was Juliet Prowse. In 1953 at the Palladium, supporting singer Tennessee Ernie Ford, were Morecambe and Wise - the first time I saw them. Interestingly, in the early 1950s, tickets for the stalls and grand circle cost £1.00.

Perhaps the most enjoyable experience that I ever had in the theatre was at the one-man show given by Victor Borge at the Palace, Cambridge Circus, when, alone on the stage with just a piano, he had a vast audience screaming with laughter. It reminded me that the first time I had ever heard of him was during World War II, when I used to listen to the American Forces Network (AFN) on the radio. They used to broadcast America's top radio shows for their troops in Europe, and I listened to them regularly. One of them was the Bing Crosby Show, and I remember that on one particular show he had started with a song, as usual, and then introduced 'a comedy act new to America'. It was the first time that I had ever heard the famous *Phonetic Alphabet* routine. However, I also remember that this new act went on for a remarkably long time, and that the final announcements came without Crosby singing again. I assumed that Crosby must have been taken ill or something. It was only many years later that I discovered that the show was the American debut of Borge, and Crosby, who apparently rarely attended rehearsals of his show, had never heard the Dane before. He was so incapacitated by laughter that he couldn't go on again, a fact which, when it reached the media, gave Borge the best publicity of his life and set him on the road to fame.

THEY

Aside from its prosaic status as a pronoun, the word 'they' seems to have taken on a whole new, sometimes sinister, meaning in this day and age. Consider how often one hears the phrases, 'they all do it', 'they say so', 'they reckon it's terrible' etc. Who are they? There is undoubtedly a stricture from 'them' about almost anything you want to do, and 'they' have opinions on every film, play, concert, holiday resort, car, foodstuff and person that you may be interested in. I used to imagine that there were three or four superior beings sitting on a high mountain somewhere, issuing directives about everything under the sun. However, I now realise that 'they' are merely an imaginary authority used by insignificant people to give support to ideas, feelings, likes and dislikes, that those people have and wish to impose on others. Therefore I strongly suggest that if you are told that 'they' don't like something, or aren't in favour of something, you take a completely opposite view, just for the hell of it. I am sure your life will be happier and more fulfilled.

TIME

As I have got older, I have found that not only does time seem to fly by, but that, perhaps not surprisingly, it becomes so much more precious. I came across a comment reputed to be have been by that remarkable man Michelangelo, which certainly echoes my own feelings about the subject. He reputedly said "There is no harm equal to that of wasted time". There is also a Latin saying "Lente Hora, Celeriter Anni", which is said to be an old person's complaint that "The hours go slowly, the years fast". I don't subscribe to the first part, but certainly agree with the second - where does the time go? Time has had a major significance in my life. Of course, we all are ruled by time to a some extent - if only in the limits set for getting to school when we are young, and to work when we get older.

With me the stopwatch has taken it a step beyond most people's deliberations with time. Originally in tenths of a second, and then, in the last 30 years, in hundredths, the timing of athletics has been of prime importance to me both in my hobby and my work. Firstly, because I enjoy the act of timing a race, and secondly, because in my early days the standard of 'official' timing was either poor and/or suspect, and, even worse for the fan, the results of that timing were often kept a closely guarded secret by the powers that be. I often crossed swords with officialdom on the matter, without letting them know that, in those early days, my results were achieved with a 15 shilling 75p surplus army stopwatch. However, I still maintain that my timings with that insignificant timepiece were as accurate, or more so, than those taken with their often £100 pieces of equipment. I say that because my timings at international occasions, such as Olympic Games and other championships, matched the official results far more often than at home meetings. Later, when I had a digital watch, and automatic timing was the official system, my timings were still remarkably close, or dead-on.

TIMEWATCH

As far as I can remember, in 26 years I only made two major errors with my timekeeping for the TV commentators. The first was at the Great Britain v Soviet Union match in Kiev in May 1976. There was only Ron Pickering and myself, and we were put in a commentary box in the roof, way above the track. We were left very much to our own devices, with no start lists nor results delivered to us throughout the broadcast. Crucially we could not see any timing devices on the ground and there was no such information on the TV monitor. At that time, I was still using my old analogue stopwatch, with a 30 second sweep, and from our eyrie the 5000m race did not look very fast. Due to the necessity of keeping an eye on the various field events going on at the same time, I lost concentration, and in the process 30 seconds. Thus, when the Brits, Tony Simmons and Nick Rose, took the first two places at the finish, Ron gave my unofficial, seemingly quite routine times. It was only at the end of the afternoon, when we descended from our isolated position to the ground floor and found some result sheets that I realised my mistake, and discovered that the British runners had run outstanding times, the first and third fastest times over the distance in the world that year. Incidentally, in that meet Paul Dickenson threw a British and Commonwealth hammer record of 73.20m - many years later he became a member of the BBC commentary team, and a colleague.

The other occasion, coincidentally affecting Ron again, was at the famous Bislet track in Oslo in 1982. Once more we were on our own, and David Moorcroft - later chief executive of UK Athletics - was expected to run a good 5000m. In fact he set a new world record of 13min 00.41sec, and unfortunately we all but blew it. This was probably the first major distance run that Ron had ever commentated on, and certainly the first he had done by himself. In my defence I was used to making out a pace chart for David Coleman, based on a set mark alongside which I would note the intervening lap times of the race going on, so that he could relate the pace to that needed for a fast time. Yet again, I was also trying to keep up-to-date with some field events. However, I should have realised that Ron did not have the same expertise as David to interpret those lap times so well, and it wasn't until almost the end of the race that I noticed that a record was in view, and that we had not commented on the possibility. Unfortunately, Ron received a lot of criticism for not commenting about the forthcoming record until the last lap, and I still feel that I let him down badly.

There were two other cases which show me in a better light - and therefore I will tell you about them. At the Munich Olympics in 1972, coming up to the last event (200m) of the five-event pentathlon, we all knew that Mary Peters had an outside chance of winning the gold medal. She had performed magnificently in the other events, and was 121 points ahead of the German favourite, Heidi Rosendahl. On an assumption of the time that Heidi would run in that 200m, I had calculated that Mary had to finish within 1.2sec of the German - probably by equalling or bettering her personal best for the event at the end of a gruelling two days, and in the cauldron of an Olympic arena. I concentrated like I had never before, and, as the starter fired, clicked my watch. Rosendahl shot ahead and stayed there, but Mary gave it everything she had, and I clocked Rosendahl with my split in 23.0sec and Mary in 24.1sec. I was pretty certain that I had timed it correctly, and shouted out to my TV colleagues that Peters had won the gold medal. Ron, as ever with great faith in me – this was before the afore-mentioned Oslo race - accepted it, but David said we would have to wait, as it was so close. The stadium held its breath, waiting for the auto-timing to show on the screen, while competitors stood around bemused, unsure of who had won. But I knew! Then the results came up on the scoreboard, and it was even closer than I had thought, with Rosendahl given 22.96sec and Mary 24.08sec - but my differential was still intact, and I was proved right. As you can surmise, it did wonders for my ego.

In Oslo in 1980, Steve Ovett was after the world mile record of 3min 49.0sec, set by his great rival Sebastian Coe at the same track 12 months previously. As the race started it became obvious that the auto-timing equipment, which had been working throughout the meeting, had broken down, and therefore I had to be sure to get as correct a time as possible at the end, especially if it was close. Boy, was it close! As Ovett finished I looked at my watch and I had 3min 48.8sec, just under the record. Ever cautious, David Coleman wanted to wait for the official result, but Ron said, over the air, that "Our statistician, Stan Greenberg, says Ovett's broken the record, and that's good enough for me". I saw my whole life flash before my eyes - my reputation, for what it was, could be ruined if I was wrong, but happily the official result came just a little later, and it was indeed 3:48.8, and I was saved.

TOILET ROLLS

There was a time when I equated the acquisition of toilet rolls with contentment. Now, before the reader thinks that I am completely round the twist, that is if he or she doesn't already, perhaps I should

TIMED TO PERFECTION
Stan Greenberg

expand on that bald statement. Years ago, not long after we were married, Carole and I visited an old friend of her father, a man who had done quite well in life. He lived in a building that was not far short of being a manor house, with large grounds and many, many rooms. As we were shown around the place, he took us into a walk-in storage area near the kitchen, and pointed out his large store of tinned foods, drinks and suchlike. In one corner he had a gross of toilet rolls, and these and his comments made a big impression on me. He noted that buying in such quantities resulted in a major saving, and it occurred to me that on an item like that, used throughout the year by allcomers, one could save quite a few bob. Thus began a quest to find room somewhere in our comparatively small house to store a gross of toilet rolls. I haven't succeeded yet, but I will never consider myself truly fulfilled in life until I do.

TOWELS

Most of us, particularly the older ones, will have holiday stories about German tourists getting up incredibly early to reserve sunbeds around hotel pools by laying their towels on them. In fact, there have been some very funny comedy sketches and routines based on the premise. However, nowadays I find that people abroad tell me that it is the Brits who are top of the league when it comes to playing that game. I pride myself that even at my age I am one of the better players, and rarely fail to get the places that we covet. My greatest triumph was at the Florida hotel we used to frequent, as the pool attendant, well rewarded when we leave, laid out towels for us before anyone else was about. My attitude has always been, if you are going to 'play' make sure, legally of course, that you win. It all comes back to the teachings of Stephen Potter and his *Lifemanship* concepts.

TRAINS

Unlike many of my friends I was never interested in train spotting, or trains in general. However, I have had a number of memorable journeys by that mode of transport. Having recently ridden Eurostar through the Channel Tunnel, I found myself comparing the unbelievable smoothness of the journey, at outstanding speed, to

TIMED TO PERFECTION
Stan Greenberg

others I had made. In particular, the trip from Cairo to Luxor, down the Nile valley in 1981. I should have been forewarned by the courier's frantic ushering to make our way to the dining car. This was before the train had even started, and the first course, soup, was served immediately. I soon found out the reason for the haste. Once the train was moving it was impossible to get a full spoon into one's mouth, as the rocking and shaking was unbelievable. Now I know what happened to all the old British hexagonal three-penny pieces - they were used as wheels on Egyptian trains. The rest of the journey was just as bone-shaking, but once in your bunk it didn't matter, although impossible to sleep.

A more pleasant trip was from Bergen to Oslo in 1956. Even in July, the snow in the mountains came close to the track, and the smell of the pines was intoxicating. The track wound its way through galleries cut out of the mountains and the views were magnificent. A few days later the journey from Oslo down to Copenhagen was memorable for an entirely different reason. Outside my compartment, by a corridor window, stood one of the most striking girls I have ever seen. She had that healthy-looking, dazzling-blonde beauty that Scandinavian girls are renowned for. On the pretext of looking at the scenery, I went and stared out of the next window, trying to think of an 'opening gambit'. The train suddenly stopped, with lots of official activity on the track, giving me the opportunity to innocently enquire if she knew what was wrong. She answered in cute, accented English, and moved to my window. We had a pleasant conversation for the rest of the journey, which passed all too quickly. She was off to Italy for her vacation, and was hoping to meet some dark Mediterranean men. I commented that all the Norwegian boys I had seen were all very tall, bronzed, blonde and good-looking. "Yes", she said, rather glumly, "that's the trouble, they all are".

Another train journey that I recall was across France and Italy one summer on the way to Rimini. It took about 30 hours and became a survival test when, in very hot weather, the train ran out of water halfway across France. At every stop, hordes of passengers would disembark and besiege any shop, restaurant or tap within reach for liquids. I began to realise what crossing the Sahara must be like.

The first double-deck train that I ever saw was in East Germany in the early 1970s. The locomotive was an enormous steam engine - bigger than anything I had ever seen on British railways. Though not a 'train-spotter' I was interested enough to take out my camera. As I settled down to take a photo I heard a voice behind me whisper urgently, "Verboten! Fotografieren verboten! ". I turned to see who had said that but there was noone nearby - something of a mystery. Anyway, I took the photo, with the engineer waving pleasantly at me from his cab, and I had no trouble. The trip itself was quite interesting, and pleasant, as this double-decker was much larger than the ones that later I travelled on in Britain, giving passengers much more room.

In 1954, after the European Championships in Berne, Switzerland, Len Gebbett and I decided to take the opportunity to visit Paris on the way back home, and booked a seat on the overnight Basle to Paris train. When we arrived at the station it seemed that we were the only people on the train, a very long one, and we found our carriage, with two seat reservation tickets hanging down forlornly - about the only ones on the train. When the train pulled out we were sitting stretched out sleepily by the window, content with life. I awoke to find a 'curtain' hanging over my eyes. As I came to, I found that the 'curtain' was, in fact, a girl's hair, a girl who was asleep in the luggage rack above me. The rest of the carriage was full of sixth-form St Trinian's schoolgirls - or so it seemed - and as I glanced across at Len, then a 32 year old confirmed bachelor, I saw that he was sitting absolutely rigid with a sleeping girl's head lying on his lap, and the rest of her laying full-length on the seat. Eventually, they all woke up, and were very pleasant, but it had been quite a shock for a couple of innocent British lads on holiday.

TRAVEL

As the reader will have gathered, I love to travel, and equally love proverbs and quotations, so that to find a proverb or quotation about travel just about makes my day. Here are a few I have noted

"The fool wanders, the wise man travels"
    Thomas Fuller
"He that travels far, knows much"
    J Clarke

"In America there are two classes of travel – first class, and with children"
    Robert Benchley

"I travel not to go anywhere, but to go. I travel for travel's sake. The great affair is to move"
    Robert Louis Stevenson

"Travelling is almost like talking with men of other centuries"
    René Descartes

"All travelling becomes dull in exact proportion to its rapidity"
    John Ruskin

"A man travels the world in search of what he needs, and returns home to find it"
    George Moore

TRAVEL IN BRITAIN

We all have horror stories to tell about travel arrangements, both public and private, and I am no exception. Perhaps not surprisingly, mine were related to athletics watching. Before I obtained a car, in 1964, Carole and I found it quite difficult to get to the White City Stadium in north London, despite not living all that far from it, as the crow flies. Unfortunately we are not crows, and had to take three different buses to get there. One afternoon we had started out late, and as our first bus entered the bus station I noticed that our next one was about to leave. I grabbed behind me for my wife's hand, and tugged hard as I ran across the forecourt towards the new vehicle. I remember wondering why Carole was pulling against me, but I was intent on reaching that next bus before it left and wrenched even harder. As I boarded the platform I turned to remonstrate with my wife, to find myself staring into a very frightened black lady's face. Carole was creased up laughing halfway across the yard, and lots of people were staring, either laughing or looking apprehensive. In my haste, I had grabbed the poor conductress's hand, and before she had been able to react in any way, had dragged her about 30 yards or so. I was very embarrassed and apologetic, and thankfully she took it in good humour.

I have noticed that most of the places I have mentioned in this booklet have been abroad. However, I have been lucky enough to visit some wonderful places in Britain. In their own way, the Lake District, the Scottish Highlands, Snowdonia , the Peak District, the Yorkshire Moors, the Chilterns and Dartmoor are superb. Among my favourite places are Stonehenge, Avebury, Tintagel and High Force waterfall. Undoubtedly, there are bigger and grander sights around the world - and many of them I have been privileged to see - but these spots in Britain have their own special grandeur and/or charm, which, I think, makes them unique.

TWIDDLING
I used to have a habit, when at a loose end, of standing with my hands behind my back, à la the Duke of Edinburgh, and twiddling my fingers. However, I was cured of this one night at the Unilever Badminton Club. I was standing with a group of people awaiting my turn on court, and was twiddling as was my wont. One of the other members was a tall, attractive, very elegant, but somewhat haughty, girl, who was the Captain's girlfriend. As she came off the court, wearing her very short skirt, she pushed past behind me, but crucially facing my back. Not realising she was there, I was still absentmindedly twiddling, and she suddenly let out a loud shriek, and loudly accused me of groping her. I was mortified - I don't think that at that stage of my development I even knew what 'groping' meant - but everyone was looking at me accusingly, and the boyfriend, an ex-Gurkha Regiment officer, looked threatening. I apologised for whatever had happened, and pitifully protested my innocence. Thankfully, after a while most people accepted my explanation. However, I got the impression that some of them saw

me in a new light. It was all highly embarrassing, and I was kidded about it for a long time.

UNITED STATES
In general terms, I don't like America very much, nor do I appreciate the general traits of its inhabitants. Having said that, I have, and I hope will retain, many American friends. I know you cannot judge a country just on its big city dwellers - in all parts of the world it is the country and small-town people who are the backbone of a nation. However, one does form lasting impressions from personal contact, and generally those impressions have not been good. Three of the cities I have visited, New York, Los Angeles and Miami, are probably the worse possible places from which to form an opinion. All three, typical examples of modern America, represent the last places on earth that I would want to live or work in, although terrific to visit.

Certainly, there are many wonderful things to see in those cities, and as a first-time tourist I was thrilled to be in each. Then, after the initial excitement, I began to note the mess, the noise, the lack of manners, the dearth of what can only be called style. If only those cities had some old-fashioned zonal planning, of the kind we in Europe often rail at. Perhaps if materialism, money, greed (whatever) was not the only apparent motive for doing things, they would be less unpleasant. Take Los Angeles for instance. The Beverley Hills and Westwood areas, where the wealthy live and shop, are marvellous, if you like that sort of thing. But the main parts of the city are a jumble, with smart office blocks adjoining 1930s Art-Deco buildings, which in turn adjoin a garage or a vacant lot. Everywhere, especially in New York, cars and other vehicles have, or take, right of way, and the resulting congestion, noise, and pollution has to be seen/heard/smelled to be believed.

Another form of noise and pollution that is not often noted, is that caused by the people. When asked for a quick impression of New York, my answer used to be "Little old ladies loudly using foul

TIMED TO PERFECTION
Stan Greenberg

language in restaurants". I had been startled by the obscene language used, by smartly-dressed, obviously well-to-do, men and women, and especially older ladies, in public places. It is not as though they were saying things in anger, but more, one got the impression, to shock, or perhaps to show that they were "with it". This view is certainly reinforced by the use of the same words, ad nauseam, in current American films and TV programs. The only time that I had heard the like before, was when I visited the London Docks as a young man, but even there the dockers would usually moderate their remarks if a woman was about. Not in New York though, since it seems it is primarily the women who are using the bad language in the first place. Perhaps, like the increase in smoking among women, it is a way of proving that they're the equal of men (a positive disease in the United States).

It wouldn't be so bad if New Yorkers didn't talk so loudly anyway. The volume of noise in restaurants can be nerve-wracking. As an inveterate eavesdropper I found that I could listen to conversations three or four tables away, and was even more bemused to discover that the topics discussed, at such a high decibel level, were often very private and personal. In the cinema sometimes it was almost impossible to hear the dialogue from the screen. Maybe that's why when they travel abroad they gain the reputation of "Loud Americans", making no concession to foreign sensibilities. In my experience, Americans rarely make concessions to anyone or for anything. Perhaps in their society such behaviour is seen as weak or sycophantic, and so they decry these traits. This might explain, at the Seoul Olympics, the American media reaction to the pleasant Korean habit of politely bowing to customers, strangers and elderly people. This was not subservience but old-world courtesy, a delight to witness and to reciprocate. Virtually all the Americans I spoke to thought it demeaning and embarrassing, although I was never quite clear who was demeaned and embarrassed.

I am appalled at the lack of basic historic/geographic knowledge in the average American. One gets the impression that only where and what America is matters, and anything about other countries or cultures doesn't. An example was my experience at the 1984 Olympics in Los Angeles. For the opening ceremony I sat between a pleasant, but excitable, Mexican-American and a middle-aged couple. A young, seemingly well-educated, twosome was in front. As the teams entered, each country's name was carried in front of them. The Mexican cheered the leading team, Greece, but queried where the next country, Algeria, was. I briefly explained, and also pin-pointed Andorra in turn. Throughout the next hour or so, he and the people around me continued to ply me with queries concerning most of the countries. They only seemed to know those in Central and South America, but not all of those either. At one point, the young woman in front turned and triumphantly put the Seychelles "in the Caribbean". When I corrected her, she asked, in awe it seemed, whether I was a professor. I commented that my young son knew where most of these countries were situated.

They are the electorate of the most powerful country on earth, whose Government takes decisions seriously affecting all of us - and they don't even know, or care, where we are. Frankly, that worries me. As I explained to American friends in Los Angeles, it was not unlike being in Moscow again. News in both countries is managed, not in the USA for the same reasons as in the Soviet Union, but effectively to the same degree. Most American newspapers I have seen seem unaware of the world outside the United States, and perhaps Canada and Central America. Foreign news on local television seems to be mainly about the next State, and Americans who may want to know about the rest of the world have to go to some trouble to find out. So they are totally unprepared for the different views held on various topics or historical events by people in other countries.

VANITY

I don't think that I am a vain man, although like anyone else I have my moments I suppose. On one occasion it nearly cost me dearly. I returned from the 1974 Commonwealth Games in Christchurch, via Mexico City. I had always wanted to visit the place, and a round-the-world return ticket gave me my chance. A main reason for wanting to go there was to visit the ancient ruins of Teotihuacan, just outside Mexico City. It was awe-inspiring, and in particular were the two pyramids, of the Sun and of the Moon. I had considered climbing the biggest one, the Pyramid of the Sun, but at the age of 43, and with the altitude at about 2240m *7300ft*, I had the sense to forget it. At least that was until a couple of young ladies in the tour group goaded me into joining them. So up the steps I went. By the time I reached the top I was bushed and had great difficulty catching my breath. I stayed up there for quite a long time appreciating the view (i.e. getting my breathing back to normality) before descending. That in its own way was almost as much of a problem as going up, as the steps are very steep.

VERNACULAR
Having lived in my early years in the East End of London, and having a number of foreign-born relatives, vernacular speech was something quite common to me. Nevertheless, I was not really ready for my first acquaintance with Brooklynese. The first time I went to New York, I took a taxi, or 'cab' if you like, from the airport to my hotel. The driver was not very talkative, which I thought was unusual. Then, as we were crossing one of the bridges, with a tremendous view of the Manhattan skyline, a flock of birds suddenly wheeled around us. He cursed, and I made some comment about the birds being dangerous, to which he replied "Yeh, der boids is moider!" As it was practically my first contact with trans-atlantic speech, other than through the cinema, I initially thought he must be putting me on. But, as he became more loquacious, I realised that it was his normal way of speaking - I had great difficulty understanding him. Mind you, he was at least an English speaker, in the broadest sense of course, whereas nowadays you are very lucky to find a New York cabbie who can speak the language at all - they all seem to be Eastern Europeans or Spanish-speaking.

VICTORY
I celebrated VE (Victory in Europe) day - at the end of WWII - in Kings Lynn, where I was evacuated. Everybody went a little crazy and my friend and I roamed around the town watching the

festivities. By chance we met with the two girls from the Public Library that most of my schoolfriends had been dying to meet, and for a shy 14 year old it was a wonderful evening. By the time VJ (Victory over Japan) day came I was home with my family in London. There was a great fireworks display on the Thames at Westminster, and my father and I went to watch it. It ended with a brilliant magnesium flare which bathed the whole city in deep purple. When it was time to go home, thousands of people were trying to get on the available public transport. Finally we decided to walk, and headed for the East End. All the way back we met various friends and neighbours who had also been at the celebrations, until there was an enormous boisterous crowd of us as we reached our locality. It was a marvellous end to a great day, and, Thank God, the final end to the war.

WANDERLUST

The definition of the word is 'a desire to travel', and I certainly have that. As mentioned before, it all seems to have started with a radio programme which the BBC broadcast on the Home Service from 1942 to 1946 called *Armchair Traveller*. The programme consisted of people reading from their own, or other writers', books about journeys, safaris, expeditions and voyages, to various wild, exotic and wonderful places. Colour was added by the playing of recordings of local sounds, and appropriate background music. Particularly, I remember one programme, which was about the Grand Canyon in Arizona, and I heard for the first time the *Grand Canyon Suite* by Ferdi Grofe. Especially I recall the highly descriptive section *On the Trail*. It implanted unimaginable yearnings in my early-teenage breast, at a time when very few ordinary people went anywhere abroad. I have now all but satiated my wanderlust, although there are still a couple of places which ......Oh well, perhaps.

WATER

I have mentioned elsewhere my love/hate relationship to water in its various forms. Thinking about it the other evening, I noted the different bodies of water that I have swum in or dipped my toes.

TIMED TO PERFECTION
Stan Greenberg

They include the North Atlantic Ocean, North and South Pacific Oceans, the Indian Ocean, the Coral Sea, the Gulf of Mexico, the Red Sea, the Mediterranean Sea; the Aegean Sea, the Baltic Sea, the Ligurian Sea, the Adriatic Sea, the North Sea, The Persian Gulf, and the Dead Sea.

Water has had much significance in my life. It is considered the source of creation in many religions, and science recognizes it as a primordial element, but I am very ambivalent about it. For one thing, I dearly wanted to swim when I was young, but never had the opportunity to learn. My father had once watched a brother-in law, an extremely good swimmer, nearly drown. Neither he nor my mother could swim, and so we rarely visited swimming pools. Dad said that I mustn't go in the water until I could swim. Catch 22. Finally, aged 16, I taught myself. One day at Margate, seeing little kids splashing about in the sea, I decided it was do or die. With the water up to my neck, I foolishly flung myself forward and thrashed about. Delightedly I found I was moving along. Soon I had developed a crude stroke (later identified as the trudgeon) but I was quickly brought down to earth, and back to the beach, by some men that my doting father had sent out to his 'drowning' son. Despite this, by the end of the holiday I was swimming - albeit in a rudimentary fashion. However, I have never been able to float. I know that it is said to be impossible not to float, but as I have proved time after time, I cannot do it. Ron Pickering and Stuart Storey, both expert swimmers, tried their darndest with me but as soon as my arms and legs stop moving - down I go. Nor can I float on my back - except in the Dead Sea. There, I lay back reading a magazine, with my toes on a level with my eyes. It is a memory I will carry forever.

As a child our house did not have a bathroom initially, so we would visit the nearby public bathhouse. The water, hot or cold, entered the bath from a main tap controlled by a supervisor in the corridor outside the cubicles. If you wanted more water you called out your request. Soon I, in cubicle number 5, realised the fun that could be had from a phantom call. Calls of "More hot number 10" or "More cold number 7", were quickly followed by screams of "No, no more hot for 10", or "No more cold for 7". The poor supervisor must have had nightmares.

Water has given me some very bad moments. Not too serious, was when I got my own house, and found to my surprise that one had to pay for water. It had never occurred to me that it was not free. Other occasions were not so minor, as when I unsuspectingly hammered a nail through a hidden waterpipe under the floorboard of the bedroom. Later I marvelled at how I moved all the heavy furniture so easily, when on a previous occasion I had been unable to even shift it slightly. However, if you have sat and listened to the steady drip of water onto your dining room table you will understand the strength that can be summoned. Another time the bathroom sink tap was left running while we were out, and we returned to find a virtual Niagara coming down the stairs. On yet another occasion the attic tank sprung a leak, and the water found the easiest exit from the ceiling - down through the overhead lamp socket in the bedroom. This wasn't discovered until we climbed into a sodden bed. So, perhaps you can appreciate why I have a phobia about water.

WATER TRANSPORT
I have deliberately used this title, as I have never quite got the hang of when to use the term 'ship' or 'boat'. Early in my life I had not travelled much by large sea-borne ships, although ironically my very first trip abroad, to Helsinki in 1952, was mainly by this form of transport. However, I have been lucky to have had a few very interesting trips in other forms of water transport. One of the most exciting was while in Christchurch, New Zealand, for the 1974 Commonwealth Games. A few of us were taken to a nearby very shallow river on which jetboats were used. These were small boats which literally skimmed over water often no more than a few centimetres in depth. It was a very exhilarating ride.

Later, on a trip to Hawaii, I was a member of the 'crew' which paddled a large outrigger canoe which rode the surf in on Waikiki beach - very thrilling and interesting, but I soon realised that I was getting too old for this sort of thing, and my shoulders felt bruised for a week. A much more relaxed voyage was in Oslo, when Carole and I were invited to join a special press jaunt around the harbour on one of the great Tall Ships, the white-hulled *Christian Radich* . It was a very civilized way to travel. Then there was the occasion, at Clearwater Beach, Florida, when we had a trip on the *Sea Screamer*, claimed to be the largest motorboat in the world. I think that the claim may not be correct, but certainly it was fast, and very noisy, and we enjoyed it immensely.

In the last few years, we have succumbed to the very popular idea of cruising. The first time was in the newly-launched P & O liner, the *Azura*, a massive 3000 passenger ship on a cruise in the Mediterranean. We did another trip in that ship down to Casablanca, and recently did a Baltic cruise in the Royal Caribbean's *Jewel of the Seas.* All three were most enjoyable.

WE HAVE WAYS
The Olympic stadium landscaping at Munich in 1972 was created with the rubble caused by Allied bombing of the city during the war. At the Games, it was embarrassing to hear one or two Britons claiming that their fathers (ex RAF) had helped build the place. However, it wasn't all one-sided. One afternoon, we were talking to the British hurdler Alan Pascoe, when the suave, urbane German TV liaison officer, a former Luftwaffe pilot, came by. Introductions were made with the information that Alan came from Portsmouth. "Ah yes", our German colleague said, "I know it very well - from the air".

WHAT MIGHT HAVE BEEN
The American poet, John Greenleaf Whittier, wrote, "For all sad words of tongue and pen, the saddest are these: 'It might have been!" Many of us can remember times in our lives when we had a decision to make, and perhaps have wondered what might have happened if we had made a different decision to that we did make. I can pinpoint a number of such times in my life, when I could have

TIMED TO PERFECTION
Stan Greenberg

taken myself in an entirely different direction to that I actually took, and sometimes I do think about what might have happened if my choice had been different. The first such decision was when I left school, and didn't take the opportunity to try for a university education. There is no doubt in my mind that if I had got a degree, hopefully a decent one, I would have been considerably better-off financially for most of my working life. Contemporaries of mine, in some cases no cleverer than I, went on to achieve distinction in various fields, and acquire fame, wealth and even titles.

Then came another turning point, when I decided to leave my first employer, and took a job with the GLC. If I had remained at Unilever, there is no way I could have taken advantage of the travelling opportunities which came with the work I did for the BBC, as I would never have been allowed the time flexibility that this required. My GLC departmental head was quite happy for me to do this extra stuff, as long as it did not affect my work for him, and I made sure it did not. The next 'crossroads' came with the offer to go to the *Guinness Book of Records*, about which I agonised before I accepted. Then, after a wonderful six years with the *Book*, I decided, against all my past ideas and experiences, to go freelance. What might have been if I had done differently at any of these points?

Well, in fact I do know probable consequences of 'going the other way' in some cases. If I had remained at Unilever, I may well have been caught up in a 'clearance' of middle management which took place a few years after I left, and which did affect a number of friends in similar positions to mine. Then, if I had stayed at the GLC, apart from missing the excitement and pleasure of being sports editor of the *Guinness Book of Records*, I would have been in serious trouble a few years later when the GLC was disbanded, and, almost certainly, I would have been out of a job in my late 40s. Lastly, if I had stayed with the *Book*, instead of going out on my own, once again I would have had problems, as, not much later, the Guinness operation was taken over by people I could not have worked with, and I would certainly have been given my walking papers when well into my 50s. One way and another, I seem to have made the right decisions nearly all my working life, and I really do believe that I have had some kind of 'friendly guiding force' looking out for me, and pushing me in the right direction. Okay, somewhat fanciful you may think, but I like the idea of it, and anyway, if it isn't that, the only alternative is that I am a genius, and that, surely, is even more fanciful.

WHISKY
I am not much of a drinker, although I do like sherry now and again, and usually have wine with a main meal at a restaurant. But when it comes to "the hard stuff" I prefer to have a glass of water. However, there was one occasion when I was very pleased to have something stronger. The World Cross-Country Championships were held at Warsaw, Poland, in March 1987, on a wet, windy, very exposed course. The TV cubicles were very small, and there was only room for the commentators in the BBC one. I had to remain outside, and the only cover I could find was a large clear plastic bag, in which I punched a hole for my head and which I draped over me. Nevertheless, by the end of the transmission I was wet and freezing, and though I found some cover in the main stand, I had to remain behind to send some details over the telephone to London. As I was shivering violently by now, I asked one of the engineers if he could get me something warm to drink - I would even have had coffee, which I hate - but all he could come up with was a glass of local whisky. Initially I was going to refuse it, but he said it would warm me so I gulped it down. It was like a cartoon, as I could feel, indeed almost see, the warmth gradually diffuse into every part of my body. I had never felt anything like it before, but certainly it warmed me up, although I thought it tasted quite awful. Remarkably, I understand, many people drink it because they like it - well, it takes all sorts, as they say.

WHISTLING
Despite being castigated by teachers, parents, bosses and friends, I have always whistled. Perhaps, as a loner when a boy, I found it very comforting to whistle to myself, especially when walking along

or in my room. I gather that, like so many other things, it is not considered (by whom?) to be good etiquette, but to be honest I couldn't care less. As long as I don't annoy other people too much, I shall whistle as long as I am able. My one regret is that I have never mastered the ability to whistle really loudly, eg to hail a taxi, with two fingers in my mouth - an achievement by some of my friends that I envy. There are some who can whistle that way without using fingers at all, just by pursing their lips - to me that is like being able to read Japanese. I took great comfort learning that the great entertainer, Al Jolson, actually resurrected his career, when his voice cracked as a teenager, by switching his act to that of a whistler until his grown -up voice matured. My older readers will undoubtedly remember a very elegant British music-hall performer named Albert Whelan, who was a very popular entertainer with his melodic whistling. Lastly, when I visited the island of Gomera, one of the Canary Islands, I was fascinated to learn, and hear, that they have a whistling language, called *Silbo*, which they use to pass messages from one part of the very mountainous island to another - similar to the yodelling in Switzerland.

WHITE CITY DAYS
The late-lamented White City Stadium was almost a second home to me for twenty years. All major British athletics meetings were held there until about 1968, when Crystal Palace took over.

I wonder how many people remember the 'Flaming Hammers' competition of 1956. The occasion was a match between Budapest and London, staged by the now defunct *Evening News*. To make the hammer event more of a spectacle, especially as the Hungarians had two magnificent throwers, the event was held in isolation, so that the stadium lights could be dimmed. A firework sparkler was attached to the hammer head before each throw - so that one could see the arc of the throw from the light of the sparkler. It worked very well for a few throws but then things went wrong. Because the visitors were so good, the judges moved nearer to the throwing circle for the British throwers. They tended to only move

TIMED TO PERFECTION
Stan Greenberg

back a little when the visitors threw, but they could follow the line of the throw in the air from the light. One of the Hungarians made his throw, and according to the light from the firework the trajectory suddenly veered sharply down to the ground. Dimly one could see judges running forward to mark the landing spot, when realisation dawned. The sparkler had fallen off - and somewhere up above them was a death-dealing 7.26kg *16lb* ball attached to a whirling 91cm *3ft* chain. To loud cries, otherwise staid British judges went scattering in all directions. Happily nothing except pride was dented, and the stadium rocked with relieved laughter. We never saw the 'Flaming Hammers' again.

The old White City track was of cinders, and not very well drained. Many was the occasion, on a typical English summer's day, when the track was inundated, creating conditions that our foreign friends rarely experienced. In one report, in an overseas publication, it was noted that the runners not only ran against the wind, but also against the tide. Sometimes there were even greater hazards. During the early 1950s the Caledonian Games Association held annual gatherings there. Mainly Highland Games events, including sheep trials and Scottish dancing, there were invitational track and field events added. In the 1951 meeting the great Scottish high jumper Alan Paterson was about to attempt a seasonal best height, when one of the sheep broke away and ran through the high jump pit. On another occasion the international hammer thrower Euan Douglas brought the caber contest to a premature end when, on his debut at the event, he tossed it rather badly. It landed flat and promptly snapped in half. Apparently this had not been expected and there was no reserve implement.

One of the greatest races ever run at the White City was the 5000m during the London v Moscow midweek meeting in October 1954. It matched the European champion, Vladimir Kuts, against the silver medallist, Chris Chataway, and I nearly missed it. I made my way there after work not expecting trouble getting a ticket. There were amazing crowds milling around and I doubt if more than ten people got in after me. I sat in the back row at one end of the ground, jammed up against the scoreboard. The race lived up to all the pre-race hype, with Kuts going straight to the front and Chataway hanging on for dear life. So it went, lap after lap, with the Soviet runner making determined bursts to break the Briton. When there was only about 50 yards left, with the crowd frenziedly chanting CHAT-A-WAY, CHAT-A-WAY, Chris slowly caught Kuts, and with a final lunge broke the tape first. The world record was well and truly broken, and I think everyone was pleased to learn that Kuts had also gained a world record, for three miles on the way. Since I had unhappily missed the first four-minute mile earlier in the year, I would have been totally devastated if I had missed this race as well. After that I always made sure that I booked tickets well in advance of a meeting.

WHITE VANS

We have all had trouble with the ubiquitous white vans which seem to dominate British roads, and one gets very wary of their drivers. Quite recently I was driving on a 30mph narrow road, when I realised that there was such a van behind me flashing his lights wildly. I assumed that he either wanted me to speed up, or let him get by, but, as there was a thick white line down the centre of the road, I decided that he would have to wait. For the next half mile or so he continued to flash me, until I thought I would have it out with him. At the first opportunity I pulled over into someone's drive and lent out of my window to give him 'a mouthful'. However, as he drew level with me, he stopped and called out, quite pleasantly, "Hey mate, your tyre is on fire". To my astonishment I then noticed thick smoke coming from my right rear wheel. As I pulled up I realised that my hand brake was still partly up, and that it must have been like that for about 2-3 miles. Happily, it was not the tyre burning, but the brake block, and after a while it had cooled down sufficiently for me to continue my journey. Herewith, I publically apologise to all white van drivers – at least until I get cut-up by one of them again.

WILSON OF THE WIZARD

TIMED TO PERFECTION
Stan Greenberg

Fictional characters can have a remarkable influence on people's lives. However, I doubt if many such characters can match the effect that Wilson of the *Wizard* had on so many people, especially in the athletics world. The *Wizard* was a boy's comic in the 1930s and 1940s. Unlike today's comics it was all narrative, with a few drawings, perhaps one per story. Also it was very well written. One particular character was Wilson. The basis of the story was far-fetched. Born in Yorkshire in 1795, and a puny child, he learnt how to lead a healthy and fit life. He also learnt the secret of longevity, for in the stories he reappears in more modern times, the 1930s, and performs amazing feats of running and jumping. I have met numerous athletics enthusiasts whose appetite for the sport was whetted by reading about Wilson, because the stories were wonderfully written, by a person very well versed in the sport.

Although most of Wilson's exploits could have been considered ludicrous in the light of the world records of the time, there was always a sneaking suspicion that they were not that impossible. I can illustrate this by one story. On the flight to Athens for the 1969 European Championships, I sat near coach and author Tom McNab, in whose bag I noticed a paperback story about the aforementioned Wilson. Eagerly I asked for it, and read it during the journey. It was called "*Wilson and the Pit of Fire*". Wilson was on the way to an Inter-Services meeting in Cairo in about 1940, when his plane was forced to land in the desert. Captured by Bedouins, who somehow knew of his exploits, he was forced to take part in an ancient ritual which entailed jumping over a very long pit of burning coals - a legendary hero had once achieved this. In the event Wilson just made it, to great rejoicing by his companions and his captors. A friend measured the pit, and found it was an astounding 29ft 6in *9.00m*, at a time when the official world record of 26ft 8¼in *8.13m* was hardly ever approached. The fascinating thing was that only the year before I read this story, the American Bob Beamon had jumped a new record of 29ft 2½in *8.90m*, almost the distance the writer had predicted some thirty years before.

WINDOW GAZING

I am not referring to window shopping here but to actually gazing out of a window abstractly, especially when at work. I am thinking of the 'art' of watching people in other office buildings, the sun shining on trees, the rain falling on those same trees, aeroplane trails in the sky, cloud formations, birds flying to and fro. Most people consider this as just plain laziness or lack of commitment to the job in hand, but I would, and have had occasion to, defend the practice. The writer James Thurber once said that his greatest problem was convincing his wife that when he was looking out of the window he was working. Personally, I have always found that I can concentrate on a problem, consider alternatives, or think of an idea, far better if I gaze out of a window. When I worked for the *Guinness Book of Records*, considering new record categories, how to check up on something, or compose an appropriate interesting entry, I would often spend quite long periods of time staring out of the window, usually at nothing in particular, to help me get inspiration. This did not go down very well with the managing director, an excellent manager and accountant, but with little imaginative flair. To him, if you did not have your head down over your desk then you were not working. Happily, when necessary, I was able to convince him that, despite what he thought he was seeing, I was working, sometimes very hard, when gazing out of the window. Even today, when putting this paragraph together, I have spent a little while staring out of my study window.

WINDOW SHOPPING

This phrase took on a whole new meaning the first time I went to Amsterdam in 1976. I was on my way to Kiev, and had to change planes, which necessitated a night in the lovely old Dutch city. My colleagues took me out for a walk, "to look in some windows" I was told. There is one area where the 'ladies of the night' display their wares in the ground floor windows of buildings. Despite my surprise, I remember that I was very impressed at how tastefully decorated those windows were. Of course, as I have noted before, I have always had an eye for 'artistic' things.

TIMED TO PERFECTION
Stan Greenberg

WINTER SPORTS

One of my great regrets is that I never tried any of the winter sports - except for a brief and painful foray at ice skating. Primarily the reason for this was that when younger I only received two weeks holiday, and I wasn't going to forego a warm summer vacation in favour of a cold one. In practice the summer holiday wasn't always so warm, but the principle was sound. By the time I was eligible for longer vacation time, I was married, with a family, and couldn't afford an additional winter break.

However, recently I recalled that once I did participate in, indeed invented, a winter sport. I refer to the rare pastime of Gas Stove Drip Tray sledding. Participation in this 'esoteric' sport has been very limited. My introduction of the activity occurred in the winter of 1941, in that famous British winter sports resort of Luton. There had been a heavy fall of snow overnight and the roads were thick with it. The street in which I lived had a distinct drop from one end to the other, and the local children, some from quite well-to-do families, appeared that morning with sleds, toboggans and even skis. I was very much out of the fun until an idea came to me. Sneaking back into the house I took the drip tray from under the gas stove and tried it out 'on the slopes'. It was fantastic - not only did it slide magnificently, but also it spun around wildly, giving a fabulous ride. Soon it became the 'in' thing to do, and offers of reciprocal rides on sleds and skis were showered on me. By the time we were called for lunch my standing in the community had shot up, and discussions were under way for a championship meeting based on length of slide and number of turns achieved.

The one black spot - indeed many black spots - on the horizon were those on the previously pristine white enamel base of the tray. The ice, and gravel surface of the road, had caused havoc to the 'vehicle' base, and my parents were, well, not happy might be a slight understatement. Nevertheless, as the damage had been done, I was allowed to use my sled for as long as the snow lasted -

though I seem to remember I used it standing up, as Dad had made sitting rather painful. The infant sport died with the passing of the snow. The development of new stoves without drip trays would have killed the sport anyway, and so a great opportunity for a comparatively cheap, but highly exciting, pastime was lost.

XENIUM
As I had to try to have at least one heading starting with 'X', I was very pleased when I came across this word, one that actually had some connection with me. It relates to something that I gave to Carole not long ago, and actually means "an offering, present, or compulsory gift, made to a ruler". I rest my case.

XMAS
I have never been a devotee of Christmas. Not, I should point out, from any religious scruples, but more from an intense dislike of what the secular side of the festival has come to be in Britain. Whereas when I was young, most of our neighbours went to church at least once during the holiday, nowadays the religious element seems to have almost disappeared. It has been replaced by a frenzy of drinking, partying and spending, that I feel sure was never intended by the founding fathers. The old-fashioned family get-together is something of a rarity now.

Personally, I have always seen Scrooge as a role model - not necessarily his meanness, but certainly his attitude of "Bah, Humbug" to the wild festivities around him. In the story, he succumbs at the end, but I have always thought that it was only because Dickens felt that he ought to fit in with society's norms, more than any true indication of what someone like Scrooge would really do. By the way, has anyone noticed that Santa is an anagram of Satan - just a thought - and, for the next one, a Merry Xmas.

X-RAYS
Having had a medical on 20 September 1949, and been passed

TIMED TO PERFECTION
Stan Greenberg

Grade I, i.e. fully fit, I was called for my National Service a month later, and reported to RAF Padgate, Lancashire, on 26 October. Soon after I arrived there I caught a very bad cold, but it didn't stop me from preliminary 'square-bashing' and an interview as a POM (possible officer material). However, when I had a routine X-ray I was recalled for another, and then another. It appeared that a shadow had been detected on my lung. I wasn't too worried, as previous X-rays had never shown anything untoward, and I was incredibly fit from all the sport I had been doing. In fact, in the evenings, to alleviate the squad's boredom, I arranged 'mini-Olympics' in our hut. Then, after more X-rays, I was told that I was to be released, and just before Xmas I was given an honorable discharge and sent home in a state of severe shock. Despite assurances, I assumed I was dying, and that certainly my active life was finished. For many months I regularly attended a local hospital, to monitor my condition - but they never seemed to find anything. Gradually I re-entered normal life, but was very upset that my RAF career had been curtailed, as from an early age I had been mad keen on aeroplanes, and had dreamed of being a pilot.

Come forward some 45 years, to the advent of a new local doctor, a lady with a more modern approach than our previous one. One of the first things she did was arrange for me to have an X-ray, relative to a blood pressure problem she had discovered. When the 'picture' came back, I was delighted to learn that nothing untoward was shown. However, she mentioned, in passing, that my old TB scar showed up. So it seems the RAF doctors were right, and I had had tuberculosis, of which I had no knowledge. It apparently disappeared as soon as I left Padgate, which was said to have been built on a swamp.

YIDDISH
I used to claim that I could speak three languages - English, Yiddish and Rubbish. While two out of three isn't bad, I could never really speak the second one, but could understand it to a certain extent. Indeed, as a boy I often visited a Yiddish theatre with my

father, and seemed to be able to follow the plot. However, on reflection, that was probably more to do with the amazing nuances of the language than with any skill of mine. Undoubtedly, it is one of the most expressive languages in existence. Soon after Carole and I moved into our house we held a party at which a very funny record of the time, *The Psychology of Yiddish* by Dr Murray Banks, was played. We found that our non-Jewish friends were laughing, in all the right places, just as much as everyone else.

No matter what country they came from, my father's generation referred to Yiddish as the mama-loshen - the mother tongue. Jews from all over Europe could converse with each other if they had picked up some of the language from their parents. Older people would often switch into it when they wanted to discuss something they didn't want the children to know about. That was the surest way to get the children to start learning. It is said that Napoleon Bonaparte used Yiddish-speaking couriers, knowing that they could get by almost anywhere. Yiddish has remarkable nuances of expression. For instance, there are a series of words beginning with 'sh' which refer to various degrees of foolishness, stupidity, and/or clumsiness etc. They are probably all interchangeable, but each has its own meaning. Some of them have entered English (or more likely American) usage, and are: shlock, shnook, shmendrick, shmeril, shmuck (not used in polite society), shlemiel and shlimazl. As an example of the nuances I mentioned, there is a saying that a shlemiel waiter accidentally pours hot soup over a shlimazl customer. So many Yiddish words and phrases have been incorporated into the native languages of England and America that a famous linguist, Leo Rosten, coined the terms Yinglish and Ameridish. Sadly, though more people than ever are using such words, the number of Yiddish speakers is getting smaller and smaller each year, and one day may go the way of Latin.

YIN AND YANG

These are the two opposing principles of Chinese philosophy, and I state what they are without making any comments of my own. Yin is the negative, dark and feminine. Yang is the positive, bright and masculine. I make no comments because I just haven't got that much nerve.

ZEAL

The dictionary definition is 'great enthusiasm or eagerness', and therefore I cannot think of a more apt word to include in these memoirs. Actually, there is another word, which somebody once said applies to people like me. It is hierophant, which is given as 'an interpreter of esoteric doctrines' or 'expounder of mysteries'. I must add that to my CV.

ZEITGEIST

The spirit or outlook of the age. Well, I am not very happy with the spirit or outlook of the current age. It seems to me that it is very mean, selfish and materialistic, much more so than in the past, or at least my past. Hopefully, things will improve as the 21st century progresses, but I wonder.

ZUCCHETTO

Just by chance, I came across this word in my recent reading. It is the name of the skull-cap worn by the Roman Catholic hierarchy on informal occasions. To those of my faith it is what we would call a yarmulke, the Jewish skull-cap. Apparently it has no great antiquity, but In the Middle Ages the Rabbis ruled that covering the head was a mark of respect and reverence before God. Thus, most religious Jews keep their heads covered at all times as thoughts of the deity may intrude at any time. Although it is customary among most Western peoples to remove headgear in their churches, it is interesting that Catholicism and Judaism follow yet another shared tradition. However, it must be said that secular Jews only wear head coverings on their (rare) visits to the synagogue. Very apropos was the cartoon in a Tel Aviv newspaper at the time of the Pope's historic visit to Israel in 1964. The cartoon showed His Holiness standing next to the President of Israel, and the comment was "The Pope is the one wearing a yarmulke". And on that happy note I end this   collection of ideas, anecdotes, thoughts and memories.

Chronology of a Life

8 July 1931 The day I am purported to have been born, in Islington, London. However, as I have indicated elsewhere, this date may be slightly incorrect.

A week or so later   First "surgery" – the least said, the better.

Just after that   First holiday, with my mother, at Margate.

1936 At 4½ years of age began infant's school

3 September 1939 Evacuated   with   primary   school   to Peterborough

Few months later   Returned home

1941-1944 Re-evacuated to, and returned home from, Buntingford, Luton, Manchester. During this time attended some dozen different schools in London and the above places.

1942 While in Luton, passed examination enabling me to attend Hackney Downs (formerly the Grocer's Company) school in north London

July 1944   Barmitzvah in Manchester

August 1944 Joined Hackney Downs School evacuated at King's Lynn

June 1945   Returned home permanently

August 1947 Passed Matriculation exam

TIMED TO PERFECTION
Stan Greenberg

29 September 1947 Started work with Lever Brothers at Blackfriars, London

31 July 1948 Attended one day of the London Olympic Games at Wembley stadium – an event which changed my life

26 October 1949   National Service enrollment in RAF

20 December 1949 Honorable discharge from RAF – TB shadow on lung

16 July 1952 First trip abroad, by boat from Tilbury, on way to Helsinki, to see the
Olympic Games

30 October 1955   First met Carole, then 15 – at family wedding

29 September 1956 My first letter published in *Athletics Weekly*

11 August 1957   Met Carole again – at another family wedding

January 1958   Founding of the NUTS (National Union of Track Statisticians)

November 1958   First date with Carole

September 1959   Carole and I engaged

Early March 1960   Acquired house – months of work needed. Still living there

4 September 1960   Married to Carole

June 1961   First flight, on a Caravelle to Rimini, Italy

21 November 1962 Awarded Diploma in Economics from the

TIMED TO PERFECTION
Stan Greenberg

University of London (3 year evening class course)

26 June 1963   Daughter, Karen, born

September 1964   Passed driving test

October 1964   First Television work – for ITV on Tokyo
    Olympics

April 1966   First publication, a booklet, *Commonwealth
    Statistics*

24 May 1966   Son, Keith, born

2 September 1967   Left Unilever Limited (formerly Lever Brothers)

29 September 1967 Joined Greater London Council (GLC)

October 1968   Worked for BBC TV – on 1968 Olympics

End-July 1970   First overseas trip for BBC (Zurich)

21 April 1972   First trip to USA – New York

19 January 1974   First long distance flight – New Zealand –
followed by first circumnavigation of the world

11 January 1976   Left Greater London Council (GLC)

mid-January 1976   Became Sports Editor of *Guinness Book of
    Records*

12 January 1982   Left Guinness, to be freelance athletics
    statistician

1982 First hard-back book, solely authored by me, published,
Guinness Book of Sporting Facts

TIMED TO PERFECTION
Stan Greenberg

1983   First edition of *The Guinness Book of Olympic Facts and Feats* published

October 1985   First US holiday trip (to Florida) for Carole and me

15 July 1986 Carole & I attend Royal Garden Party in grounds of Buckingham Palace

September 1988   First stay at Sheraton Sand Key, Clearwater, Florida

February 1992   With the receipt of a portable Toshiba PC from the BBC, I became computerised.

1992   Diagnosed with high blood pressure (not necessarily connected with previous item).

August 1994   Last major champs with BBCTV – Commonwealth Games. First flight in First Class on return journey from Canada

July 1996   Became a pensioner

October 1996   First trip to Las Vegas for Carole and me

September 1998   Recalled for very last BBC work – World Cup, Johannesburg

June 2000   Evidence of prostate cancer discovered

May 2001   Last working trip abroad – Doha, Qatar

April 2003   Long awaited trip to Machu Picchu, Peru

October 2008   Twenty-second and last time to Clearwater

TIMED TO PERFECTION
Stan Greenberg

June 2010   Our first cruise - Mediterranean

September 2010   50th wedding anniversary

July 2011   Celebrated 80th birthday

August 2012   Attended Olympic Games in London – my 9th

September 2015   Celebrated 55th Wedding Anniversay in Las Vegas

January 2016   My 35th trip to Las Vegas

INDEX

TIMED TO PERFECTION
Stan Greenberg

Lightning Source UK Ltd.
Milton Keynes UK
UKHW02f1612080118
315759UK00005B/133/P